## Praise for *The Concubine's Children*

"A perfectly wonderful book. As a work of history and memoir, *The Concubine's Children* has the narrative flow of fiction; as a work of invention, it has the persuasive force of the truth. It deserves a large and admiring readership."                    —*The Washington Post*

"In telling this complicated family story, Ms. Chong remains unfailingly honest . . . [she] details the treatment of women in her family without trivializing Chinese culture or underestimating its internal logic."
                    —*The New York Times Book Review*

"[A] superbly told saga."                    —*Publishers Weekly*

"Even better in form and content than the fictionalized works of Amy Tan."                    —*Library Journal*

"An incredible story."                    —*New York Newsday*

"An eloquent, unsentimental act of love, prompted by the writer's contagious desire to make sense of her origins."
                    —*Kirkus Reviews*

"A beautifully rendered tribute . . . this moving celebration of the values of family and tradition will make you ponder your own roots and loyalties."                    —*New Woman*

"Heartwrenching but ultimately uplifting."
                    —*The Cleveland Plain Dealer*

PENGUIN BOOKS

THE CONCUBINE'S CHILDREN

Denise Chong is an economist and writer whose work has appeared in various magazines and several anthologies. She lives in Ottawa with her husband and children.

DENISE
CHONG

# THE CONCUBINE'S CHILDREN

PENGUIN BOOKS

PENGUIN BOOKS

Published by the Penguin Group

Penguin Books USA Inc., 375 Hudson Street, New York,
New York 10014, U.S.A.

Penguin Books Ltd, 27 Wrights Lane, London W8 5TZ, England

Penguin Books Australia Ltd, Ringwood, Victoria, Australia

Penguin Books Canada Ltd, 10 Alcorn Avenue,
Toronto, Ontario, Canada M4V 3B2

Penguin Books (N.Z.) Ltd, 182–190 Wairau Road,
Auckland 10, New Zealand

Penguin Books Ltd, Registered Offices:
Harmondsworth, Middlesex, England

First published in Canada by Penguin Books Canada Ltd 1994
First published in the United States of America by Viking Penguin,
a division of Penguin Books USA Inc., 1995
Published in Penguin Books (U.S.A.) 1996

1  3  5  7  9  10  8  6  4  2

THE LIBRARY OF CONGRESS HAS CATALOGUED THE HARDCOVER AS FOLLOWS:
Chong, Denise.
The concubine's children/Denise Chong.
p.  cm.
ISBN 0-670-82961-7 (hc.)
ISBN 0 14 02.54277 (pbk.)
1. Chan, Sam.  2. Chinese—British Columbia—Vancouver—Biography.
I. Title.
F1089.5.V22C564  1995
971.1′33004951′0092—dc20
[B]  94–28442

Printed in the United States of America
Set in Adobe Garamond

*To the memory of my Dad*

# ACKNOWLEDGMENTS

THE CONCUBINE'S CHILDREN began as a magazine article that first appeared in *Saturday Night*. Its editor, John Fraser, made everything seem possible, and Barbara Moon's advice about story-telling reverberates with me still. Both envisaged and encouraged a book. From that point, I owe thanks to my editors at Penguin and Viking Penguin. Iris Skeoch was an early enthusiast and Mindy Werner and Meg Masters kept their faith in me and were critically and personally supportive, especially in the notes we traded about our pregnancies and the babies we had along the way. In the research of the book, many—family, relatives and others—candidly shared their recollections, and they deserve thanks. I am most grateful to my mother. As we retraced her family's footsteps, she never tired of my questions and she willingly—and vividly—replayed the past for me. I also owe special thanks to my brother Wayne, whose sense of humor was as valued as his tape-recorder and notebook on our travels in China. Diana Lary provided insights on Chinese history; any mistakes are my own. I shall remember the making of this book as a family effort; my husband, Roger Smith, and I discussed the manuscript over our infant son's colicky protests. Our young daughter perhaps cared the most, asking often, "Is the book finished?" The truthful answer is probably that such a book is never finished, but that there comes a time when the story is ready to be told.

*L*ONG AFTER MY grandparents, Chan Sam and May-ying, had passed on, I would often return to the cedar chest upstairs in my parents' bedroom in our home, open the bottom drawer and take out the pile of old black-and-white photographs there. Each of those photographs was a formal portrait, taken when Chan Sam and May-ying wanted to record a moment for posterity. Each was intimate enough to be a powerfully suggestive voice from the past, but also distant enough to stir curiosity. These were the only artifacts of their generation; anything else of value had gone the way of the pawnshop.

My mother had tried to hold shut the door on the past. But that door was pried open thirty years after Chan Sam's death, twenty years after May-ying's, when she and I took a trip to China in 1987. There, in the village of my grandfather's birth, was the storeroom of the past: his house, a few treasured relics and photographs. What would prove to be of most value for this book was a small packet of letters that my grandfather had written to his wife and son in China in the last four years of his life, all that was left of four decades of correspondence. My Uncle Yuen, having twice lost earlier letters and photographs from his father, first to looting Japanese soldiers and then to the Communists, had to be persuaded to part with the remaining letters long enough for me to have them copied. Fortunately, in them, my grandfather had recounted for his son his early history and reflected upon his life.

To recover the family's past in Canada, I myself was not enough of a living link. I had known my grandfather only as a young child, and my memories of him were fragmentary. I had known my grandmother longer, but by the time I was either interested in the past or had the necessary courage to ask her about it, she was long gone. And so, I had to rely upon my mother's memory.

What she first spilled was a mud puddle of emotion. Only with discipline and patience did she and I begin to order the past. In plumbing the depths of her memory, I was also able to find my way into those of May-ying and Chan Sam. The very nature of their immigrant past and of the old Chinatowns—the poverty, the lack of education, and the claustrophobic existence of being excluded from the larger white society—lent itself to a legacy of oral history. Most of Chinatown's inhabitants had only "chat" to pass the time, and consequently their stories, enlivened by vivid accounts of conversations, were repeated again and again. What my mother overheard of her parents' stories formed some of her earliest memories.

Retracing the footsteps of the family involved collecting other stories of their time. Chan Sam's generation had passed on but a few among May-ying's contemporaries were still alive. My mother's friends were the last generation of children to be raised in Vancouver's Chinatown, and they remembered it well. In addition to gathering information from personal interviews, I relied upon published works of others and public archives.

It was not easy to find physical evidence of earlier generations. Nanaimo's old Chinatown was already gone, burnt to the ground in 1960. In Vancouver, I stood at the wicket where Chan Sam once bought passage to China; I sat at the counter at the B.C. Royal Café, where May-ying once worked; I climbed the dark staircases of the rooming houses where my mother once lived. But in the echo of my footsteps, the wicket was torn down, the café was closed and the rooming houses were overtaken by a skid row drug culture. The decline continues as the newest wave of Asian immigrants, those with money enough to flee Hong Kong before it becomes China's in 1997, bypasses the old Chinatown in favor of setting down roots in the flourishing suburbs. I found the south of China to be changing even more rapidly. On the first trip to see our relatives, we reached my grandfather's village only after traveling three hours along back roads; on the second, an hour's ride by jet-foil took us to a terminal ten minutes from the village. Even as I researched and wrote the book, I felt as if the window of opportunity to get a glimpse of the past was closing.

Once my research was done, the challenge was to press it flat onto the pages of a book. Taking on such a responsibility was daunting. There are as many different versions of events as there are members of a family. The truth becomes a landscape of many layers in an ever-changing light; the details depend on whose memories illuminate it. I felt strongly that the book should be a "family project;" I needed also to feel that those who were in their graves were somehow behind me. Above all, I wanted to be true to the individual lives of the family. It seemed that the most fair and honest way to do that was to tell the story as an omniscient narrator. This involved some necessary interpretation of events and some reconstruction of dialogue. I approached it as one might approach the task of restoring a painting—the original canvas was someone else's. Of course, in the very act of writing a book, I myself bring another shading of truth.

A comment on Chinese names and places and the romanization of Chinese words: for simplicity, I was guided by the most common or local usage. Thus, I refer to Kwangtung instead of Guangdong, because that was how the Chinese province was known to Chan Sam's generation; similarly, I use Mao Zedong over Mao Tse-tung, the former being the common usage during the span of my book. There is no standard romanization of Cantonese words and names; I spelled them as best I could phonetically. And finally, "dollars" refer to the Canadian dollar. Once fixed at parity with the American dollar until World War One, it subsequently fluctuated between roughly parity and some ten percent less until the mid 1970s, but since then to as low as some seventy cents American.

Denise Chong

# THE
# CONCUBINE'S
# CHILDREN

# CHAPTER ONE

IN A SMALL village in China, the concubine, pregnant, consults a blind fortune-teller, whose predictions are considered to come closer to the truth than those of a sighted one. He tells her that the child she is carrying is a boy. A concubine is supposed to produce sons; Leong May-ying has failed her husband, Chan Sam, twice already. She decides this long-awaited son should be born not in China but in Canada, the land the Chinese know as "Gold Mountain."

Some years pass. The child is almost of school age. Chan Sam wants to follow the custom among Chinese sojourners abroad of taking children home to be educated in the motherland. He also longs to see his first wife and to stand on the soil of his village; since he first left China for Canada twenty-one years ago, he has been back only twice for brief visits. The concubine proposes that he alone go to China and that the child remain behind in Canada with her. Chan Sam agrees, but on the condition that, to give purpose to his visit home and to bring honor upon his name, he raise a roof over the family while there.

The predicted son, the one who came to Canada in the womb

and whose stay in Canada was bargained for a house in China, was my mother.



Fifty years after Mother's father, my grandfather, built his house in the village of Chang Gar Bin in Kwangtung province in south China, Mother and I stood in its front reception room, together with her sister and her half-brother. It was spring of 1987. My Aunt Ping had announced that she and Yuen had something to give back to their sister, and Yuen motioned the two of us to follow him upstairs. Mother wondered aloud to me: "What on earth could they have of mine?" As a young child growing up in Canada, all that she knew she had shared with the family in China were letters of formal greeting to her two elder sisters, Ping and Nan, and to the other mother there. To her father, at whose insistence she had copied out the Chinese characters, these letters were a show of respect; to her, they were little more than an exercise in Chinese brush-writing.

Climbing the stairs behind Yuen was not easy; we had the sensation he was going down instead of up. My uncle was born with his feet bent backwards, and in the rural village life in China then, no one his mother put her faith and money in could right them.

At the top of the stairs was a vast floor space, interrupted by three beds, each shrouded in mosquito netting. Yuen led us to the far corner into a small room. In the decaying wood of the screens that enclosed the room, gouge marks were still faintly evident where decorative porcelain panels had been lifted out. Ping intoned: "This was supposed to have been a room for guests. *Baba* said that he wanted a place to entertain friends and relatives, a place to sip tea together." Like her brother, she never missed an opportunity to pay homage to the grandeur their father had intended when he built this house. To Mother and me, the room looked to be a storeroom. It held an inventory of junk: a tall, rusted metal crib with broken springs, crockery topped with split corks, an RCA Victor phonograph that had probably been silent for decades, an assortment of cracked straw baskets.

Yuen rummaged around and finally handed Mother a faded

bundle of brown cloth. Ping led us out to the balcony where the sun afforded better light. The bundle, shook out, fell into the shape of a coat, a child's perhaps. With sure hands, Mother reached slowly for the collar, found its black velvet trim. She threaded her arms through the sleeves and drew the coat over her shoulders, exposing knees and wrists that betrayed when she had last worn it. But the ill fit fell away when she pulled the sides of the collar together to wrap her neck in velvet. It was as if the coat, in its last performance, in forbearance and forgiveness, had itself restored the two halves of the family—one in Canada, one in China—to one.

Mother had been a girl when she'd last worn it. With its velvet trim and chamois lining, the brown bouclé knit coat had been a rare extravagance of her mother's. She had purchased it on Vancouver's fashionable Granville Street, several blocks from Chinatown where the two of them lived. Mother had paraded Vancouver's sidewalks in it, arm-in-arm with her girlfriends. Never had she guessed that it had lived out its life in China, that her mother had given it to her father to include in one of his regular care packages to his other family there.

Ping had sashayed along the village paths in it, enjoying the taunts of the other villagers: "*Faan-gwei neu.*" The coat that labelled her "the foreign girl" had passed from her to Yuen, and when he outgrew it, it had been kept in safekeeping for more than forty years, away from looting Japanese soldiers, Communist vigilantes and the moths of time, stored along with Ping and Yuen's hopes that Mother, their sister, was still alive in Canada.

I had known all my life there might be relatives in China. As a child, I was curious about a photograph of two young children. It lay loose among a pile of other black-and-white photographs in the bottom drawer of the cedar chest upstairs in our home in Prince George, a logging town in northern British Columbia.

If I stared long enough, the two girls blinked. They had to: how could they not, waiting so long for their sister? I sometimes imagined that they had just run in from school to be told: "Your little sister, she's here! Quickly! Get ready to greet her!" She's the one they've heard about but have never met, who was in the womb when their mother left China without them. Hurriedly, they roll their socks to their ankles, smooth the fronts of their dresses. The older grabs the younger's wrist, and they stand, ready to be presented. And there they stay, trapped in time for a moment that will never come.

I knew in reality one was dead. The younger died a teenager. For all my family knew, the other was dead too. Contact, forsaken when Mother's parents separated and her letter-writing sessions with her father ended, had been entirely lost when the Communists took over China. But like indelible ink, the words that invariably ended my mother's sad tales of her childhood could not be blotted from my conscience: "I had nobody." Whenever I looked at that photograph, I wanted to believe it didn't have to be so.

I didn't need to use my imagination as much for other family photographs in that drawer. I had known my grandfather and his concubine, my grandmother, in real life. Nowhere in the drawer was there a photograph of them together. The only portrait of him had a melancholic air, showed him with his jaw set with age and worry. I know Mother didn't cry at his funeral—I was only four but I remember being there. I myself had adored him. "Do I look like him?" I wondered, tracing his jawline, retracing my own. I was not so bold as to think I resembled any image of my grandmother. She wouldn't entertain such closeness to me, or so I thought.

In person she scared me; I much preferred the silence of her photographs. They were proof of how, in her time, she had been one of the prettiest women in Chinatown. "It was a known fact," was how Mother put it. "Everyone told me, 'May-ying is so beautiful.'" It was perhaps the most generous thing she said of her mother. While my grandmother lived, I was always to think of her as beautiful; I took it to be an absolute truth. Somehow I thought it made up for everything that went so wrong for her.

# CHAPTER TWO

*M*AY-YING TRACED a part down the back of her head, bound the hair on each side with a filament of black wire and twisted it into a chignon above each ear. Then she unpinned and combed the curls framing her forehead. She assessed the finished look in the mirror: a girl of seventeen looked in; the reflection was supposed to pass for a woman of twenty-four.

It had been Auntie's advice to wear her hair up to add years to her face. May-ying set her dangling earrings swaying, the tear of jade on each side following the gold ball suspended between the links above. The earrings, along with a jade pendant, had been her mother's; she had taken them off to give to her child when they'd said goodbye forever. In the years since, May-ying had kept them safe. Now that she was leaving her girlhood behind, she knew she should guard no other possessions more carefully. As long as she had her jade and gold near, the souls of her ancestors would do all they could to keep harm from her path.

She stood up, turned away from the mirror, smoothed the *cheong sam* over her girl's body and went to sit for her portrait as the wife of a man she had not yet met.

⟞⟶⟝

May-ying had never expected that she would have a say in whom she married; no girl or boy did in traditional Chinese society. Marriage was a union between two families and was too important to be left to the whim of the young. Love was not a consideration; in fact, it was seen as a threat to the husband's family, as undermining the authority of the mother over her new daughter-in-law. Parents, in arranging their children's marriages, were most concerned about avoiding any mismatch between the two family backgrounds that might create problems, envy or embarrassment between the families. That was best ensured by a matchmaker, typically an elderly lady from one of the surrounding villages. As well as asking the gods to pronounce on the auspiciousness of a match, she would act as messenger in negotiations over the dowry (if the girl's family was better off than the boy's), or (if his was the better-off family), the bride-price to be paid.

Auntie was not May-ying's real aunt. Born in 1907 into the Leong family, May-ying came from Nam Hoy, one of four counties that comprised the city of Canton and its outskirts, in the province of Kwangtung in south China. As such, she carried a strain of superiority; the people from these four counties were the original native Cantonese, whose dialect and ways were considered more refined than those of peasants further afield. But May-ying's first fall from grace was to be born a girl. No one is glad when a daughter is born; a girl is "someone else's," a mouth to feed until she marries and goes to live in another household. Sons, on the other hand, live at home even after they are married. May-ying's double curse was to be a girl born into a poor family, although not so poor that they drowned or abandoned her at birth.

She stayed with her family until she was perhaps four; she could remember her mother trying to apply the first bandages to bind her feet. The practice of binding a young girl's growing bones had been dying out in China, especially in the south where the peasant economy needed girls and women to work in the fields. But some clung to the practice as a way for their daughters to escape becoming beasts of burden. Diminutive feet, the ultimate sexual allure, would have elevated May-ying into a social class where women were artful objects. When hard times struck, as they surely would, and the family was without rice, her mother might have hoped to sell her daughter as a child-bride, to have some say over her future husband. It was not to be. Because of May-ying's cries of protest, her feet were unbandaged. "Auntie," a stranger, bought her as a servant.

When May-ying turned seventeen and of marrying age, she was ready to be sold again. Auntie was aware that her girl-servant's looks would command a high bride-price. No man or woman who first came upon May-ying could help but stare fixedly at this tiny figure of a girl, who stood no higher than the average person's chin. Her delicate features, the bright round eyes and the much admired heart-shaped mouth, were set in pale skin that had retained its translucence because Auntie's chores had kept her out of the fields and out of the baking sun. But for her unbound feet, she had the body and features much imitated in Chinese porcelain dolls.

May-ying had been squatting over a basin in the courtyard washing Auntie's clothes when she was summoned inside. A stool was offered, tea poured. May-ying was immediately suspicious; a mistress does not serve her servant.

"*Ah* Ying, I have found you a *ho muen how,*" Auntie declared.

A girl expected there to come a day when she would hear these words, announcing a good doorway to another house, that of her future mother-in-law. The question was where; she wondered if she would be staying in Auntie's village.

"Where is it, Auntie?"

Auntie hesitated. "It is in *Gum San,*" she said.

"What?!" May-ying could not believe her ears or bite her tongue. "What am I hearing?" Gold Mountain was another continent, a foreign land of white ghosts. Her tone said it was unthinkable that she would be sent to live in North America. "I don't want to go!"

Auntie had expected the news to come as a shock. She herself had been persuaded only when she saw the bride-price offered. She took it as a sign that the claims of prosperity in Gold Mountain were no exaggeration.

"The man is from Heung San," Auntie said, naming the province's county of rice farmers, further south along the Pearl River estuary. "He has been living in *Gum San* for some years. People living in *Gum San* have wealth and riches; they have to push the gold from their feet to find the road." She met May-ying's eyes. "I am only doing what is best for you. I want you to have *on lock cha fan.*"

May-ying heard the echo of these words in her head. Her mother had used these same words of farewell. She too had wished her a life of contentment, a life never short of tea or rice. It only reminded May-ying of that tearful parting.

In a flash of temper, May-ying kicked the table legs. He's only a peasant, she said. Why couldn't Auntie find a boy from a decent family near Canton? She shoved the table top, splashing tea. She repeated that she did not want to go, that she did not want to eat rice from a strange land. Auntie was dismayed; she had warned May-ying many times that her quick temper would enslave her to her heart.

Auntie had to shout to make herself heard: "You are not going for good." May-ying glared and waited for what had been held back. "He has a *Dai-po* in Heung San," Auntie continued, "and he wants to have a *chip see* in *Gum San.*"

The effect was more cruel than if May-ying had been told no family would have her. Stunned to hear that she was to join the household of a man already married, that she was to be a concubine, at his whim and in the servitude of his wife, May-ying knew it would be taken as a mark against herself. No decent girl became a concubine, married off in shame without wedding or ceremony. On the other hand, the more concubines a man had, the more prestige and social status he garnered. His parents chose his wife, but he himself recruited his concubines, often from a face he fancied in a brothel.

May-ying's ebony eyes flashed a familiar accusing look at

Auntie. "Then I might just as well stay in China and be a prostitute," she snapped.

At such a stinging rebuke of ungratefulness, such disrespect for the match she had made, Auntie thundered back, "I will not hear any more of this nonsense. When I say go out the door, you will go!"

It was early in 1924 by the western calendar when May-ying was married off. Her rebellion was useless; in the Confucian way of thinking, a girl has no authority of her own. She does as she is told. The choice was that or suicide. The village gossip would cast Auntie as the tyrant and May-ying as a girl wronged only if she took her own life, if her body were discovered floating near the stilt-houses over the Pearl River at the village's edge, or hanging from a beam in Auntie's house.

Auntie grew excited about helping May-ying make preparations to leave. She engaged a photographer to record May-ying's new identity. The photograph had to conform with the age on the false birth certificate. Perhaps feeling guilty that there would be no wedding biscuits to distribute to the villagers, no double-happiness cutouts to hang from the doorways of her house, Auntie hired a tailor to sew two *cheong sams* for May-ying as her going-away present. May-ying's outburst forgiven if not forgotten, Auntie reveled in repeating tales of Chinese men going to Gold Mountain and harvesting the money trees and coming home rich men with prestige. She imagined May-ying, once she came back to China, living in one of the large houses of the wealthy, where the rooftops are all that is visible over the wall around the compound. She imagined a harmonious household, where the man's first wife, instead of being jealous, encouraged concubinage. "She will choose you over the other concubines to serve her," said Auntie. "She will prefer you to occupy the master's bed, you will be the one to produce the sons."

A Chinese knows only one thing for certain: that danger and evil spirits lurk everywhere. According to Chinese belief, jade and gold are the only talismans, and the more they come handed down, the more power they have to bestow good luck. May-ying's dangling earrings had been worn by her mother. The pendant, a flawless baize-green jade inlaid in gold, had been retrieved from the coffin of her mother's mother, and was even more precious. She left Auntie's house as she had left her mother's, with these pieces sewn inside her clothing.

May-ying's outward journey began by sampan, hailed from among the many plying the Pearl River. After a day downstream, slowed by the crowd of boat people living on the river, she and the middleman accompanying her arrived in Canton. There, May-ying had her first glimpse of the ancient trading city, flag-stoned lanes choked with shops selling everything from firecrackers and ready-made herb preparations to sandalwood and rattan. On the train trip from there to Hong Kong, she peered out the window as rice fields gave way to a city hinting of people with greater ambitions. The man delivered her to an address on Des Voeux Road, and another man there delivered her to the ship. The officers of the Blue Funnel Steamship Line found her papers in order, stamped them and accepted her for passage.

After eighteen days at sea, the ship steamed into the port of Vancouver. Mountains and sea seemed to diminish man's efforts at fashioning this young cityscape. Among the wide-eyed disembarking passengers was a tiny girl, who, but for her mature hairstyle, looked too young to have left home. Her birth certificate said she was born in Ladner, British Columbia. The fertile farmland of the Fraser Valley just outside Vancouver was dotted with Chinese laboring in the fields for white farmers. Presuming she was one of the new generation of Chinese born in Canada, immigration officials accepted her false papers, and the girl who had left her Chinese homeland as Leong May-ying was waved through as the woman Chung Gim-ching returning to her native Canada. "Such a pretty girl alone?" asked the interpreter. No, she was being met, she said, by her husband.

One Chinese man waiting for the passenger ship to dock at the pier at the foot of Granville Street stood out from the crowd by virtue of his nearly six-foot frame. He had a body that was all limbs, long even in his fingers, which gave his every gesture an elongated emphasis. A fedora graced his head, and he was attired in a custom-tailored three-piece gray suit. His shoes and wire-rimmed glasses were polished and his black hair meticulously combed to expose a high forehead, a physical trait the Chinese considered a sign of intelligence. He owned two suits—one gray, the other brown—and two fedoras. Believing one's appearance mirrored one's inner mind, his appearance today was, as always, immaculate. His manner, like his dress, was sober and serious. At thirty-seven, he was a year younger than the city of Vancouver.

A few Chinese were among the waiting crowd of whites, some of their faces familiar to Chan Sam. But he had no desire to squander time in conversation with someone to whom he had no loyalties. He returned to studying that day's *Chinese Times,* to a report of a speech given by a Canadian-born Chinese in Victoria calling for political reform in the homeland. He underlined the characters he did not know; in this way he added two or three new characters each day to his written vocabulary.

The dock scene was a marked contrast to what it had been like when Chan Sam himself had first stepped onto this same pier in 1913, eleven years earlier. Now, the Chinese dressed in western dress. Then, he was one of the few among his compatriots who had spilled off the packed freighter not in mandarin-collared jackets, pajama-like trousers and sandals. Chan Sam had arrived in a western tailored suit. But it had made no difference to his reception; along with the other arriving Chinese, he was herded into a dock-side low brick building to spend three months in quarantine behind barred windows and under guard. Despite their protests that they had already stood naked in a line for examination by the white doctor onboard ship, the men were fumigated with sulfur, and so were their belongings. Inside the packed and filthy "pigpen," as the Chinese called it, amid the noise from trains rumbling into the adjacent western terminus of the transcontinental railway, it had been hard for them to keep fast their belief in Gold Mountain's fairy tales, spun from men before them who'd gone to make their fortunes.

They were men from the delta of the Pearl River in Kwangtung province, where seafarers were folk heroes. In the eighteenth century, Canton had been the only Chinese port open to foreigners. Ever since the arrival there of foreign traders offering to exchange opium from India for Chinese silk and tea, distant shores had meant adventure. In 1848, gold was struck in Sacramento, California, and the race was on across the Pacific to Gold Mountain. More Chinese left in 1862, in a second dash for gold up British Columbia's Fraser River to Barkerville. Many, when pushed off the better claims by white prospectors, stayed on to cook and wash clothes, and early Chinatowns sprang up and thrived. Anti-Chinese feelings intensified, and whites up and down North America's west coast began lobbying local governments—state, provincial, municipal—to stem the flow of arriving Chinese and to make it clear to those already there that they were unwelcome. In the 1870s and 1880s, there were limits on the number of incoming Chinese per boat, bans against hiring men with pigtail-length hair and against the use of poles to carry baskets. There were special taxes levied on the Chinese for school and policing, employment, laundry, shoes and even cigars. Worse was to come. Chinese were soon barred from becoming naturalized citizens, from owning land, from working on public works.

Such distaste for the Chinese presence did not deter white contractors who were looking for cheap labor to carve out the great transcontinental railways across the United States and Canada. Their governments bought their claim that the Chinese would work for much less and were more reliable than the available white labor, mostly Irish. Though many Chinese, assigned the most dangerous jobs, died building the railway, racist resentment sped along the newly built iron rails. Whites in the east railed against the inevitable eastward settlement of a race they condemned as alien, steeped in moral depravity and degradation.

The Chinese continued to arrive — fathers, uncles, sons and brothers of those who had come before. One was Chan Sam's father. His voyage from China to San Francisco was financed by his clan society in his home county. During his sojourn abroad, he met his own expenses and his wife's at home and still returned home for a visit every third year, three times in all. To further distinguish his name, he more than repaid his debt to his clan society by soliciting overseas donations to help build an ancestral hall.

Luck was with him in that he first landed in America before the United States Congress passed the historic Chinese Exclusion Act of 1882. That act gave in to the most fanatical of those lobbying against the Chinese presence and slammed the door shut to new arrivals. Only diplomats, certain scholars and import-export merchants holding temporary visas were to be allowed in. The effect was to condemn Chinese men already in the country to a life abroad without the possibility of their families joining them. The male-female ratio in Chinatowns, already primarily bachelor societies, would change only with the birth of their American-born children. Lest any Chinese try to sneak in by way of Canada, the Americans posted guards at the border.

In 1888, Chan Sam's father was back in China cradling him, his firstborn child. That same year, Congress suddenly declared void all Certificates of Return, which had allowed previous sojourners to reenter the United States. Chan Sam's father was grateful that his years abroad had been fat. He had made ten times what he might have had he not gone, enough to buy some thirty *mau tin* (one *mau tin* equals less than one-sixth of an acre of cultivated land), enough to have a second child, a third and a fourth.

The only door to the mythical Gold Mountain that the Chinese could still pry open was Canada's. But the Canadian government, aware that some Chinese saw it as a back door to the United States, sought to act in concert with the Americans. In 1885, it tried to put off the average Chinese laborer by imposing a fifty-dollar head tax upon entry. Merchants were exempted for fear they'd go south of the border. In 1904, in the same year that the United States extended its Exclusion Act indefinitely and broadened it to apply to Hawaii and the Philippines, then American possessions, the Canadian government raised the head tax to five hundred dollars.

Chinese men were desperate enough to leave China that they found ways to raise such sums. In 1913, when Chan Sam crossed the Pacific, he was one of seven thousand coming to Canada that year, a new high. Such numbers dismayed even the Canadian Chinese Benevolent Association, headquartered in Victoria's Chinatown, Canada's oldest. That year, in an urgent circular to Kwangtung province that was posted in county magistrate offices, the Association painted a picture of the Chinese in Canada as jobless, hungry and cold: "In a nutshell, it is better not to come." The Association's fear was that the Canadian government would overreact to the growing number of arrivals by driving out those already here. Exclusion was the Association's worst nightmare.

In Chan Sam's time, the destination of choice was Vancouver's Chinatown. The community had boomed along with the city. But so too had anti-Chinese sentiment. Within the four to five square blocks of Vancouver's Chinatown, some three to four thousand Chinese, mostly men, lived and worked in virtual isolation from white society. No self-respecting white would be seen anywhere near Chinatown, believing it to be populated with shifty-eyed, pigtailed Chinamen of the Fu Manchu and Charlie Chan movies that would later show in North American movie houses. The appetite for painting the Chinese as villains grew when First World War veterans came home to a depressed economy. Newspapers and politicians alike pandered to public hysteria, accusing the Chinese of stealing jobs from Canadian fathers. Chinatowns were denounced as dirty and disease-ridden, as centers of gambling and crime. Vancouver's was depicted in local newspaper editorial cartoons as a congestion of rooming houses, of unmarked doorways to a labyrinth where lascivious Chinamen smoked opium, lay with Chinese prostitutes, fed on rats and enslaved white girls. No one saw the contrasting truth, that there were, among the bachelors, a few upstanding families living there. These included the wives and children of the merchant class who could raise the money to pay for the five-hundred-dollar head tax on each family member, who could install them above their ground-floor businesses, and who could afford to send their children back to China for part of their education. Selling out their business was always an option too, if Canada got unbearably inhospitable, to pay for the family's passage home.

In 1923, the Canadian Chinese Benevolent Association's worst nightmare came true. That year, the Canadian Parliament went the way of the American Congress and passed its own exclusionary law. The date the Chinese Immigration Act went into effect— July 1, the day the nation's birthday is celebrated—the Chinese marked as "Humiliation Day." In reply to such hostility, many Chinese men went home for good. After ten years abroad, Chan Sam too could have abandoned his plan to sojourn abroad. But to do so would have led to a loss of face, for which he could not look himself in the mirror. Some might have called his pride a character flaw, except that showiness was almost expected of those coming back from Gold Mountain—a sign to others that the dream of riches abroad was still alive.

❦

Had fate and blunder not conspired, Chan Sam might have been living out his future at home instead of trying to fashion one abroad. His first misfortune came in his boyhood. Like any schoolboy with big ambitions, he had dreamt of one day passing the civil service examinations, which would have opened the door to a respected post of privilege as an imperial court official serving the Qing dynasty, or even the Empress Dowager herself. But his father died, and at the age of twelve, he had to quit school. As the eldest son in a family of four children, he became the new head of the household.

"Tiles over one's head, and soil under one's feet" was the peasant's lifelong dream. The house of Chan Sam's family gave no indication of his father's Gold Mountain success. The squat, two-room adobe house—the first room was the sleeping and eating quarters, the second was for a cooking hearth and crude washhouse—was like any other in Chang Gar Bin, a village of fifty or so households crammed together as tightly as cauliflower heads. Owning a plot or two of land was what separated one peasant from another. A man rented however many *mau tin* he could afford and prayed to the gods that he could keep starvation from his doorstep with what was left of the harvest after paying rent to the landlord (50 to 60 percent of the annual harvest, often exacted years in advance), taxes (about one-sixth of the price of the crop) and interest on his debts. Peasants were China's poor; its city-dwellers were relatively better off. It was they who were the biggest landlords, the landowners with tracts of thousands, often tens of thousands of *mau tin*. It was they who had the money, and they, by virtue of their positions as high officials or military officers (positions money bought and held), who had the backing of police or hired troops to collect rents by force or to take what collateral they could find.

In the nineteenth century, one in three peasants died landless. A peasant's entire cash wage for six to eight years might buy one *mau tin*. The poorer peasant might own five or six *mau tin*, possibly enough to keep two from starvation, but not from hunger. A middle-class peasant might own four times that. Others with the income to spare sought to buy more land to rent out, hoping it would get them through the hard times. Therein lay Chan Sam's father's reward for going abroad; his thirty *mau tin* was enough to raise him from a poor peasant to a middle-class one. Though it was stretched among three inheriting sons, it might have been enough to keep alive a father's wish that the next generation would escape impoverishment.

For years, the teenaged Chan Sam hoed, planted and harvested the *mau tin* himself. The county was surrounded by waters draining into the Pearl River estuary on one side and by the South China Sea on the other, with a system of canals connecting villages like Chang Gar Bin. It was once ideal rice-growing land. But this teeming land was now so tired, so crowded. At the turn of the century, the number of people living in an area of Kwangtung province not much larger than the San Francisco Bay area had a third the population then of the United States and four times that of Canada. Feeding so many mouths was too much to ask of the soil. Chan Sam had to toil laboriously, carrying buckets of water on a split bamboo pole, spreading night soil to still the threat of starvation swirling in the soil. Thinking his younger brothers might show more inclination to hard work if it were less back-breaking, he sold some *mau tin* for four water buffalo.

He could not know that anything he tried would be undermined by the growing political and economic chaos in the country. Weakened by corrupt mandarins, challenged by secret societies and dissident officials, the Qings were powerless to subdue widespread rebellion and riot against their imperial dynasty. Frustration spread like a cancer. Even as the young Chan Sam took on his father's legacy, the only secure livelihood was banditry. Armed gangs roamed the land. They were made up of the very poor, dispirited youth, unemployed soldiers and malcontents. Entire families and even entire villages formed or joined gangs. Government troops themselves behaved as bandits; what others called stealing, they called "confiscating."

Chan Sam's hold on subsistence began to slip while his responsibilities grew. He was a husband—at sixteen he had taken his mother's choice for his wife—and the father of a daughter. He had to hire extra crop-watchers for his fields at night. He took his turn sleeping in the damp fields, and like every man and boy of Chang Gar Bin, he took his turn keeping vigil atop the village's watchtower from dusk to dawn. Similar towers, financed by clan landowners, rice merchants or ancestral halls, rose above every village in south China, giving the countryside the look of medieval England. The more elaborate had guns mounted at several sentry positions on their castellated tops. Chang Gar Bin's had a strong door and a walled-in viewing platform built to the height of the village rooftops. Night in the village brought two sounds. The tok-tok! of the *mook-yue*, the clap of a wooden fish that was served at a poor man's banquet as a substitute symbol for the real fish he couldn't afford, signaled all was well. The sharp note of the *di-da*, a flute-like instrument, warned of bandits approaching and was a call to take refuge in the tower. The danger was in being left behind when bandits struck. For any man or boy, it was certain enslavement; for a girl or woman, most probably rape.

In 1909, when Chan Sam was twenty-one, the Empress Dowager died. Upheaval ensued, and in 1911 the fledgling

Kuomintang—the National People's Party—won a minor skirmish that allowed Sun Yat-sen, the party's founder, to declare himself the provisional president of a new republic. He was traveling out of the country at the time and was as surprised as anyone.

In reality, however, the country had fallen into the hands of warring warlords and local strongmen. The wealthy retreated behind the walls of their compounds, hired more soldiers and bought off anyone more powerful who had managed to survive elimination. The very poor had no choice but to grimace against fate. Those who could raise money did what their fathers had once done and went abroad. And so Kwangtung province became the spout of the teapot that was China, pouring forth men like Chan Sam, neither very poor nor very wealthy. They went to feed the ache of hunger and hope, to seek the stability missing in the homeland. Some sojourned in Hong Kong, some in southeast Asia. Others, like Chan Sam, chose Gold Mountain.

An old lady in the village, a relative of his father's, lent him the seven hundred dollars for what the Chinese called the "traffic fee" to go abroad: the five-hundred-dollar head tax and another two hundred dollars to cover the boat passage and expenses while he looked for work. "Return home in brocade," the old lady said. Chan Sam made a promise to his wife that he would struggle and save, that he would remit enough to cover her expenses at home. He pledged to return before too many years for a visit, and one day, to come home for good.

Chan Sam was lucky to find work immediately, despite the economic gloom that pervaded Vancouver. Still, there were almost always jobs for the Chinese, either in Chinatown, or else the menial, poorest-paying or the most dangerous jobs on a sawmill floor, a mine or a farm. Certainly the white owners of the sawmills along the Fraser River, the canneries on Burrard Inlet and the vegetable and pig farms just outside Vancouver saw the advantage of hiring Chinese foremen to find them cheap Chinese labor. What work a man got depended solely on his connections and how much money he had to set them in motion. In

Chinatown, a job was both a privilege earned and a favor granted. Outside Chinatown, a man got nowhere without an "in" with a Chinese foreman.

If there was one Chinese law of the universe, it was loyalty to *gee gay yun,* to one's own people. In the homeland, it was to family, village and clan—sometimes one and the same. In the new world, where connections were spread more thinly, a man's demonstrable loyalties were to an extended family—to men not only from his own clan, but to men from the same locale in China. If there were few from his clan, then the shared locale was extended to include men from the same county, or from a group of counties. Chan (also anglicized as Chen or Chin) was not among the more common surnames, like Wong, Lee or Mah, whose clan societies were well established in Chinatown at that time. A man without a clan association to help him get a job had to know where to go to be looked after by his own. Chan Sam found a foreman of the mill from his home county and got work as a sorter and a tie-up man, catching and bundling shingles coming off the line. He learned why it was work a white man avoided when a flying shingle severed the top of his middle finger.

He worked eleven-hour days, six days a week. The Chinese, only too grateful to have any work at all, were not complainers. At Chan Sam's mill, the Chinese were third on the pay scale behind whites and Hindus, earning a fraction of their pay. They paid room and board; others did not. Their bunkhouses were segregated from whites, and they were expected to survive on salted fish, soup and rice. Whenever Chan Sam tired of the abuse that came from the white man's mouth, he reminded himself that one week's wages could buy one *mau tin* in China. But expenses made it difficult to save. He cut costs by coming back to Chinatown on his one day off a week and during the off season, where he shared the rent on a bunk at a tenement complex. To cram in more bunks, rooms were crudely partitioned, windowless and no bigger than six feet by eight, with makeshift bunks three deep on each side. Like a game of musical beds, there were more bachelor men sharing the monthly rent than there were bunks.

The typical bachelor's entertainments were afflictions Chan Sam shunned. The ratio of men to women fell from twenty-five to one to ten to one within a decade of his arrival. But on the streets, the ratio was dramatically higher. "Decent" women—the merchants' wives—rarely ventured beyond the walls of their family home. A laborer, on the other side of the social chasm from a merchant, called a rooming house home and rarely even saw a woman or girl, unless he fraternized with the white prostitutes in the skid row area bordering Chinatown, or unless he frequented the tea houses, all of which employed waitresses. Chan Sam was faithful to his wife and policed himself on all matters of vice. He rarely even entered a gambling den and certainly never even passed by one on payday. He would take an occasional whiskey, but he regarded drinking, like gambling, to be addictive. Such moral caution and frugality enabled him to remit money to keep his wife at home, and within three years of living abroad, to send money home to repay his debt to the old lady and to start saving for his family's future.

He had been in Canada five years when he received news that his wife had died. Numb with sadness, he spent some of his savings to buy a ticket home. He would visit her grave and erect an ancestral tablet there, so that future generations could worship her soul. Bad news came on top of bad. He came home to find his brothers, both now married, deeply in debt. At first sorry that the *mau tin* had not been enough to meet their families' expenses, Chan Sam soon found out to his chagrin that they had also spent all the money he had remitted home instead of repaying the old lady for the traffic fee she had lent him. He admonished his brothers. "Your conduct is not good," he said. They asked him to lend them more money. Chan Sam pleaded that he could not on account of his plans to open a business upon his return to Canada.

He could be absent from Canada one year without having to again pay the head tax. Before the year in China was out, he did the sensible thing of taking a "replacement wife." Huangbo was plain, quiet, unassuming and kind. At twenty, she was old to be married off and happy to have her future provided for, if by a widowed man twelve years her senior. Chan Sam pledged to care for her as if she were his first wife. He asked her to be dutiful in helping work his share of the *mau tin,* in raising his deceased wife's daughter until marrying age and in keeping the home for an absent husband. When the time came for him to leave, she was pregnant; once back in Canada, he learned that their baby girl had not lived long.

In 1919, he and a couple of his bachelor friends opened a small storefront in Vancouver's Chinatown. They had rented space at the east end of the three long blocks of Pender Street, Chinatown's main artery, to sell miscellaneous Chinese dry goods, one of many shops that did the same. But their idea was to rely on the loyalty of the patronage of their own people, the moral contract that kept dozens of other storefronts in Chinatown in business. It provided an adequate income.

His brothers wrote to ask if they had best come to Canada. Chan Sam remained optimistic about life abroad: "It is not easy to save money, but making a living here is better than making a living by cultivation in the homeland." Without consulting him, the brothers sold the four water buffalo for their traffic fee money. Abruptly, exclusion came in 1923, and their plans to come had to be canceled. "You sold the only productive asset!" Chan Sam wrote his brothers when he found out what they had done. The *mau tin* that had not been lost to mounting debts were eventually unable to support two families. One brother decided to leave for a country that would have him. Using Chan Sam's name and the *mau tin* as collateral, he borrowed money from the bank and a rice shop to pay his passage and to start a business in Havana, Cuba. At the same time, he had Chan Sam lend him the same amount and more. Other than one miserly gold coin sent from Cuba to the wife and daughter he had left behind, the brother was never heard from again, leaving Chan Sam to clear up his bad debts.

The money that Chan Sam, feeling guilty for being duped himself, sent to his brother's abandoned wife left him anguishing about his own. He himself had to make a choice. The Canadian exclusion act required every Chinese in Canada, born there or abroad, to register with immigration authorities and to state whether they were staying or leaving. Prospects for Chan Sam's shop on Pender Street were not good; exclusion would choke Chinatown's growth. By day and night at the shop, his friends gathered to talk of the growing numbers registering to leave. For many, years, possibly decades of separation from their families stretched behind and ahead. Chan Sam did not know how much exile he himself could or ought to endure. Fighting loneliness, worry and homesickness, he lay awake nights wondering if his wife, Huangbo, and other villagers were still alive. He was thirty-six and had yet to father sons. The exclusion act allowed absences of two years, but spending money on a visit would only postpone the day he went home for good. He pondered a way to ease the pain of his solitary life: he decided to take another wife.

A friend of a friend knew someone returning to the homeland. "Can you find me a *chip see?*" Chan Sam asked. The request for a concubine was not unfamiliar among married Chinese men abroad. The wife in the village, the one chosen by their parents, was the "At-home Wife." The concubine, sent from China, joined the man abroad and the two lived together in the foreign country as man and wife. Those who wanted to observe western customs legalized it with a marriage certificate, but few saw the need, for within the Chinese notion of the family, the At-home Wife had her husband's first loyalties.

To bring his plan to fruition, Chan Sam needed money and the birth certificate of a Canadian-born Chinese about the same the age as his imported concubine. In short order he was put in touch with an agent who dealt in "paper families." He bought and sold birth certificates of people already dead, of people who had left Canada with no intention to return or who, for a price, could be convinced to stay away. He offered Chan Sam the birth certificate of a woman born in Ladner, outside Vancouver. Nothing was said of what had become of her.

A decade earlier, Chan Sam's traffic fee had been seven hundred dollars. To acquire a concubine, the price was more than triple that. On top of the bride-price, most of that was the cost of the birth certificate and the fees of middlemen in Vancouver, Hong Kong and China. It was not the kind of money that a man like Chan Sam, a peasant minding a storefront, had.

The Blue Funnel Steamship stood dockside. The building known as the "pigpen" was boarded up, but it served to remind Chan Sam again of his first reception. He turned his attention to the arriving passengers as they began to disembark. He looked for a face that matched the photograph of May-ying.

He heard the murmurs of approval from other Chinese men before he himself caught sight of a porcelain doll come to life. He recognized the dangling earrings and the hairstyle, the two chignons over the ears. He stepped forward into her path.

"I'm inviting you to *dim sum*," Chan Sam told May-ying as they stood on the pier, having barely made their introductions. The teenaged girl strained to understand the thick peasant accent. She caught the words *dim sum*, a phrase borrowed from Canton's social custom of tea houses. Going to sip tea, she thought, was a kindly first gesture from this older man who was her new husband. She gave a quick smile and tried to hold back a laugh of girlish delight.

Chan Sam hailed one of the waiting taxis. He had decided before setting out on foot from Chinatown that they would take a taxi back. Usually he walked everywhere.

From the pier it was a short, ten-minute ride east along Pender Street to Chinatown. Their taxi skirted the city's financial district. Its tall stone buildings and the rhythmic flow of streetcars spoke of ordered calm. On the other side of the tram lines that ran between New Westminster and Vancouver, the western architecture suddenly gave way to a dense conglomeration of two- and three-story brick buildings bedecked with an assortment of awnings. Two tiny alleyways off Pender, Canton and Shanghai Alleys, both of which had been privately developed, were congested with tall, narrow tenements, dozens of businesses, shops, restaurants, even a public bath and an opera house. May-ying was vaguely reminded of buildings she had seen in Canton.

They alighted from the taxi at the corner of Pender and Carrall, where Chinatown first began. The tidal waters of False Creek had left sludge along these shores that repulsed all other settlers but the Chinese.

"We're going upstairs, over there," Chan Sam said, pointing to a second-story sign across the street. "Peking House," it said in Chinese; in English, "Pekin Chop Suey House." The ground floor was occupied by a boot-and-shoe shop and by a Chinese grocery store. The building was Victorian on three sides, but on the fourth side, overlooking Pender, its facade was Italianate, with curved arches and wrought-iron railings enclosing recessed bal-conies. In south China, the doors to these balconies would have been left open to circulate air in the day's heavy heat. Here they were closed.

May-ying followed Chan Sam through the crowd of men milling on the sidewalk. Some were leaning against the buildings or in doorways, some chatting to pass the time; many of the younger ones were smoking. All stared at the new face in town, that of the tiny young girl. All wondered at the mismatch: Chan Sam was tall, older; she was so short, and so young. They watched as the two of them climbed the wide stairway to the upper floors.

The owner of the tea house saw them come in and strode up. "*Ah* Chan Sam, *Sin-sang*," he said, using the title for a gentleman. "You are here!" His voice was too loud, even above the din of chatter from people sequestered behind half-curtains drawn across lines of wooden booths.

May-ying hoped the ebullient greeting hinted well at her hus-band's status in this new land. Chan Sam beamed; he was proud to introduce her. The owner led them to a booth adjoining a table where some staff were eating, outside the swinging doors to the kitchen. "Today is a special day," he said, "a day for a feast."

A waitress, a pretty girl perhaps not much older than May-ying, placed before them bamboo basket after basket of hot steamed morsels, rice dumplings of shrimp and minced pork, small porcelain dishes of bite-sized spareribs, stuffed bitter melon, dishes that could be found in tea houses in Canton. To wash it down, there was a choice of teas: jasmine, chrysanthemum or "six contentment," a mixture of several teas.

At the end of the meal, the owner parted the curtain and stood before them. "Everything taste all right?"

"Very tasty, very tasty." Chan Sam reached into his trouser pocket and made an elaborate gesture of reaching for money.

"No, no, put your money away." The owner slid onto the bench across from May-ying and poured a cup of tea for himself.

Then Chan Sam told her: "*Ah* May-ying, this gentleman is your new boss."

# CHAPTER THREE

WHEN THE OWNER took his leave of them, Chan Sam told May-ying that she was under contract to the Pekin tea house until she'd worked off what it cost to bring her to Canada. It would take her almost two years.

"Whatever have I done in my previous lives to deserve this?" May-ying thought to herself. She said nothing, but her bright eyes dimmed with resentment, which Chan Sam mistook for confusion. He put on his fedora.

"It is not that difficult," he said, "to bring to the table what the customers order."

In an earlier time, it had been government contractors seeking men to lay rail who had procured labor from China. Now the owners of the five or six tea houses in Vancouver's Chinatown, like tea house owners in most other Chinatowns, relied almost solely on agents to recruit—some said kidnap—girls and women from China to work as waitresses. They were forbidden by a Vancouver city bylaw to hire white women, and at the same time, they could find virtually no local Chinese help. Certainly no merchant would allow his wife or daughter to be a *kay-toi-neu*. To the

Chinese way of thinking, a "stand-at-table girl" was considered to be almost one and the same as a prostitute, someone who wooed men to spend money. When exclusion turned the labor shortage into a crisis, the owner of the Pekin could easily see that he and a poor man dreaming of a concubine could make a deal to their mutual benefit. He came to Chan Sam's aid.

May-ying worked six, sometimes seven days a week. Her small, narrow figure could be seen moving purposefully between her lodgings at Chan Sam's shop at one end of Pender Street and the Pekin at the other end. She worked a nine-hour split shift, sometime between one in the afternoon and three in the morning, or later. By day, she passed scores of bachelor men sitting outside on the sidewalk. To pass idle time, they would drag out an empty orange crate, turn it upside-down and watch the comings and goings on Pender. When May-ying came into sight, they stood up. "*Ah* May-ying!" several would holler, gesturing and watching until she disappeared from view. They took such liberty because, out alone, she was considered "loose," a woman for whom the usual propriety was unnecessary, not unlike the solitary white women who lingered near Chinatown, working as prostitutes and trolling for Chinese customers. Because of that, a wife or daughter of a merchant would never venture out of her home unaccompanied without the family's designated "Uncle"—a family friend—by her side. The bachelor men never spoke to these women directly; they only nudged each other, naming who was passing by.

There wasn't a female in Chinatown who wasn't known. The most familiar faces were those of the four or five waitresses employed by each of the tea houses that lined the upper floors of buildings along Pender. The bachelors had nicknames for them all: there was Fire-Engine Mah, Soft-Cooked-Bean Fong and Three-Thumbs Yee. Back in Canton, tea houses were the traditional male refuge, a gathering place for men to wander into on their own and it was the same in Chinatowns abroad. Customers at the tea houses took from the bite-sized *dim sum* choices their first food of the day, sometime after noon, perhaps over a newspaper, and their last, the late *sew-yeh*, the traditional sociable light meal taken around midnight, in the company of other patrons, who came streaming in after an evening at the gambling dens.

As much as the food, the men were drawn by the waitresses, who were a tonic for the loneliness of their lives. They were invariably young and pretty. The more glamorous its waitresses, the better a tea house could withstand competition. The waitreses themselves competed for customers and tips. They painted their faces and perfumed themselves, walked about in high heels and hats. They dressed in the *cheong sam,* dress normally saved for special occasions, like a clan banquet or a portrait sitting.

May-ying enjoyed the vanity of carefully applying the white powder on her face, of staining her lips red, of dabbing flower-dew water behind her ears. She enjoyed shopping, especially for purses and for shoes; clerks who fitted her size three feet marveled at how small and dainty they were. Her diminutive size and beauty were her trademarks, which drew customers to the tea house like moths to a flame. However, her job required much more talent than Chan Sam had suggested. Bringing food to the table was indeed not difficult; the real art of the tea house waitress was her ability to entertain with witty conversation. Once the food was brought, the patrons expected their favorite waitress to join them. "Sit down! Sit down!" they urged. "Have a drink," they said, pouring the scotch whiskey they had brought with them. "Have another, don't be modest," they would insist.

In Canton, where the tea house was as much brothel as salon, when the dining was over, a waitress might disappear with a man behind a brocade curtain in the back. In Vancouver's Chinatown, if one disappeared with a customer, it was only after hours. May-ying soon grasped the art of entertaining her customers on shift. Her girlish laughter chased her wit, and her love of repartee was genuine. She was restrained about the invitation to drink with the patrons, tasting but hardly swallowing—even small amounts of whiskey had a strong effect on her small body.

With Chan Sam minding the shop just blocks away, May-ying ignored the customers' flirtatious advances at the end of her shift. Other waitresses who did not were the single ones or those whose husbands were out of town, either at mills or canneries up the coast during weekdays or on the farms until winter. These waitresses often circulated after hours. They joined a game of mahjongg, went to the gambling dens, went to men's rooms or brought men to their own. Such socializing was as much for the company as to keep their tables full at the tea house.

However morally strict Chan Sam or May-ying were, the rest of Chinatown would judge her as no better than her own people, the circle of tea house waitresses. As young girls, these women might have imagined an ordered Confucian society of house and household, of having to test their compatibility with only the likes of a mother-in-law. But all that was dashed when they were brought to North America solely for the profit of their work. There were recruits younger than May-ying; Shortie Lan had passed her thirteenth birthday aboard ship. The reality of their new lives came home to them in the confession and gossip within their circle. There was talk of rebellion against their husbands or the men who had brought them there, of running away. Some brought word of other waitresses once on the tea house circuit who had left one man for another. Pregnancies were common, mostly unwanted ones. Some waitresses had a string of children by different men; most boarded out some if not all of their children.

There were the days when waitresses came to work with especially heavy powder on their faces. When washed off to be freshly reapplied, it revealed the bruises of their men's anger against them. No matter that a waitress didn't like the work or the life that came with it, the men to whom they belonged liked the money too much. A waitress received a monthly advance of about twenty-five dollars a week. A male laborer's wage was by comparison no more than fifteen dollars a week, often as low as eight. On the first of every month at the tea houses, some men showed up themselves to collect their waitresses' pay, not trusting them to hand it over. They left the waitresses their tips, which was often all they had to support their children.

The young May-ying was tossed between the contradictions of her life as a lowly waitress and her wish to do honor as a wife. Her frustrations were not something she and Chan Sam discussed. A new husband's few words to his wife did not go beyond whatever was necessary to keep the woman in her place. A wife did not ask questions of a husband when obedience was always the answer. However May-ying felt about her lot, she was bound to the Confucian sense of social order that had crossed the Pacific with her. It struck into women the fear of divorce, of being "outed" from a man's household. A divorced woman disappeared into social oblivion, both in her earthly life and her afterlife.

May-ying knew no other way but to dutifully work out her contract to the Pekin. The owner held enough of her wages to recoup the money he had paid in Chan Sam's name to bring his concubine to Canada. May-ying's tips were hers; she gave them to Chan Sam. She had only two personal necessities, money to spend at the herbalist and money to make offerings to the resident effigy god at the temple. In China, she had observed the traveling herbalists as they squatted over their sheets of red paper, demonstrating old and new remedies made from thirteen essential herbs: what to use if one's legs were numb, if one couldn't raise an arm, if one had phlegm, if one was old and coughed at night, if one's back and head ached, if one had bad nerves, if one had to strain to urinate, if one had just had a baby, and so on. In Chinatown, May-ying's intuitive understanding of herbal medicine astounded even the dispensing herbalists, who themselves had accumulated their expertise from years of study, reading and practice.

She was just as religious in her appeals to the world of the supernatural to take care of her in this world and the next. Most Chinese abroad were lapsed believers, but May-ying regularly sought and took guidance from the gods and goddesses. She honored them by worshiping at the makeshift temple in the living room of a dingy house at the edge of Chinatown, near the Vancouver Gas Works. There, she lit incense and made offerings of fruit and biscuits. Chan Sam tolerated this preoccupation of May-ying's, but he himself was a strict follower of Confucius, who said that one should revere the gods, spirits and ghosts of the supernatural but also keep them distant. He too sought guidance for his own conduct, reciting to himself what he had learned as a schoolboy from the *Confucian Analects* and the *Book of the Golden Mean,* classics which were supposed to reveal their deeper meaning as one went through life.

Chan Sam remained singleminded about his purpose in Canada, and he began to realize that his decision to take a concubine had also been a good investment. He husbanded the income from May-ying's tips and from his shop to meet the expenses of the household in Canada and remit money to offset the expenses at home. He saved what was left. In China, his At-home Wife, Huangbo, tended a small plot of rice, kept the floors swept and fed the pig her scraps from the table. Having buried the infant daughter of Chan Sam and herself, and having married off the daughter of Chan Sam's first wife, she had her own gaze fixed only on the day her husband would return for a visit. Only then, she believed, would she have a chance to fulfil her duty of bringing forth the next generation, and, more importantly, the male heir.

"What I am doing is the so-called 'making a mountain by accumulating the sand,'" Chan Sam liked to say to May-ying. She did not question the necessity of remitting money to China to keep the household that she would one day join. But the decision to do so was not hers; everything accumulated since marriage was the husband's, including May-ying's income, however hard-earned. All that she as a wife owned was her personal clothing and the jewelry she brought to the marriage. Like Chan Sam, she held their life in Canada as temporary, and so she accepted its sparseness. In the cycle of her life and her afterlife, she expected to be repaid for her wifely sacrifices by being looked after in her own old age by the sons of the household and, in death, by having her tomb swept and her ancestral spirit worshiped.

⟡⟡⟡⟡

Had he been at home in the village with two wives, Chan Sam would have been the envy of every man; there was not another man in Chang Gar Bin with such a household. But here in Chinatown, he couldn't repress a nagging feeling that he was a man wronged. He did not like having to share the company of his concubine with the regular customers of the Pekin tea house. He did not frequent such places, his self-imposed penury denied him a meal out. Only on her day off did they take a meal together. The other days May-ying took her meals at the Pekin. Every Chinese establishment provided its employees two meals a day; even grocery stores and poultry shops had a cook out back for that purpose.

Chan Sam kept to his bachelor's routine of old. When business at the shop got slow, especially during the week, when most single men were working out of town, he would wander across the street to the Kuomintang building, the Canadian political headquarters of the Chinese Nationalist League. He hoped to find among the men milling about his own people, men from his county. Though compared to a big-time merchant he was a nobody, among his own people he was respected for having a storefront in Chinatown and for knowing how to read and write Chinese. They liked to talk about another of their own kind—Sun Yat-sen, the Kuomintang's founder, who was from their home county. They talked about the troubles at home and about Sun's dream of bringing modern government to China. When he died of cancer in 1925, they felt as if they'd lost a member of their own family. In his honor, the home county was renamed Chung-san, after Sun's familiar name.

If Chan Sam wasn't at the Kuomintang building, he could usually be found a block away on Main Street, at the house where his clan society met. When he signed up in 1919, he was the 1,091st clan member to do so. A new four-story building, largely financed by members' donations, was going up on Pender. When completed in 1926, it would be the tallest building in Chinatown, the cornice on its facade reaching higher than that of any other clan building. The clan was proud, if not large.

Chan Sam used to go to the *Chinese Times* building to read that day's edition taped to its windows. But the newspaper office was across the street from the Pekin. He avoided that corner because of his discomfort at the sight of the men coming and going from the tea house, knowing that one reason they went was that May-ying was working there.

As the debt for May-ying receded, Chan Sam contemplated his next move. He must have been tempted to keep May-ying waitressing, as exclusion had intensified the competition for waitresses. The moment the door shut on Chinese immigration, any single girl or woman in Chinatown was getting marriage proposals from both men and boys. As many left the profession, wages were bid up to the dizzying height of thirty-eight dollars a week, and any tea house would have hired May-ying on her own terms. But Chan Sam wanted May-ying out as much as she did; he had yet to father a son. She became pregnant with their first child.

Chan Sam decided to open his own family-run business. He bought out his partners. He put a display of his best-selling dry goods and confectioneries in the window. In front of the partition dividing the shop from their living quarters, he put four tables, with four stools around each. He lined up chairs along the wall. He set up a concession, with some tobacco and cigarettes, melon seeds and candies, oranges, Chinese patent medicines and favorite brews, some glasses for tea. A kettle sat on the potbellied stove in the middle of the room. Then he put word out that he was ready to host rounds of mah-jongg.

The clack of mah-jongg tiles was constant in Chinatown. Most everybody knew and played the game. Parlors like Chan Sam's were not for the likes of merchants and their families. They played in the privacy of their homes, which were big enough to entertain a foursome. Their womenfolk squeezed in games between chores, between hanging the mustard greens out to dry or stirring the tubs of salted fish. Evenings were spent playing and eating; whoever didn't play cooked. Friends brought their children, babies were nursed at the tables. It was the loners, mostly bachelor men looking to join a foursome, who went to the mah-jongg parlors. One of the more popular places in Chinatown was the White Lamb, a bookstore with tables for mah-jongg out back and on the "cheater" floor, a floor installed between the ground and second floors to give extra space while avoiding paying the city its extra taxes. Another was Sing Kee Confectionery, which had tables in the back. The back room was known simply as

"Grandfather Eng's," after its host. Both hosts—at the White Lamb and at Sing Kee—were among Chinatown's best players.

The owners of the parlors did not share in the winnings but took a nominal fee upon each completed round, when the play that began with the easterly wind came back to where it had started. Depending on the players' generosity, the mah-jongg parlor usually got something extra. The players would decide the maximum win on each game. A dollar or two kept it interesting enough; if anybody wanted to gamble bigger sums they could play the game at one of the gambling dens, where there was always at least one table going.

The piddling sums won and lost at the mah-jongg parlors didn't concern the city's vice squad. They were more interested in the gambling dens, where whole weekly paychecks and more were regularly won and lost at the big games of *fan tan* and dominoes. The Chinese did their best to disguise their locations, moving them from one apparently vacant rental space to another, or else running them out of basement rooms, accessed from the street by a series of locked doors. Mah-jongg parlors in contrast were both a shop and a social club.

❧

On a late summer's day in 1926, a Chinese midwife was called to the back of Chan Sam's mah-jongg parlor. She delivered a baby girl into May-ying's arms. Her father gave her the name Ping, in remembrance of his deceased first wife.

On the day of the Full Month, when it was safe to assume the baby would live, May-ying's waitress friends came to offer gifts of money inside red envelopes. They were served hard-boiled eggs that had been tinted red, as well as a broth of pigs' feet boiled in rice vinegar and ginger and another of chicken with dried fungus. The broths, which were supposed to get rid of any blood clots and strengthen the bones of the new mother, were the traditional food offering on the Full Month. "Next time a son, May-ying," some had said when they left. Admittedly, May-ying was disappointed that the firstborn was not a son. But a girl, one strong enough to survive her first month, was at least proof of her fecundity, and reason enough, she thought, to mark the occasion with a formal photograph. The young mother took the babe in her arms and walked down Pender to Yucho Chow's, one of two photographers in Chinatown.

Mother and baby looked the picture of innocence and light, the babe-in-arms in a pale bonnet and long matching dress threaded with satin ribbons and trimmed in lace, the mother in a flowing silk, cut in a Chinese style. The photographer had chosen a plain setting: the mother on a simple armchair beside a table on which sat a bamboo basket, a single silk chrysanthemum tied round its handle. Had it been a boy, he would have chosen more elaborate props. Yucho Chow's photographs came in a popular postcard size, imprinted on the back with space for correspondence and a stamp, with "Made in Canada" in fine print across the bottom. May-ying put one in a cardboard frame, which she stuck underneath the frame of a small mirror on the wall at the back of the mah-jongg parlour. Chan Sam did not order one to send to his At-home Wife.

Ping was a happy and lively child who was quick to laugh, a characteristic of her mother's. Chan Sam was the more lenient parent. He could not even bring himself to raise his voice to his child. If at mealtime the child asked for her favorite—McCormick's salted Jersey Cream soda crackers floating in hot boiled water with a spoonful of Eagle Brand sweetened condensed milk—it pleased him to oblige her. May-ying herself indulged her daughter in her own image. She made sure Ping was well presented; the two of them sometimes looked as fashionable as the brunette mother and daughter mannequins in the display windows of Woodward's Department Store just north of Chinatown. On strolls through Chinatown, the child delighted men sitting outside with stern pronouncements of "Dirty!" pointing to where the refuse of sidewalk commerce—vegetable trimmings, chicken feathers, broken crabs' legs—had been washed short of the gutter. She was her parents' pride, and for May-ying, Ping was proof that it was untrue what people said and liked to think, that waitresses made unsuitable mothers.

Within a little more than a year, a second child was on the way. May-ying hoped it was a boy. She beseeched the temple gods to bestow such good fortune on her. A son would confirm her usefulness to the family in the eyes of Chan Sam and the At-home Wife. Huangbo, as the first wife, would also be considered the *Dai-ma,* the first mother. Any children in the household, including all those born to the concubine, were hers, as if she had given birth herself.

All the wives of a household would breathe a sigh of relief when the first son was born. The absence of a male heir would break the family lineage, would leave no one to look after the parents in their old age or to worship them after death. Their spirits and those of all the family's ancestors would be under a curse, at risk of turning into ghosts, condemned to wander the supernatural world as beggers until they eventually faded away. The moment a son was born, the family could rest easier that tragedy had been averted.

In 1928, the concubine failed, as she herself believed, to deliver her worth for the second time. The sister for Ping was named Nan. Nan was a calm and quiet baby, and her arrival on the scene was uneventful. This time, there was no trip to Yucho Chow's on Main Street.

❦

Chan Sam was an ordinary mah-jongg player at best, but one of his ideas was to get May-ying to get the patrons coming in and staying long enough to fill the till. It worked.

When presented with the new challenge of learning mah-jongg, May-ying excelled. With her quick mind, she was able to sense the odds of waiting for a tile, of knowing when to change her hand, or, in the parlance of the game, knowing what to hold to "eat." "For May-ying, the tiles are transparent," players who tried to outwit her would say. Chan Sam did not have the temperament for the game. He either could not or refused to see the futility of the hands he kept, and consequently he suffered heavy losses. And he did not see that stopping the game, saying he was having no luck, was poor sportsmanship.

May-ying was also the better host. From the gamblers who frequented the Pekin, she knew the best players and how to make up the foursomes. The patrons trusted her to keep the tables honest and to mediate disputed wins and losses. She was also better at conversation with customers between rounds and with customers who weren't playing. It got so that Chan Sam, rarely called upon to be a fourth, was left to the books and to minding the girls, who usually played or napped nearby.

Feeling left out, he occasionally positioned his stool between two players' shoulders, an acceptable vantage as long as the observer kept silent about play in progress.

However, Chan Sam often clumsily imposed his welcome. He'd say something like, "What a good hand you have!" to a player. Murmurings of reprimand around the table would silence him for a few games. He invariably blundered again. He'd address another player: "At last, you've got your tile, the one you wanted!"

In that instance, it was not that player's choice to pick up the tile that had been discarded. As usual, it was May-ying who had to move quickly to appease the irate customers at that and every table in the parlour. She would often call out to Chan Sam from across the room, "Don't open your mouth! The players don't like it; they have to concentrate."

Chan Sam did not see himself in the wrong. "I'm not telling anybody what tiles are in their hand," he protested. He cut May-ying short. "*Gum gee!*" he yelled, pointing his finger at her and proclaiming what came out of her mouth to be nonsense.

The scene was repeated, again and again. May-ying's temper flared, and he brought an end to their exchange by reverting to his village slang. Still, instead of biting her tongue, May-ying found she couldn't help but protest his stubbornness, in business and at home. As for the business, either Chan Sam had to stay away or the customers would. Eventually, Chan Sam had trouble meeting the rent.

<hr />

The most recent reply from Chan Sam's wife at first appeared no different than previous letters. Written in the schoolmaster's hand because Huangbo herself could not read or write, it began as usual. Addressed "My beloved husband," it informed him of having received his latest remittance and, as usual, enclosed a receipt. Chan Sam had already received two receipts, one from the banking institution in Hong Kong to which he had sent his draft, and another from the broker in the market town of Shekki, which served several satellite villages including Chang Gar Bin. A courier had carried the draft from Hong Kong to Shekki. Every time the broker there received a draft, which was about every two months, he would travel twice the sixty li (about twenty miles) to Chang Gar Bin and back, first to get Huangbo's signature on the promissory bank draft, and then to return from the money-changing shop, where he had exchanged the draft for copper cash strung on a hemp cord.

Whenever Chan Sam wrote to his wife, he had but one thought in mind: to bridge the distance between himself and the village. He asked after her and his kinfolk, about the house, about the security of the village. Had the bandits been kept away? How much grain did she have in reserve? Was water draining from the dirt floor? Had the termites come back into the house? His queries helped to transport him, in spirit at least, back to the village.

Her letters would append at most a line or two to the receipt she sent back. She'd tell him she was fine, that he shouldn't worry about her, and then pass on news of any births or deaths or marriages in the village.

But this reply was out of the ordinary. "I am happy my husband is not alone," she wrote. There was more: "I am wishing good health to the concubine and the children." Chan Sam was stunned to see the words *chip see* on paper. He had not told Huangbo about the concubine and his Gold Mountain household. He knew he should, but he hadn't known how to couch it. The longer he waited, the harder he found it was to break the news. It might have been different if he could have softened the blow with the announcement of a son. But twice, that had not happened. He had decided to wait until he could also announce his next homecoming.

Someone else had been before him with the truth. Chan Sam faced the realization that Huangbo could do one of two things to save face: either pretend her previous knowledge of the concubine and feign pride that her husband had the stature afforded by two wives; or condemn his betrayal in a statement of suicide. He was terrified she would choose suicide, which would bring shame upon himself and his family.

So in 1928, just months after Nan's birth, Chan Sam strode into the steamship ticket office at the back of a store on Pender, money in hand to pay for third-class passage for himself, May-ying and their two daughters for a sailing from Vancouver to Canton. "I'm not the kind of man who thinks only of making money and does not miss my wife at home," he told himself. As he waited for the agent to book space, he cast his eye over the mail arrayed in the heavy cloth pockets of a bag on the wall. The letters were all from China—some from years ago—sent by relatives hoping someone coming in to buy a ticket might recognize the name of a man who had come to Canada and hadn't been heard from again.

It had been ten years since Chan Sam last bought a passage home; this would be his second trip in fifteen years. Though it was inadvertently Huangbo who was forcing him to wind up his business and to bring his other family home from Gold Mountain, he was at peace with himself, believing that having the family under one roof would put Huangbo at ease. May-ying was happy to take the girls to China, to replace the faraway notion of At-Home Wife and *Dai-ma* with the reality, and to see the house where both women would live out their lives. What Chan Sam wanted most of all to assuage his guilt was for Huangbo to see his face. He believed that she would see that, as a husband, he had been honest and true to her, that his wife came before his concubine.

Chan Sam also felt the pull of China and thought its future had never been brighter. An overlord had finally emerged—the Kuomintang's Generalissimo Chiang Kai-shek. Born in the same year as Chan Sam, Chiang had succeeded to the leadership upon Sun's death, and in two years had accomplished the seemingly impossible. From his military base in the extreme south, he had moved his troops northwards to Peking, toppling rival warlords who were too busy eliminating each other. When he proclaimed himself head of a government of a unified China, Chinese newspapers abroad heralded it as the coming of age of a modern China. It was a sentiment echoed among foreign traders and governments alike.

Still, Chan Sam could admit to a tinge of regret that he was leaving without having found the end of the double rainbow in Gold Mountain. Why couldn't he have had the luck of a man like Yip Sang, the man best known by the Chinese across Canada as the agent for the Canadian Pacific's Blue Funnel Steamships Line? He had come as a teenager and turned his wits from washing dishes to making his fortune on salt herring. His property, Chinatown's first brick building, was actually two buildings, connected by a walkway, with a total of nine floors. His was also a house of many wives. All of his four wives, with twenty-three children among them—nineteen of them sons—were installed in separate apartments on separate floors. It was so large a household that there was even an in-house newspaper.

If luck should turn against him in China, Chan Sam had one last chance to chase the Gold Mountain dream that Yip Sang had found; his certificate of return was good for an absence of up to two years.

From the steamship office, Chan Sam went to make final arrangements with the shipping company that was to take delivery of the goods he'd purchased, crate them for shipment and deliver them to the pier, to be put on the same sailing as his family. Chan Sam had spent days assembling the goods to bring home. He had combed the second-hand stores on Main Street for household goods and gone to the public market at the end of Market Alley, where there were good buys to be had on everything from cast-iron pots to garden tools. He had also gone to the white department stores, and gone from floor to floor, including the basement food floor in Woodward's, to choose some indulgences that might help Huangbo better accept the concubine. He remembered the old lady's words: "Come home in brocade." Anything less would lose face, not just for himself, the family, and his neighbors, but for his entire village. "Bring so much," he joked with the man at the shipping company, "as to reach the roof of the cart and make the ox carrying it sweat."

In the dirt courtyard outside her house, Huangbo sat on a footstool facing the gate, fanning herself against the tropical heat and humidity of south China. For the last three days, from early morning to dusk, she had sat there, waiting both patiently and anxiously for her husband to walk through his gate. She had hardly closed her eyes in sleep since the day the schoolmaster read her the letter from Chan Sam with the news he and his concubine and children were coming home. Along with his homecoming, the news that he was returning with savings enough to buy some land became the talk of the village.

The house had been swept of any lingering evil spirits and was ready to receive him. Huangbo had replaced the old faded strips of red paper hanging from the front door frame with new ones. Across the top was written "The officials in heaven bless us all." The banner down one side said "Five kinds of fortune and luck come into this family." Down the other, she had replaced the saying "Dragon and phoenix are in good health and good term" with "Flowers of the same stalk love and care for and share with each other." As a further gesture to her husband of her acceptance of the concubine, she had arranged for a girl in the village to pour tea at the homecoming. Tradition held that the concubine, being beneath Huangbo in rank, should pour tea for the first wife as one of her first acts of respect. But Huangbo wanted her returning husband to see that she accepted the concubine's admittance into the household as a done deed.

For Chan Sam's Canadian family, the almost three-week journey, by steamship to Canton, ferry to Shekki, then by hired motorcar to his village, took them back to a world far removed from Canada. From Shekki, there was no paved road, only the rutted cart path through the rice fields, eventually skirting the steep, scrub-covered hills, pock-marked with shacks and hovels, and finally narrowing into a footpath leading to the windowless adobe walls of the backs of houses, the village of Chang Gar Bin. The coughing putt-putt sound brought villagers running; few had seen a motorized vehicle before. The cry "Chan Sam has arrived home!" shook the village.

Inspiring as much curiosity as the car, atop which goods and baggage were tied, was the sight of the family emerging in western dress. May-ying was immediately dubbed "*Faan-gwei-po.*" With her pale skin, her dress and shoes, she seemed more a "foreign lady" than Chinese. All eyes turned to the contraption being unloaded—another vehicle on four wheels, into which the two children were put. Women and girls in the crowd, seeing the foreign lady's children bouncing in the comfort of this overseas pram, suddenly felt the weight of the babies and children on their backs, tied there with a knotted length of rags. Eventually all eyes came to settle on Chan Sam. His face was shaded by a fedora, but there was no mistaking his tall figure or his village dialect as he greeted his kinfolk.

Chan Sam led his overseas family through the village square. The old banyan tree there offered the first shade. At the watch-tower, he left the main path, turning down another, at the end of which was his house. A procession of villagers followed, some carrying the family's baggage; others collected as he went. They were bursting with pride. "Chan Sam has the Gold Mountain walk," they said to each other.

Upon the sight of her husband, the woman in the courtyard came to life.

"*Ah* Huangbo," he greeted her, touching her outstretched arm. "So many years, so many years, but the heart is the same."

She wiped tears from her eyes. Her soft voice was barely audible. "*Ah* Chan Sam. I am content now. Just to see your face makes me happy."

Huangbo turned to the small woman who'd come in the gate behind him. The two women could not have looked more different. One was tall, the other tiny; one had skin darkened and wrinkled by the sun, the other's was like pale silk. One was dull in her cotton tunic and pants—once black but faded from the sun and years of washing to the same color as the gray adobe bricks of the house behind her—and plain-looking with her hair combed back and pinned behind her ears. The other, in her flared dress, nipped in at the waist, her hair bedecked with a satin ribbon, was a splash of color and style. "*Ah Dai-po*," said the concubine, receiving a nod from the Number-One Wife in return. She pushed her eldest daughter forward to her Number-One Mother: "Greet your *Dai-ma*."

Inside the cool house, Huangbo introduced May-ying to the most venerated members of the family. She led her before two large paintings of figures clothed in robes and seated in chairs. They were Chan Sam's father and mother. Beneath the paintings was a small worship table. May-ying knew what was expected. She clasped her hands and bowed three times before each portrait. She took the offering *Dai-po* had waiting and placed on the altar a pair of chopsticks, three cups of tea, a bowl of persimmons and five rice cakes—the mother's favorite during her earthly existence. Lastly, she lit the three sticks of incense. Only then did husband, wife and concubine sit down to take tea.

On the following day, one porter after another came from Shekki pulling cartloads of crates piled high. Villagers who came to pay their respects and join in the revelry of the homecoming had to negotiate their way around the crates, some still unpacked, that spilled onto the courtyard. The small house—the one room with a partition separating front from back and the other room with the basin and hearth—already bulged with foreign riches.

"What a good husband and father Chan Sam is," the villagers said.

They admired the foreign-made furniture. There were three large wall mirrors and two dressers—a tall one, and a commode dresser with drawers on either side and a three-way mirror in-between. A stool went with it. Of particular fascination was a metal crib, for no villager could believe the luxury of furniture for children. Chan Sam engaged a local carpenter to fit a board between the crib's high rounded ends, to turn it into a bunk bed for his two daughters. The girls each had with them their down comforters, made in Canada.

Chan Sam had a love of clocks. Though hardly necessary to a peasant's life, to him they were the important symbol of a gentleman. He brought home several, including a large mahogany Regulator wall clock, and two smaller ones of jade and gold. He brought wool blankets that were the trademark of the Hudson's Bay Company in Canada, the country's oldest store.

The villagers were invited to sample the family's favorite overseas foods. There were crates of sweetened condensed milk, crackers and raisins—all Ping's favorites—Horlick's malted milk and some unlabeled tins, which were canned salmon bought from the back door of a cannery in Canada. Chan Sam went on a round of visits through the village to pay his respects, leaving behind tins of biscuits and candies, the standard show of generosity. For Huangbo, Chan Sam had a special personal gift. It was a tin whistle, the kind with a clear, piercing toot, with a silk cord so it could be hung round her neck. She knew the sentiment it carried, that he was there at her calling.

The villagers had already scouted out for Chan Sam what parcels of land were available to buy. Despite the weakness of the world economy turning the Chinese exchange rate in his favor, he was not able to buy as much land as he had hoped. Land-buying by the rush of sojourners returning for good had bid up prices for what little was available. He bought twenty-eight *mau tin*, the average-sized family farm in south China. They were three separate plots, two each of ten *mau* and a third of eight *mau*, one near the school, a second against the side of the hills and a third outside the village near a temple. Many family holdings were fragmented into even smaller plots and often more widely dispersed. For the time being, Chan Sam needed two of those plots to sustain his family. Until there were more mouths to feed or ill fortune struck, he could afford to rent out the third to a tenant farmer.

In Chinese, home and family are one and the same word. The character is a pig under a roof, a symbol of contentment. For Chan Sam's family, however, things didn't go quite right.

For Huangbo, neither her position as *Dai-po* nor the eight years she had on May-ying were any guarantee of authority. Her gentleness was ripe for taking advantage, and she was no match for May-ying, who found her easier to outwit than obey. The two began quarreling, and invariably Huangbo would end up crying. When Chan Sam came home from working the fields and asked Huangbo why she was sobbing, she said the concubine was "cranky." When he confronted May-ying, she almost boasted that she could make *Dai-po* cry. He pleaded with the two of them to live in harmony, but it did no good.

Chan Sam eased the situation at home by enrolling May-ying in the local primary school. She was one of the few females. Most villagers believed schooling was for boys, not girls. But Chan Sam also saw a chance to put in practice the progressive views of the Kuomintang's new government. Besides, the school was conveniently located. In his youth, the closest school had been several villages over. The one built in the village in 1915 was Chang Gar Bin's first modern building, with a four-columned rotunda, from which flew the sun of the Kuomintang's flag.

Huangbo minded the children, but she still expected May-ying to help with most of the household chores—most concubines were expected to do all the work of the household. May-ying did what she thought was her share, less than one-half.

"Don't be so unreasonable," Chan Sam pleaded with her.

"Going to school is hard work!" May-ying retorted. "You tell *Dai-po* to go to school, and I'll stay home and bring water from the well, feed the pig and go look for rice worms under the stalks." The thought was ludicrous. *Dai-po* had broad and strong shoulders, but not the mind for learning to read and write.

"May-ying is just so stubborn," Chan Sam would say.

There was only one issue on which the two women stood united. Chan Sam, thinking he'd found a way to keep the household happy and garner more prestige for himself, came home one day and said he was thinking of taking a second concubine. May-ying, he said, was gone to school each day. What help was there for Huangbo? "I have two daughters," he said. "I should have one wife each at home to look after them." To his surprise, Huangbo and May-ying cried on each other's shoulders. He hastily backed down. Neither wanted another, younger girl to vie for his attention. Nor did they want competition for the honor of producing the first son and heir. It held greater significance for May-ying as the concubine than for Huangbo, for Huangbo would still have the satisfaction of being addressed as the mother. Besides, Huangbo, at twenty-nine, was getting on in her childbearing years, while May-ying, at twenty-one, was still ripe.

Huangbo retained one wifely dignity. She slept in the privacy of the back of the house, and usually in the company of Chan Sam. The concubine slept forward of the partition, in the front room, which was crowded with furniture, there being no other place to store the overseas dressers and no wall space big enough to hang the large mirrors. The children's crib was shifted to the back only if Chan Sam wanted to lie with his concubine. Within months, the household was expecting.

May-ying continued to go to school, pregnant. Her routine was changed only in the different seeds and roots, bark and flowers she bought from traveling herbalists to nurture her pregnancy and which she herself often peeled, scrubbed or roasted, and then boiled for hours to take in a soup. At the temple, where followers came day or night, she faithfully paid her respects and left offerings to appeal to the gods for a boy.

A few months into her pregnancy, she took it upon herself to consult a soothsayer a couple of villages over from Chang Gar Bin. "Blind as I am, I see the world better than you do. When you are lost, let me tell you where to go," proclaimed the characters surrounding the white-bearded immortal painted on his box. The blind man spoke at length. From time to time, May-ying nodded her head. At last, he took his shaker of sticks, shook one loose, fingered the character. He told her what she had hoped to hear: "You are carrying a son."

In the eighth month of her pregnancy, May-ying went to Chan Sam. She had made up her mind. She wanted the family's first son born where her daughters had been born: in Canada, not in China. She also argued that a son born with a Canadian birth certificate would always have the choice of living abroad.

Chan Sam, though dismayed at a soothsayer's superstitions meddling in his life, was torn. May-ying was right, but at the same time, a son's filial duty was at home, to the first mother. And yet, a tradition of going abroad had been established for two generations; a third might be needed to secure the family's fortunes at home.

Huangbo meekly protested the risks to the pregnancy of the long sea voyage. In truth, she herself did not want to be twice denied—a son and a husband. In the end, only the pregnant May-ying and Chan Sam were to go; the daughters Ping and Nan would be left behind in the care of *Dai-ma*. The decision to leave them behind was made in the interests of their schooling. Ping was now of school age. Educating children in the homeland, for the first years of schooling at least, had been the accepted thing to do among families sojourning abroad. Parents feared that filling children's heads with a white society's curriculum and a foreigner's language first might turn them against going back to China.

On a spring day in 1930, Chan Sam said goodbye to Huangbo. He promised to do his best in this next sojourn abroad to finance an early homecoming. In her goodbye with Ping, May-ying left her a sepia-toned photograph of the child in her mother's arms, showing her where it was imprinted "Made in Canada." Promising one day to return, she told her to be obedient and to look after Younger Sister.

Only Huangbo, a child in each hand, had tears at the farewell. The waiting motorcar's engine coughed against the dust and heat. The villagers shook their heads at the sight of the pregnant "foreign lady" leaving home, to ride the waves and the threat of miscarriage. Few believed the baby would survive.

Three days after the boat docked in Vancouver, a healthy baby was delivered on the second floor of a tenement building on Market Alley in Chinatown.

# CHAPTER FOUR

THE BUILDING AT number 79 was midway down the two block-long Market Alley. Tucked in behind a taller building on Pender Street, the flat-roofed tenement stood across from the back of the Empire Hotel. The hotel's garbage cans were popular with vagrants from skid row.

May-ying and Chan Sam were back to the living conditions they had known when May-ying first arrived in Canada: a rather squalid rooming house, where the kitchen and bathroom were communal facilities. Though they at least had an outside room on the second floor with a window that overlooked Market Alley, the alleyway itself was dark, dank and unfriendly. There was the odd Chinese tenement or shop, but only where there was space behind the backs of existing buildings, and where the white owners would let the Chinese build. Owners on the north side of the alley were determined to keep Chinatown from expanding in that direction.

It was in that rooming house on the first day of spring in 1930 that May-ying gave birth. The midwife announced it was a girl. So great was May-ying's disappointment that she could hardly bring herself to look at the useless girl child. She wondered what she had done to anger the gods. She had made the long journey from China, endured the rough passage at sea and, for the third time in her life, had been denied the joy of looking at a son.

On the day of the customary Full Month celebration, several of her women friends from her waitressing days came by. May-ying talked about the birth of the third daughter, who was named Hing. "The labor was so bad, as the baby was coming out, I wanted to give her one push with my foot," she said. "I didn't care if she died."

Just when everyone was saying their goodbyes and heading down the staircase to the outside alleyway, there was a gasp and commotion as the infant suddenly fell from her mother's grasp and tumbled and rolled halfway down the stairs. Years later, one of the women, Lee Yen, told Hing, "Your mother dropped you." She arched her penciled-in eyebrows and added, "You weren't hurt, but you could have been killed." At the time, the woman, along with everybody else who was there, said it was just an accident.

⁘

Chan Sam's decision to abide by May-ying's desire to return to Canada looked like a mistake. Having wound up his life there once before, and having invested virtually all his savings in land in China, he had no collateral in Canada to either take out a loan to buy back the old lease on his mah-jongg storefront or to reestablish himself in any other business.

He tried his connections at various sawmills to once again get work bundling shingles, the dangerous but better-paying job for the Chinese, but his connections were themselves out of work. Not one of the mills on the tidal flats of the Fraser River where he once worked was in operation. Their saws had been silenced the year before. There was no saying when they might start up again, for by 1930, the Depression was upon the land. The Chinese sank like stones to the bottom of the labor pool; eight out of ten of the thirteen thousand residents of Vancouver's Chinatown would be unemployed before the year was out. Owners of mills, mines and canneries that did manage to stay in operation did what the politicians preached—put white men, Canadian fathers living here with their families, ahead of Chinese men, bachelors who sent money out of the country to families abroad.

Chan Sam watched the sidewalks of Chinatown fill with unemployed men like himself. For a short while, the Chinese Benevolent Association set up a bureau to place Chinese in the few white-owned businesses that dared risk the harassment from hiring non-whites. Chan Sam could offer them nothing; he had no command of English and no skills.

As the weeks of unemployment turned into months, the relationship between Chan Sam and May-ying chilled. Without the foil of Huangbo's presence, it became a cold silence interrupted only by recrimination. He reminded May-ying how her insistence on returning to Canada had divided the family. He felt badly about leaving Huangbo, whose manner and subservience he preferred. Though an apology was expected, May-ying had none, for she pitied her own situation. She was the less-favored wife and the mother of two absent daughters, with the bad fortune to have had a third. Wondering again what the gods were asking her to atone for, she clung ever more stubbornly to her worship of them.

Chan Sam was plagued with regret about being in the wrong country at the wrong time. The Depression hung over most of the world, but at home, the Pearl River delta area was going through a brief but relatively prosperous boom. The *yuan,* China's main currency, was based on silver, and when silver prices plummeted in the crash of stock markets around the world, the *yuan*'s devaluation had lured overseas Chinese investment to south China. In Chang Gar Bin, some peasants, in their heady economic euphoria, coupled with the hopeful political climate fostered by Chiang Kai-shek's government, were borrowing to buy *mau tin.*

If he'd been desperate, Chan Sam could have borrowed against his *mau tin* or perhaps sold his Gold Mountain extravagances to provide the passage home. But villagers would scoff at the notion that the future abroad was dimmer than theirs in China. And to have money sent from China to Canada would have unraveled

Chan Sam's reputation, built upon years of exile from his homeland, as a provider for his family. A laborer in Canada who had a
job could still earn in a day what a peasant in China could earn in
a month. Though poor in Canada, the laborer was, in the eyes of
his relations at home, wealthy. Chan Sam did not even consider
the possibility of turning around and going back. His pride
demanded that he only show his face again at home when he had
something to be proud of; if not the son predicted by the concubine, then a new abundance of material goods and money from
Gold Mountain.

When the money he had brought to finance his search for
work ran out, Chan Sam borrowed here and there from friends in
Chinatown. But everybody was hurting. When the situation
looked bleak, he suggested to May-ying that she consider selling
her pendant. Anyone who saw it on her always remarked on it.
"See how beautiful the shade of jade is in the light?" May-ying
would ask, proud to show it off. When she would explain that it
had been buried with the dead, people immediately offered to buy
it. "I'll never sell it," she always said. She cursed Chan Sam for
even thinking she could part with it.

The baby Hing was three months old when May-ying left Chan
Sam to mind her as usual while she stepped out. She was off on
her regular errands to buy fresh food for that day's meals, or to
visit the herbalist. When she was gone longer than usual, Chan
Sam grew suspicious. The baby had filled her diapers, and changing them was not a man's work. Annoyed, he wrapped up the
baby and went looking for May-ying. She was nowhere to be
found, and no shopkeeper could say he had seen her. As the hours
passed, Chan Sam came to the realization that May-ying was not
coming back, that she had run away.

He went to Lee Yen, the same woman who'd been at the baby's
Full Month and seen her fall from her mother's arms. Long before
May-ying's time, Lee Yen had been one of the earliest waitresses
at the Pekin tea house. She'd stopped working only when she
married the head cook. But she never turned her back on her

waitressing past, keeping her trademark penciled-in eyebrows and her friendships with the waitressing circle, to which she had become something of a den mother.

Lee Yen was as certain as Chan Sam that May-ying would show up somewhere on the waitressing circuit. Other than Vancouver's Chinatown, there were only two others large enough to support tea houses. Both were on Vancouver Island, less than half a day away by ferry. One was in Victoria, the provincial capital. Its once-dignified Chinatown, which dated from the gold rush days, had been in decline since the turn of the century, when Vancouver became the destination of choice for arriving Chinese. The other was in Nanaimo, a coal-mining town whose frontier Chinatown bustled on weekends when the Chinese miners spilled out of the camps.

On the third day of May-ying's absence, the baby developed a fever. If this had been China, had the baby been a boy, a doctor would have been called, but sickness in a baby girl was allowed to take its course. Chan Sam went to Jang Noong, the one friend that he and May-ying shared. This gentle man with the shape of a baby Buddha was a cook on the coastal tugboats. A regular patron in the days of the mah-jongg parlor, he had adored and spoiled the concubine's two daughters, Ping and Nan. Chan Sam confessed that he was angry at May-ying, but he had to find her because the baby was sick: "May-ying would know what to give *Bebe* for fever," he said.

The idea of running away had been planted in May-ying's mind in the days at the Pekin, in the talk she overheard from other waitresses. It saw the sunlight when she had last confided in Jang Noong. He had lent a sympathetic ear to her ever since the days of the mah-jongg parlor, when May-ying's complaints about her husband's clumsy interference with play would spill over to how difficult it was to live with a man so stubborn.

Days ago, when Jang Noong dropped by to see May-ying and the baby, May-ying talked with bitterness about how her life with Chan Sam abroad was one she'd never wanted. She talked of the Depression and how unhappy both she and her husband were; he could not find work, nor would he consider turning around and going back to China. Jang Noong, knowing the feeling of longing to be home with one's wife in China, had sympathy for Chan Sam, but his heart also warmed to May-ying's lament. Talk turned to Nanaimo's Chinatown, where the Chinese, among the poorest abroad, lived happily with less. He told her its few merchants must be doing well; the owner of the tea house there was building larger premises. He could tell even as he spoke the words that May-ying was already planning to run away.

Jang Noong, thinking May-ying would want to know if her baby was sick, divulged her whereabouts to Chan Sam. "You will have to swallow your pride and go after her," he counseled, hoping he wouldn't be too hard on her.

Chan Sam bundled up the baby and headed for Nanaimo's Chinatown. He had never been there before; he'd had no desire to, his impression being that it was backward, small and boring. From the ferry dock, he walked uphill a mile or so, crossed the railway tracks and continued until he came to Pine Street. A makeshift fence stretched across the street, and in front of a gate was a city sign: "No thoroughfare." The unsightliness of the odds and ends of lumber hammered together to make a fence was improved only by the overgrowth of weeds. He opened the gate and passed through.

Pavement turned to dirt, and as he crested the hill, Chinatown lay before him. Pine Street ran another two hundred or so feet before it ended in a dead end at the edge of a bluff. The street looked like the set of a western movie. It was lined on either side with unpainted one- and two-story wood-frame buildings, some with false fronts, all with overhanging balconies that sagged and careened. The entire scene was bleached by the sun. There were no signs hung out. Stores were identified by what was painted in Chinese characters and sometimes English on the building fronts or on panes of glass in the doors. A lone maple interrupted the plank sidewalk on one side. An old man on a bench painted with the advertising slogan "Players Please," the cigarette known to the Chinese as "Sailor Mark," directed Chan

Sam to Chinatown's tea house.

Chan Sam found May-ying upstairs at the Canton House. When May-ying had appeared in Nanaimo's Chinatown looking for a job at a tea house, wagers were taken among the other staff as to when Chan Sam would appear. There wasn't a woman on the waitressing circuit without a man keeping tabs on her pay.

He couldn't say much, not in public: "*Ah* May-ying, *Bebe* is sick with fever." The public demeanor of both showed no hint of trouble between husband and wife. She took the baby in her arms. She felt her forehead. She examined her tongue. "Poor little thing," she said. She led the way to a staff house beside the Canton. From her purse she took a black, urn-like container, no bigger than a thimble, and counted out four minute grains of Six Saints Medicine. She closed the baby's mouth gently around each and left instructions as to when to administer the next dosage. "I have to get back to work," she said, adding that she'd be back when the tea house closed.

It was almost three in the morning before she reappeared. "Get in here," Chan Sam said. He pulled May-ying through the doorway. She waited for a blow to come, but none did. Instead, he proceeded to lecture her. "For a daughter to grow up without a mother's care is to grow up no better than a worm," he said. He opened his lectures with whatever Chinese proverb he thought applied.

He was talking about Hing, of course. But to May-ying, who still thought of Hing as the son she was deprived of, his words stung her where she felt most vulnerable—in leaving Ping and Nan behind in China. They'd been four and two when she'd said goodbye, younger than she herself had been when her mother parted with her.

Chan Sam saw her crestfallen face. He moderated his tone and tried a gentler approach: "*Ah* May-ying, if you are the one who can find work, then we should consider ourselves lucky. When I can find work, then we will both save for the day we can go home and take it easy again, when we can have the three girls together and be one happy family."

May-ying had expected Chan Sam to talk of a husband wronged; he did not. But uppermost in both their minds was how easy it had been for her to find a job. The three of them, Chan Sam, May-ying and the baby went back to Vancouver. Chan Sam didn't want to live in Nanaimo's Chinatown. There was nobody from his own clan living there. He preferred Vancouver, where he could be closer to his own people, and he was certain one of the tea houses there would hire May-ying.

The China House in Vancouver took her on. But, like every other tea house along Pender, it was struggling to stay in business. As the Depression worsened, it halved the waitresses' wages. The business provided by the meal tickets handed out by the Canadian Benevolent Association to starving Chinese men helped keep its doors open for awhile, but in 1932, the China House could hang on no longer and closed for good. By then, destitute Chinese men, most of them elderly, were begging in the streets, gambling on a helping Chinese hand. The first Chinese deaths from starvation finally forced the provincial government to show some concern. It funded the Anglican Church Mission's soup kitchen in Chinatown, but it expected a Chinese to be fed at half what it cost to feed a white man on relief. Some destitute Chinese said they'd rather starve than accept relief.

Fortunes in China fell even more brutally. The Depression came to China in the winter of 1931-32. The brief boom in the Pearl River delta came to a sudden halt. Squeezed by falling rice prices and rising costs, and having made foolhardy decisions to buy more *mau tin* on credit, many peasants found themselves in debt as never before. Word from Chang Gar Bin was that the misery of the turn of the century, when whole villages fell victim to starvation, had come back. Chan Sam needed no reminder that, despite the difficulties in Canada, nowhere could it be any worse than in China, "the sick man of Asia." To him, the family's duty in Canada was clear: to sacrifice for the family at home. He and May-ying returned to where they could live more cheaply. They went back to Nanaimo, and May-ying went back to working at the Canton.

Nanaimo's Chinatown itself had been reincarnated three times. When landlords raised rents out of reach or put the land up for sale, the Chinese had been uprooted, each time clearing new land further up the hill. In the late 1920s, hundreds of Chinese miners were laid off and several Chinatown merchants went bankrupt. The Chinese land company that owned Chinatown's eleven and a half acres was itself threatened with bankruptcy. The remaining merchants set up a non-profit company and appealed to Chinese across Canada to buy shares so that they could buy out the land company and save their Chinatown from extinction. In 1929, after enough Chinese had dug into their pockets, Nanaimo's Chinatown was back in business.

If the rents the Chinese charged themselves were dirt-cheap— less than a third of rents in Vancouver and as little as five dollars for a small house—so were services basic. There was no money for improvements. Some of the town's population of three to four hundred that huddled around the stretch of Pine Street that was Chinatown still had to use outdoor privies; the only indoor plumbing was at the two tea houses and the few family businesses that could afford to put in septic tanks. Potholes rutted ever deeper into the dirt road, and nobody seemed to bother about keeping the dust down. Not that there was much traffic in or out, other than Mr. Elliott's horse and buggy once or twice a week to deliver 4X-Bread to the restaurants and to a couple of families who had picked up the western habit of toast in the mornings. Neither the city nor the province concerned themselves with public works, mainly because of the peculiarity of the city boundary, which left one side of Chinatown's only street within city limits and the other outside, under provincial jurisdiction. Both administrations largely ignored Chinatown's existence. Not even the city police bothered to come around, to case out the gambling joints or to check Chinatown as a source of bootlegged liquor.

There was a convivial atmosphere in Chinatown on account of the extraordinary generosity that had saved their town. "Where there's a worm, there's a leaf to help," people liked to say. The pos- sibility of disappearing off the map had brought everybody closer together; everybody appreciated that they depended on everyone else for survival. Even the poor and unemployed who came here had a sense of contributing to the community. If as many as fifteen got together and pooled their relief money, they could afford to rent a small house—primitive to be sure—and still have money left to hire a cook. It was this very characteristic of togetherness that put May-ying at ease, and left Chan Sam uncomfortable.

Working at the Canton took her into the bosom of a family business, headed by Chinatown's most respected citizen. Wong Wah Soon, the benevolent, well-liked herbalist turned restaurateur, was generous even to those who did not patronize his tea house. Every Chinese New Year he ordered Chinese sausages, dates and sugar cane from Vancouver and delivered them to men on relief. "Men still have to eat. If they have work or no work, they still have to eat," he told his wife and eight children, who all helped out, cooking and baking, tending the vegetable garden and chicken coop out back, carrying wood up the back stairs, washing and ironing the white tablecloths.

In keeping with this philosophy, as Vancouver's tea houses were shutting their doors, Mr. Wong built newer and bigger premises for the Canton. There was enough business that a competitor, the Nanking House, was built. Some time after Chan Sam and May-ying's return to Nanaimo, a third, Goong Nam House, opened. The tea houses were Chinatown's largest buildings and also served as rooming houses. The tea rooms were upstairs, and downstairs, there were ten to fifteen rooms available to rent for less than fifty cents a night.

May-ying quickly proved herself to be one of the Canton's best assets. To the patrons, she was the tiny waitress, the one with the fair skin, bright eyes and the dangling jade-and-gold earrings. To the Wongs, she was ever punctual, polite and soft-spoken, someone who minded her own business, who never complained about the long hours and hard work, who was never mad at anybody. The chefs, who were notoriously temperamental and had to be assuaged by a bottomless glass of whiskey as they cooked, never had a word to say against May-ying. On weekends, when there

wasn't an empty booth between Friday evening and Sunday afternoon, May-ying had customers lining up for her tables.

The simplicity of life in Nanaimo suited May-ying. Children
could play on the street without fear of cars, and though merchants' wives would not socialize with waitresses, they didn't mind
if their children were friends. No one was ever going to have to beg
for their next meal, for food was plentiful and fresh. There was a
garden behind every store and family home. Two pig farmers lived
down the back lanes—cured pork was available every day of the
week, fresh pork twice a week and barbecued pork on Sundays.
The local Cowichan Indians came into Chinatown and laid out
fresh shiners and rock cod, alongside hand-knit sweaters, right on
the sidewalk in front of the gambling joints. As for May-ying's
own needs, there was a herbalist, but no temple. But what made it
easy for her to live there was having her own people there, men
who came from Poon-ye, a county neighboring hers in China.
One of the small houses along Pine was a house of Poon-ye men,
some of whom worked at one of Nanaimo's coal mines. The people who ran the Goong Nam tea house and Tong Yick general
store were also Poon-ye. May-ying had ready-made friends, and
help if she needed it.

The sense of belonging that May-ying enjoyed escaped Chan
Sam. For him, Nanaimo brought an unshakable boredom. He was
a good and caring father to Hing, but he longed for other dimen-
sions of respect. He thought it beneath him to be consigned to
the company of idle men, unemployed like him, who came to
Nanaimo. He had none of his own people here. Accustomed to
choosing his friends from among those who convened at the clan
building or the Kuomintang building in Vancouver, he did not
have the graciousness to extend friendship to strangers. Instead,
he hankered for the respect and admiration he had from Huangbo
and the villagers of Chang Gar Bin. As if to remind himself of his
stature among his kin at home, he was acutely self-conscious of
his demeanor; he avoided lingering too long on the benches or
walking aimlessly along Pine Street.

With the discipline of keeping in mind his future in China

came a longing for a wifely relationship. Rarely was there intimacy between him and May-ying, and when there was, she made sure no pregnancy ensued. After any relations, she promptly douched herself with a purple dye. If she thought she had to make doubly sure, she had someone get her some deer placenta to ingest, to bring on a miscarriage. They both knew they could not afford to feed another mouth in Canada, but Chan Sam often thought about how Huangbo must long for a child of her own. He thought about how time for her was running out with each passing year. May-ying, still holding fast to the importance of a son in the family, seemed to voice what would suit them both, often telling him: "You should go back to China and bring forth a son."

If Chan Sam's body was in Canada, his heart was in the village. He became more devoted to Huangbo, faithfully writing letters to her. May-ying's emotional bond to the village was with her daughters left behind. Though literate enough to make out a few words here and there, she could not write a letter or decipher one without help, and she relied on Chan Sam to keep in contact with them. Letters from Huangbo in China were, as ever, little more than the formality of announcing the receipt of his latest remittance; they included greetings from Ping and Nan, but little more. Every time one came, May-ying would say, "I wonder how the two girls are doing." Chan Sam would express a longing "to walk awhile" at home. As if he needed some distant star upon which to fix his gaze, Chan Sam held out hope that economic conditions in Canada would improve and allow them to save enough to return home by the time Hing was ready to start school. That was the understanding, that as parents, they honor their youngest by taking her to China for her first schooling.

May-ying diligently stocked the cardboard carton under their bed with "things to send to China": used clothing, tea towels or kitchen scrub brushes, food tins, anything that might have another life. From time to time, she knit sweaters to send to the girls. More than once she bought a dress from downtown Nanaimo that was big enough for Ping, that Nan could grow into, that Hing herself might wear if the family were together again. In

Hing, she was reminded of her absent daughters. The youngest had some of the lighthearted gaiety of Ping, and some of the serenity of Nan.

Every two months, or more often if he could manage it, Chan Sam sent home what money he could manage from May-ying's wages and tips. As she'd done before, May-ying abided by the practice. As always, it was reason enough that she saw China as home and Canada as but a temporary exile, but as long as her two daughters remained unmarried, she also accepted responsibility for them.

Other overseas Chinese were not so accepting about relations at home. "It's enough to send *lishee* for the New Year," they told each other as they sent a token amount of money in a red envelope and hid behind the excuse of the Depression in Canada. Done once, it turned their heads from their familial obligations easily enough. But not Chan Sam. He kept his eye on the fortunes of China and Canada. China's economy would be dealt another blow when the United States devalued its currency and, by an act of Congress, artificially raised the price of silver. Silver flowed out of China as it had in the days when it went to pay for opium. Exchange rates were affected and parts of the urban economy collapsed. For Chan Sam's family, any imbalance could only be righted by greater sacrifice in Canada. Though the total value of overseas remittances to his home county dropped drastically (from 1930 to 1931 it fell by a third; by 1933, total remittances would be only only one-fifteenth what they had been in 1930), he remained one of the dwindling faithful.

Mr. Wong was someone Chan Sam looked up to, and one of his few associates in Nanaimo. Enjoying the prestige of the invitation, Chan Sam occasionally joined him for a game of mah-jongg at the back of the Canton tea room, even though Mr. Wong sometimes set the stakes dangerously high. The others making up the foursome were the Chinese baker from the Plaza Hotel downtown and a Chinese chef who cooked for crews on the Canadian Pacific Railway. Chan Sam could bring Hing without having to worry about her; she was fussed over by the Wongs. The older brothers of the Wong children would carry her about on their shoulders, and let her help refill the soya sauce containers and play out on the balcony. The men could get on with their game, played over an amiable glass of whiskey.

Chan Sam also went to hear what Mr. Wong had to say about news in China, and to talk about the news of China in the Chinese newspapers. They each read two, one from Victoria and one from Vancouver. Chan Sam, who never saw himself joining the larger white society, had little interest in the newspapers' campaigns for equal access to unemployment relief and welfare for whites and Chinese in Canada, or for other rights due them as residents and citizens. The future that preoccupied Chan Sam was China's; he cared only about developments at home that might affect his house, his *mau tin* and his kin left behind.

Like other overseas Chinese, he hoped most for stability in the homeland. Despite the factional fighting within the Kuomintang—some of which was being played out in the United States and Canada, as it remained primarily an overseas-funded party—Chiang Kai-shek represented the one hope for uniting China. Chan Sam was comforted to learn that Chiang's campaign to exterminate the Communists, led by a young Mao Zedong, had the Communists in retreat.

More valuable to the overseas Chinese than newspaper reports was the firsthand word of travelers returning from China. During his recent visit home to Kwangtung, the most traveled-to province, Mr. Wong had bought a business as an investment. Although Chan Sam had done better than most of his class by having gone home to buy a few *mau tin*, he found himself dreaming of the sequel, of building a new house for his family there. For most sojourning peasants like him, the only house they managed to save for was their last—the coffin in which they would be laid to rest. But in Chan Sam's mind danced images of large, tall mansions that he had seen in the south of China, whose flourishes of western architecture identified like pins on a map the husbands and fathers who had proven their worth and more by going abroad.

In Nanaimo, there were enviable men like Mr. Wong, and then there was most everybody else. Chan Sam watched Nanaimo begin to empty of unemployed men like himself. They dug up from their back gardens their Ogden tobacco tins containing whatever savings they had to show for their sojourn in Gold Mountain. For them, it had come down to swallowing the shame of going home poor or going home dead, their bones dug up and cleaned from the grave and crated for the last boat ride home. But even the Chinese society that paid for bone shipments, normally every seven years, had halted shipments during the Depression, not even bothering to crate the bones in the meantime. The men in Nanaimo began to wonder what honor there was in one's bones waiting in a gunnysack stored in a pile in the bone shed down one of Chinatown's back lanes.

When the provincial government offered in 1934 to pay a one-way passage to China for the destitute unemployed, the infirm and the mentally handicapped, on the condition that they never return to Canada, many took the offer. Chan Sam stayed on, preferring to hold on to his aspirations to climb up, rather than down, the social ladder.

⋖⦁⦁⦁⦁⦁⦁⦁⦁⦁⦁⦁⋗

Chan Sam never did concentrate at mah-jongg. While playing at Mr. Wong's table, he noticed the attention paid to May-ying, the customers vying for her attention and clamoring for her to speak to them. By himself again back at their lodgings in an A-frame house next door to the Canton, he became possessed with the thought that the customers shared more affection with May-ying than most husbands shared with their wives. Jealousy and sheer boredom drove him out to the balcony or to the side window to stare across at the Canton. From either vantage point, it was possible to see the comings and goings below and to pick up tidbits of conversation coming from the tea house's open balcony doors.

May-ying did not need to look to know what he was doing there. "I know he's spying on me," she told the other waitresses. "He pretends to look at the potted chrysanthemum or the lily outside on the balcony." It fed her appetite for retaliation, and tempted her to give him something he could really worry about.

There came a day when he was expecting her home between shifts and she did not appear. His immediate suspicion was that she had succumbed to the temptation of the gambling houses. There being nothing else to do for entertainment along Pine Street, most everybody gambled a little at Chinatown's three or four gaming houses. Gambling in Nanaimo carried little of the stigma that it did in other Chinatowns, if only because the profits went back to the company that ran Chinatown. Chan Sam, who had prided himself on never having crossed the threshold of what he regarded as vice, decided to go prove his suspicions. He took Hing in hand and they went to each gambling parlor in turn, pushing open the door with its window painted dark green, peering inside for May-ying.

In one, he heard her name being called out: "*Ah* May-ying! You're so clever—pick another win!" Over the heads of the crowd, through the cigarette smoke, he saw the ribbon tying her hair back: there she was at the *fan tan* table, the center of attention. With the assembled gambling crowd, he watched as the boss lifted the brass shaker off the pile of porcelain buttons and, with his curved stick, began paring them away four by four. Hardly was he halfway through the pile when May-ying proclaimed the winning gamble: "Three porcelain buttons left!"

Chan Sam whispered in his daughter's ear and pushed her forward. "*Mama?* Come home," Hing said. Everyone turned at the child's voice; children were not seen in such places.

Once they were behind the door of their rooms, it was May-ying who had the first say. "I don't need anybody to look after me!"

"Bull-lo-shit! People who go into the gambling dens do not think of the future!" he said angrily. "Go in there and you will sink into vice. What do you want gamblers' company for, all that smoking and drinking?" He grabbed the collar of her dress with his two hands, shaking her in frustration because she did not appreciate the risk of gambling away the savings that represented their passage home.

Unexpectedly, May-ying retaliated as if in a fight to the death. In a temper, she turned wiry and strong. Her fists pummeled his chest, her feet flailed at his shins. He dragged her, kicking and screaming, into the front room where they wouldn't be overheard by neighbors on the other side of the back-room wall.

"*Baba,* don't do it. Don't do it." The child was crying hysterically and clinging to his trouser leg. The two parents froze, and the heat of the argument passed.

"One must be clear about what one loves and hates," he said to his concubine, teaching her as he had taught himself.

May-ying's tone was dismissive: "You pile your proverbs one on top of the other; you might as well build one house on top of another."

<hr>

When Hing was almost five, it was time for her to start Chinese schooling, the signpost that pointed Chan Sam's Canadian family back to China.

Realistically, the day when he, the concubine and their third daughter should pack up in Canada and return to China had not come. The Depression had not lifted either here or at home. The Chinese side of the family had come to rely ever more on the Canadian side, on what May-ying made as a waitress. Ever more *mau tin* was needed to keep a family fed, which, if Chan Sam were to wind up their lives abroad tomorrow, he could not afford to buy.

It was May-ying who suggested that Chan Sam go home alone for a visit.

He gave her the opportunity she had been looking for when he happened to mention that, according to his duty as a good father, he should be taking their youngest back to the village soon for schooling. "You and I are just discussing this," he told May-ying, lest she cut him off. "That's all, we are just talking," he said, as if talk was only a way to pass time. He named other fathers and uncles he knew who were doing the same, who were taking their children, nieces and nephews back to China for a year or two. Their wives, he said, were not accompanying them home; they remained in Canada, awaiting their husbands' return.

May-ying had already understood why he really wanted to go. "*Ah* Chan Sam, it is about time you walked in the village again. You should go yourself, go see how the girls are," she said. Then she added, "You should go to bring forth a son into the family."

"But, if you do go," she said, having also thought about this before, "I want Hing to stay here with me, to keep me company."

May-ying had been looking for some relief from his stultifying presence in her life. She longed to get out from under his prying eyes, from his proverbs that buffeted her this way and that, as if neither he nor she had an original thought of their own.

Chan Sam could not resist the thought of going, for all the reasons May-ying mentioned. He was conscious that time was short for Huangbo, now in her late thirties, to bear a child. He had also often wondered if the girls, Ping and Nan, almost nine and seven, were applying themselves to their schooling. But he disliked the idea of going without Hing; that had never been the understanding about what was best for her education.

Whenever May-ying took a stance, she was like a driven woman who could not be steered off her course. Having made the decision that Hing would be born in Canada, she was now convinced it was propitious to have the child remain with her.

"Hing is all I have here in Canada," May-ying said. It was true; what had she here—aside from her jewelry—but her child?

"I would be lonely by myself," she continued. "You have already taken the two girls back to the village. I think I should have the last one here with me." It would not cost much, she insisted, to keep Hing with her: "She can eat at the Canton. Mr. Wong would be happy to provide Hing's meals as part of my contract."

The mention of Mr. Wong brought a self-satisfied look to Chan Sam's face. He now saw a way to bring a grander purpose to his visit home. "Then I would like to go home to build a house," he said. "The present house is much too small."

May-ying nodded in agreement. "Yes, yes, by all means, go to build a house."

Chan Sam continued, his enthusiasm growing. "I will require more money than the sum I have saved, but not too much more because I can do a lot of the work myself, and the villagers can help. I will just have to feed them two meals a day and they will do it for practically nothing. A dollar can go a long way in China, not like in Canada."

May-ying asked Mr. Wong for an advance against her wages to finance Chan Sam's trip home. He was happy to oblige, for she was a good and trusted employee.

Families made an event of coming to the Vancouver pier to say goodbye. May-ying and Hing were in the crowd, enjoying the festive atmosphere. Chan Sam could not be picked out among the ship's passengers—he was on the crowded lowermost deck in third class—but he was waving, both his hands in the air.

As he'd prepared for this visit home, he'd been a different man, buoyant and more agreeable. He would not return until he had completed the house, which he expected to take one full year. To stay at home much longer would be seen as a financial burden on his family there, but if he chose to stay longer, his certificate of return to Canada was valid for four years; the length of absences for Chinese residents from Canada had been extended by the government from two years since the onset of the Depression.

He had been optimistic that the economy would reverse itself by the time he came back, that he would return to find a job. "When I save enough again, you and Hing and I can all go back together and *tan sai gai*," he had told May-ying. It was just an expression, but that was what he believed, that one day his entire household—wife, concubine and all their children—would take it easy, that they would all be sitting on top of the world.

He'd had to make a few trips from Nanaimo to Vancouver to arrange the shipment going with him. In it were the necessary gifts for the family, including a red wagon for Ping and Nan, a wind-up Big Ben alarm clock for each of them—the kind with a loud tick-tock and a large face, on a two-legged stand, made in Peterborough, Ontario—and two RCA Victor phonographs along with some Cantonese opera recordings, made in New York by famous opera stars. One phonograph was for Huangbo, the other was for his new godson in Shekki, who was already rehearsed to bow before him in a ceremony of reverence.

The most essential part of his shipment were tools required to build the house. North American tools, even those as basic as spades and saws, would be better than the tools made in China that he would have to buy or borrow. Better tools, he reasoned, would improve the workmanship. In his mind, the house was already rising, and standing for generations to come.

Smoke billowed from the steamship's blue funnels, and the ship's whistle sounded the moment of departure. Cheers erupted, and passengers on the decks tossed rolls of colored paper streamers anchored to the railings over the side of the boat. May-ying waved, but her mind had already turned to the revelry of conversation and gossip that would last into the night in the room of a waitress in Vancouver's Chinatown, where a few old friends were to gather. Hing, who understood vaguely that *Baba* was going away to build a house, was busy trying to catch the rainbow of streamers spiraling down, hoping some passenger would toss one far enough to land on the pier instead of in the water.

# CHAPTER FIVE

C HAN SAM SIGHED and said how much happier he was to be back in the village. Huangbo's head, like a blade of grass bending with another in the wind, nodded agreement. "Rice from the village tastes better," she said.

As she had done for her husband's previous homecoming meal, Huangbo had bought the best food money could buy, the rare *tin guy*. The family sat down to dine on the several tiny chickens, so tender they ate them bones and all. There was not the usual clear broth to finish the meal. Instead, Huangbo prepared Ping's favorite western food. From Chan Sam's crate of foods from abroad, she took a tin of sweetened condensed milk and a box of crackers and served crackers floating in steaming milk. The family would taste such western foods again, but never *tin guy*, for this homecoming—though no one thought so at the time—was to be Chan Sam's last.

There was hardly enough elbow room in the cramped house for the four of them to bring their rice bowls and chopsticks to their mouths at the same time. From every corner spilled the necessities of a peasant family's everyday life—crockery jars, hoes and scythes, a spinning wheel, a loom for weaving cotton, baskets of all shapes and sizes. Overhead, from bamboo poles tied end to end with hemp, hung yet more baskets, pots, straw hats, clothing and cloths, to be taken down with a hooked pole when needed.

Amongst the clutter, Chan Sam's eyes found the overseas furniture that he had brought home on his last trip. He saw the two dressers back to back. Straw mats half covered them. Stacked on top of the dressers was the metal crib, and inside it was the pram, both showing rust. Everything was layered in dust. Chan Sam noticed that not one of the overseas clocks was on display, and still in their shipping crates were the three large mirrors. He vowed that the new house would have a proper place for the necessities and the luxuries, from the crockery to the wall clock.

Every villager in Chang Gar Bin knew Chan Sam had come home to build a house. They congratulated each other that their village could boast one husband and father who had kept his head above water. Gloom had otherwise beset the village as peasant after peasant, unable to pay back loans at interest rates of 30 to 40 percent a year, lost to creditors their rice seedlings, pigs, furniture and tools. For many, it had come down to selling even their tea and the last of their unmarried daughters, anything to avoid surrendering their *mau tin.*

The Depression saw the price paid in Shekki for the villagers' best grade of unhusked rice fall below what they needed to meet rent and taxes. To worsen their burden of debt, the array of new taxes had multiplied wildly as the Kuomintang military authority governing Kwangtung pushed ahead with its new programs. Soldiers from various levels of government kept coming to Chang Gar Bin to proclaim and collect new levies in a confusing variety of currencies. On top of the heaviest-ever land and harvest taxes came a transport tax on rice sent to mills, a levy for road repair around Shekki, a tax for county watchmen and police, a provincial survey tax and even a village tax on pig butcherings.

Chan Sam's faithful remittances had not always kept hunger away from his wife's door, but they had at least kept creditors at bay. He had not lost one of his twenty-eight *mau tin,* a holding second only to that of the local grain dealer. The dealer, who held one *kung* (one hundred *mau tin*), had built himself a new house, the first to be built in recent memory in Chang Gar Bin. Tall and narrow, its three rooms were stacked one atop another, like a column of Chinese characters. But the villagers dismissed the dealer as not one of them; he kept his first wife in a grander home in Shekki and kept his second wife in the village. The villagers held out the house-building plans of Chan Sam, a peasant like themselves, as a greater achievement. Not only would his house be the first built by a peasant of their generation, it would be the first house to testify to the wealth to be found in Gold Mountain. It would bring Chang Gar Bin renown among the surrounding villages of the county. Among the men of Chan Sam's time, not one in ten who'd gone abroad had managed to send enough to keep their families intact and alive; most returned broken and became a charge upon those left behind. That was not Chan Sam's way, said the villagers of Chang Gar Bin. He had earned face by having the good moral character to worry and care for his family left behind. The news of his house-building had come at a time when the rice gruel on everyone's table was so watered down it was almost tasteless. His news gave hope to all that after bitterness would come sweetness.

<hr />

In the bosom of his Chinese family, Chan Sam settled into a happy harmony, cherishing his home with the devotion of a model husband and father. In his first days back, when he had time away from the preparations for the house-building, he hovered over Huangbo. Feeling sorry that her work seemed so tiring, he even helped with some of the womanly chores. He would take the pole from Huangbo's stooped shoulders to carry water from the village well, rice stalks from the fields for the hearth or grain from the granary to the courtyard, where it was spread to dry in the sun, then swept together and winnowed. In concern for her safety, he had put a stop to her forays into the hills surrounding Chang Gar Bin to dig up bamboo shoots that had just broken ground, to collect herbs or to gather wire grass to make into brooms. Never mind that other women in the village did the same; the hills were dangerous, inhabited by beggars and ruffians, Chan Sam said. "Buy what you need," he said. When money could not buy a broom, because every household made them for themselves, he said he'd have a better one sent from Canada. Sure enough, an overseas broom eventually arrived. With its straw tightly compacted and neatly trimmed, it looked to Huangbo as if it would take years of sweeping to wear out.

Once at home, Chan Sam vowed to do what he could to assure himself during his absences that his family would not fall seriously ill. He told Huangbo that his greatest fear was always that she or the girls might succumb to the three sicknesses that often swept the villages. Every time the "waking of insects" season arrived in China—after the floods and rain—the sound of mosquitoes carrying malaria buzzed in his bad dreams in Canada. Before leaving Vancouver, he had made inquiries about what western medicine could do for the disease known at home as the "moist evil air" sickness, and had obtained a prescription for quinine sulphate. Knowing that Huangbo would not incur the expense of seeking the advice of a doctor in Shekki—no villager did unless the person lying on their deathbed was the father or the first son—he gave her the bottle of fifty large white capsules, instructing her to administer them to herself, Ping or Nan if a high fever persisted. Two other diseases concerned him less. No villager needed reminding to boil water and cook food to avoid the "flowing-stomach" disease, dysentery, but they had no answer for the "spitting-up-blood" disease, tuberculosis, which lurked in the dampness and moisture stored in the crumbling bricks of the walls of every peasant's house. Chan Sam would see to it that his new house was made of bricks as hard as stone.

He wanted a full report about how Ping and Nan were doing in school. Huangbo reported that she dutifully sent the girls off six mornings a week at half past eight and they returned each afternoon at half past four. Chan Sam, bearing a gift of persimmons, paid a visit to the schoolmaster. The schoolmaster declared Nan to be one of his favorites because she was both quiet and

clever. Ping, he said, was as noisy as a boy. She did not take learning seriously and shrugged off her mistakes. Mindful of what
Chan Sam had made clear to him in a letter from Canada—
"However difficult, I am going to cover all school fees and expenses involved in my daughters' education"—the headmaster said he
felt compelled to report that the two girls did not show up every
day. Attendance was irregular among all the village children,
mostly depending on whether they were needed for chores at
home or whether the expense of brushes and paper could be met.
But when there were only two or three girls enrolled among thirty
boys, the absence of Chan Sam's daughters was noticeable.

"*Baba,* my head is made of wood; I don't see how I can ever
remember enough characters to be able to read and write," Ping,
giggling, told her father.

He asked where she and Younger Sister went when they left
the house with their school books under their arms. Ping confessed that when she didn't go to school, she took Nan down to
the canal and to the fields, where they passed the hours trapping
toads and crabs. So as not to arouse suspicion at home, she made
sure they returned home at the proper hour.

It is not only Nan who is clever, thought Chan Sam. "*Baba*
will help you learn your characters," he said, "but you must
promise me that you and your younger sister will not stay away
from school."

Every day after school, until the house-building began to con-
sume almost all his waking hours, he took paper, ink and brushes,
which he'd brought from Canada, out to a bench in the courtyard. Ping set out the Big Ben alarm clock her father had given
her and set the alarm for a half hour later to signal the end of the
writing lesson. Each day was the same: Chan Sam selected a few
characters and taught his daughters the order of the strokes,
building each character as meticulously as he would soon build
his new house.

<hr />

There was business to take Chan Sam to Shekki. He had to receive
his new godson in a ceremony, and to deliver the phonograph. He

also had a gift for the child of his eldest daughter by his deceased wife. By tradition, a visit to a daughter who had left the family was rarely, if ever, made. He went only out of sentiment.

His main business in Shekki, however, was to arrange the house-building. His first inquiries were to seek out draftsmen who could design and build the kind of house he wanted. The ideal for both rich and poor was "many generations under one roof and feeding from the same hearth." Chan Sam's was not to be a mansion of the monied and powerful, however. Their houses were walled compounds, with inner and outer courtyards, separate quarters for the various wives and their children, the servants, tutors and guardsmen, and separate buildings to house an ancestral hall, a study room, a music room and so on. Nor would Chan Sam's house match the size of what returning merchants had built, but it would speak of the same experience of having gone abroad. On his travels through the Pearl River countryside, Chan Sam had committed to memory houses that added western architectural touches, whose balustrades, porticos and balconies decorated at least two stories, sometimes three. In his mind, he imagined these houses, built by overseas fathers like him, standing in judgment of the generations of squat, crumbling one-story adobe houses huddled at their feet, offering proof that going abroad was the only hope of raising one's family above the peasant class.

There was no such house within two villages of Chang Gar Bin, and no one from the village had been in a peasant's home that had an upstairs. The site Chan Sam chose to build his new house, on one *mau tin* of his holdings, was five minutes' walk from the old house, on the side of the village furthest from the hills. It would be the last house at the village's edge, offering an unobscured view south over the canal to the expanse of fields and countryside beyond.

Not a day went by, as Chan Sam awaited the first workmen to arrive, that he didn't walk the path from the old house to where his new one would rise. He'd stand on the site enjoying the vista, imagining the perspective from a second-floor balcony; his two stories would stand as tall as the grain dealer's three. He walked in and out of an imagined doorway, thinking of how the coolness inside, afforded by tall ceilings, would offer respite from the searing noon day-heat outside. He saw in his mind's eye the main portico and the two lesser entrances on either side of it opening onto the front courtyard. He envisaged the windows, wanting them to be both high enough to guard against thieves and large enough to afford a view. There would be neither doors nor windows in the wall hugging the back property line—not least because one couldn't have good luck come in the front door only to have it escape out the back—but also because Chan Sam did not want a view of the village.

With the draftsman's plans in hand, he paced them out. They included a front courtyard with a well—a welcome luxury for the women of the household—and a separate shed for the storage of grain and for the pig, so it could be moved out of the kitchen. Chan Sam moved the bamboo markers for the house further and further out, each time adding more string to stretch between them. He had complained that he could hardly stretch his arms out between the walls of the old house. In his new one, he wanted to be able to stroll in a leisurely way across its breadth, without the congestion of others of his household coming and going. He rehearsed by standing in what would be the large main reception room, turning through a doorway on one side into a lesser reception room, retracing his footsteps and passing through to the other side, across a walkway and into a room for the kitchen and wash basins. When he was finally satisfied, the floor space, including the upstairs balcony, totaled almost four thousand square feet.

Chan Sam, Huangbo and the concubine would have the two bedrooms downstairs behind the reception rooms. The children—the three daughters and the son he hoped to bring forth with Huangbo—would sleep upstairs. Eventually, the upstairs would be taken over by the son and the daughter-in-law—the bride chosen for him by his parents—who would care for the three aging parents. For good luck, Chan Sam had included a second staircase, in hopes that the next generation might beget two sons. Thinking ahead, he decided it would be better if each of his grandsons and their wives enjoyed separate access upstairs.

Chan Sam delayed breaking ground until after the fall harvest when the men in and around Chang Gar Bin would be available to work for a small wage. It did not take long for work to fall behind schedule. Chan Sam had not brought enough tools from Canada, and he refused to use the Chinese tools he judged inferior. Bricks were made on site, but work proceeded excruciatingly slowly. The workmen watched perplexed as Chan Sam, who rolled up his sleeves alongside them, took a blunt axe handle to test each batch of bricks being turned out. He shook his head at how easily they crumbled. He complained that they were full of air holes, which to the workmen were how bricks were supposed to look. To achieve the stone-like quality he wanted, the kiln had to be heated so hot that the amount of fuel consumed made the laborers gasp. To them, it was like money being burned.

When it came time to steam-dye the bricks in the kiln, each time the workmen went to seal it, Chan Sam was not satisfied that they had poured enough water through the soil on top. More steam turned bricks a bluish-grey; such lustre in a house spoke of the wealth of its occupants. The hundreds upon hundreds of buckets of water that consequently had to be shoulder-poled from the canal to pour into the kiln, as well as the labor involved to sand each brick individually, as Chan Sam insisted upon, required extra laborers. He found them in Shekki's marketplace, men and boys each squatting behind an upended brick, which was the way they advertised their trade. He also had to buy the extra tea and tobacco that was provided as part of their contract. The building site in Chang Gar Bin, with the laborers' makeshift bamboo and straw huts built on stilts over the canal, and the canteen that churned out their two meals a day, looked more like an army encampment than a modest peasant's house-building.

⟨⟩

As the house began to take shape, villagers and workmen alike saw it as a testimonial to the man himself. They saw him as a husband and a father who had realized a peasant's dream of soil underfoot and tiles overhead. "Chan Sam will leave a good name for a hundred generations," they said. The most faithful in the crowd of villagers watching the progress of house-building were his daughters, Ping and Nan. The two sisters came to the worksite before school, after school and on their day off. Taking turns pulling one another in the red wagon their father had brought from Canada, they bumped down the path from the old house. They parked the wagon at the edge of the worksite, sat in it, moved it when they wanted a different view, all the while admiring their father as the sweat poured from his brow.

As her husband's reputation grew, Huangbo's nature was to retreat more into the role of the model Chinese wife, ever more humble, yielding, diligent. She observed the house-building with her customary reserve and posed no questions about what she saw as her husband's business. She seemed not to know that the money supporting the family and financing the house-building came from the concubine. Even if she'd been told, it would have made little impression, for as a woman, she too saw everything accumulated in marriage as the property of the husband. Just as her sacrifice to the family was to endure an existence more like widowhood than marriage, any sacrifice on the part of the concubine would be considered just and honorable, and expected.

Huangbo had, however, felt a sadness for Chan Sam, and she carried it as if it were another wifely duty. She was sorry that he had not been rewarded with a concubine more worthy of him. His letters home had not betrayed his unhappiness, but once within his own four walls, he bemoaned how cranky and argumentive May-ying could be with him. "May-ying is not like a lady," he said, complaining that she did not know her place. He told Huangbo of May-ying's fondness for gambling. "She is a woman who is more like a man," Chan Sam said. Huangbo clucked her tongue, and shook her head.

The children, Ping and Nan, could not help but overhear what was said of their birth mother. This talk began to drown out what few memories Ping had of her. One of her earliest memories was of walking on a sidewalk with her mother in Vancouver's Chinatown—there were no such things as sidewalks in the village.

She remembered arriving in the village in a motorcar with her Canadian family, and she could picture both mothers together. She recalled a feeling that the pretty, younger mother was the triumphant one, the other the vanquished one. But from what she now overheard of talk about May-ying, she sided with Huangbo. Both sisters, having already spent more of their lives in China than abroad and having been raised by their Chinese mother, had to be reminded of their foreign origins. There were the care packages that their father sent from Canada, which occasionally included a dress that their mother had picked out or a sweater she had knit. Whenever they were out in their overseas dresses or playing with their overseas toys—the pram and now the wagon—mothers and children called out after them: "*Faan-gwei-neu, Faan-gwei-neu.*" The sisters rather enjoyed the taunt of "foreign girl," taking it as a compliment to the worldliness shared with their father.

Though Huangbo loved Ping and Nan as her own, she longed for a child to replace the one she had lost. In Chan Sam's absence and with each passing year, she thought of the Chinese saying, of "fallen flowers carried by the flowing water of age." She was nearing forty, and if a child was not born on this visit, by the time of his next, she would most certainly be too old. One purpose of her husband's trip home was to father a child; hopefully she could give him a son.

Before Chan Sam's return, she beseeched the gods to use their influence. At a local temple, she lit three sticks of incense, placed them in the sand urn and lit the oil lamps on the altar. She placed a coin into the temple-keeper's hand and signaled that she wished to have the gods speak. He handed her the wooden *bei.* Her first toss onto the dirt floor had been smooth, smooth. The gods were laughing at her. She bowed her head the customary three times again before taking a second toss. It had come up round, round. This time the gods refused to speak one way or another. On the third and last toss allowed, the combination finally came up right: smooth, round. The gods had nodded favorably.

With the house-building proceeding at a snail's pace and money being paid out like running water, the cache of money Chan Sam had brought to China was soon gone. The house stood only half finished. However, he paid the wages due to each worker, and he promised that work would resume when more of his money arrived from Gold Mountain. The villagers were disappointed, but saw no disgrace in the work stoppage. Had Chan Sam discarded his fanciful plans on account of having run out of money, he would have been liable to the damning charge of "no concern for face," and proper social behavior was to preserve what face one's family had. As it was, the villagers likened the entertainment of Chan Sam's house-building to a Chinese opera, where one often had to attend several performances to view an entire story.

Just as he had promised, another installment of money arrived from Gold Mountain. Steam again rose from the brick kiln, mortar was gently slapped and scraped between each new brick, timbers for the roof creaked under the ax and saw. But as sure as the moon waxed and waned, the pattern was repeated. Work slowed as money ran out, revived when money came in. There was, for example, a yawning gap between the solid stone double columns of the central portico until there was money to raise the twin portals of the massive cinnabar-colored door onto its wooden peg hinges. The second-floor balcony door opened dangerously to a naked ledge until there was money to cast the cement balustrade and install the railings to surround it. The roof remained half covered in baize-green glazed ceramic tiles until money arrived to have the rest delivered from Shekki.

Throughout these interruptions, Chan Sam maintained an air of calm. One reason was that, as the house rose, so too did China's economic situation unexpectedly improve. In 1935, the year of Chan Sam's arrival home, a move by Chiang Kai-shek's government to replace its silver-based currency with a managed currency mildly invigorated the economy. The next two years brought favorable weather and bumper crops. Come harvest time, the villagers helping build the house would put down their masonry and carpentry tools, pick up the scythe and hoe and head for the fields. The happier economic outlook was making everybody better off. It only strengthened Chan Sam's resolve to stay with his costly house plans, if only to ensure his stature as Chang Gar Bin's most prominent peasant. Certainly Huangbo did not mind the fits and starts in the house-building; the longer her husband stayed at home, the more fulfilled was her own life.

⟶⟶⟶

In contrast, the longer her husband stayed away, the more accustomed May-ying grew to a new-found freedom. Letters from Chan Sam were the only reminder that it was temporary. The men at Tong Yick store who, being her own people, would help her in whatever way they could—lend her a few dollars, keep her mail for her or read and write her letters—told her when a letter from Chan Sam had arrived. The first brief note from him told of his safe arrival and of finding the At-home Wife and her daughters Ping and Nan well. May-ying had someone at Tong Yick pen a reply, sending her respects. She expected a second letter from Chan Sam to come within the year, to announce the completion of the house and the timing of his return to Canada. In the meantime, she found it rather easy to put him from her mind.

Certainly she knew he was happiest back in the village. Every sojourner liked to say so himself. Of the two women in Chan Sam's life, it was Huangbo who could make him happy. May-ying herself spoke highly of her as "a good and decent woman." Almost as if she were acknowledging her own inadequacies, May-ying began to behave during her husband's absence in ways that were at odds with the proper and decorous conduct expected of a Chinese wife. Perhaps it was inevitable, for the Confucian ideal was asking the near-impossible of a waitress on her own, living in a claustrophobic Chinatown.

She began to spend money in ways that Chan Sam would have kept a tight rein on. He was painstakingly thrifty. On her own, she was not so inclined to deprive herself. She hadn't much to spend—Mr. Wong docked each of her paychecks to pay down the loan that financed Chan Sam's visit home. But hardly had he left when she began to live according to the rhythm of the life of most people in Chinatown—within a cycle of spending, debt and borrowing.

She indulged herself with outings to Victoria and Vancouver. Such day or overnight trips between the three main Chinatowns of British Columbia were a common pastime among the Chinese. Still shunned by the larger society, they had no choice but to stay within their own circles. At least once a month May-ying took the train to Victoria to visit friends and to worship at the Tam Kung temple, one of the oldest and most venerated Chinese temples in North America. There she regularly sought the advice and favor of the resident gods. On overnight visits, May-ying would ask a friend to put up her and her daughter, or else she'd take a room in a rooming house. For five-year-old Hing, these visits occasionally offered the reward of another waitress's child to play with while their mothers chatted or played a round of mah-jongg.

For both mother and daughter, a favorite Vancouver friend to call on was Jang Noong, the cook. He was the same friend who had helped Chan Sam find May-ying when she'd run away to Nanaimo. So gentle was his nature that he avoided using a knife in preparing certain leafy greens for cooking. "It scars them; better to break leaves by hand," he explained to May-ying. She was carefree and laughing in his presence. Her daughter looked forward to Jang Noong's organized outings. Both enjoyed most the times he would hire a driver from Tom's Taxi on Pender to take the three of them on a drive around Stanley Park. They would picnic on a bench against the backdrop of the city skyline or of the ocean and mountains, or on the green where the cricket players assembled near Brockton Point.

In her solitary life in Nanaimo, May-ying's taste for gambling developed into a habit. She was enough of a regular to have a line of credit at the gambling halls. That she gambled was not held against her, not even by her employers, with whom she had an outstanding loan. The Wongs had great sympathy for the waitresses who worked only to hand over their pay to a man. Knowing Chan Sam was not on the scene, they felt May-ying simply did what most men on their own did—indulged in one of Chinatown's few diversions. The difference was only that she usually had Hing by her side. But, though most Chinese would think it immoral to have children present in a gambling den, Nanaimo's gambling patrons ignored the girl's presence. And so Hing became as much a fixture as her mother in those smoke-filled rooms, by day and night.

The only times Chan Sam's name crossed May-ying's lips were in exchange for the gossip of the men in other waitress's lives. When the shifts ended at the three different tea houses, the waitresses would retire in twos and threes to one or another's rooms. If May-ying was among them, they went to her room so that she could check on the sleeping Hing. Her friends sat themselves on the bed, making no effort to avoid waking the child. Most of them, May-ying included, would light up cigarettes. Everybody would talk. Each one had the same litany of complaints: they were hard up and short of money; they were having problems with the men in their lives.

"The trouble with Chan Sam," May-ying was fond of saying when her turn came, "is that he always has to be Number One." What peeved her most was how difficult it was to make him see anything her way. "Talking to Chan Sam any which way, coming or going, is useless. He doesn't hear what I'm saying. Every time he opens or closes his mouth to me, it's '*Gum Gee!*' or 'Bull-lo-shit!'"

"How frustrating," others murmured.

"Such a man could make one sick enough to die," they said—which was what they always said of each other's men.

At one of these sessions, just months after her husband had left, May-ying brandished a second letter from him. Assuming it brought word that Chan Sam was returning soon, the waitresses struck up a chorus of sympathy for the end of May-ying's run of freedom. She silenced them. "He's not coming back yet," she said. "He hasn't finished the house. He needs more money." She showed them what the letter said: "See if you can raise the money and send it to me." The waitresses snorted in disgust and asked what she was going to do. May-ying was already thinking aloud.

"Naturally, I'll send him what he's asking for. I'll borrow. Anything to keep him in the village and out of my way," she said to nods of encouragement.

The next letter from Chan Sam was the same, and the letters that followed were just as brief. Each asked her to send more money so he could finish the house. The sums asked for might not have seemed very large in themselves, but they represented a claim on her future spending money. Therein lay the difference between the sojourner's pennies saved abroad and spent at home in China—the poorhouse abroad became a mansion at home.

To May-ying, what Chan Sam was asking for was the price of postponing the day of his return, which she was willing to pay. She did not go to a bank; the Chinese had no need of banks; they had each other. Money was lent to friends with no questions asked and on the understanding that it would be repaid as quickly as possible. There was no such thing as interest. The favor was always returned. To answer Chan Sam, May-ying relied upon the generosity and trust of Mr. Wong, her loyal friend Jang, her waitress friends and their friends. One flamboyant waitress, Yoong Fong, a sometime Chinese opera star, leaned on her boyfriend and eventual second husband, who had a produce store on Commercial Street in the heart of white Nanaimo. Yoong Fong was generous enough that May-ying gave her the honor of receiving Hing as her goddaughter.

May-ying had a little extra income in commissions she'd made from selling lottery tickets. The most common gambling game in every Chinatown was a "pigeon lottery," a game where winnings were paid based on how many characters inked out on an eighty-character sheet matched the ten drawn. Draws were five times daily. Virtually everybody played for a chance to win some of the jackpot. Most adults would bet just enough so that the winnings would pay for a meal of several courses for themselves: a little more could win enough to entertain a couple of friends. The jackpot would build up when nobody won, and was sometimes as much as thousands of dollars, more than enough to go home to China and retire. Often other adults let Hing ink out their sheet.

"Plant in spring, Sow in winter," the first column of rhyme on the sheet, were the first Chinese characters she learned to read.

Neither her wages nor these lottery commissions met Chan Sam's demands. As the house in China rose, her own financial security became ever more fragile. In a growing recklessness, she began to sink into a more desperate existence. She succumbed to the gambler's conviction that the next win was going to be the big one, that the next win would make up for the last loss. When she didn't have enough credit to play the big sums expected at the *fan tan* table, she changed her game to mah-jongg, where the stakes were lower and where skill played a bigger role than luck. But even there, her shrewd playing was often undone by not knowing when to walk away from the table.

As she became more desperate, May-ying finally went the way of many waitresses—when her shift was over, she no longer refused all the advances of her customers. Men had always been attracted to her. Now, in her mid-twenties, May-ying had exchanged youthful prettiness for beauty, girlishness for woman-hood. With her husband away, bachelor men saw her as "available." She weakened to several men, all of whom she knew. Her motive in these casual liaisons was mainly to help ease her financial problems, yet it was not prostitution in the strict sense of a simple, quick exchange of sexual acts for money. The men would generously pay a gambling debt here or there or give her money to "buy herself something." Some may have been satisfied with physical gratification, some may have hoped for more, for a romantic love. May-ying must have suffered some inner conflict over juggling these men, for she tried to keep her encounters secret. At the tea house she kept the customers vying equally for her attention. And however much she carried on, each night she was always back in her own room, tucking herself into the three-quarter bed beside Hing, who she assumed was fast asleep.

It would be hard to imagine, however, that May-ying did not give some thought to whether her husband might ask where the money she sent was coming from, except that he had never demonstrated a head for money. Despite good intentions, Chan

Sam had bungled most business decisions. In his dealings with his brothers to manage the inheritance of his father's land, he had exhibited unplumbed depths of gullibility. In taking a concubine, a stubborn assumption of chattel. In building a house, a weakness for show. Whatever ability he demonstrated to be frugal and to save, he saw no contradiction in his extravagant spending on Gold Mountain goods to bring home to the village or on the house he was building there. For May-ying, gambling and men were the answer to extending her freedom from his presence. If she needed any other justification, there was the unerring notion of sacrifice for the good of the family.

<hr>

As the house-building entered its second year, Huangbo had only one nagging concern; though her bed was not empty, her womb remained so. Just when the exterior of the house was nearly completed, however, the gods found their propitious moment to reward her.

Chan Sam was already fairly bursting with pride at the accomplishment of his house. The windows gleamed with the first glass seen in the village, and in front of the glass was wrought-iron grating instead of the usual wood that thieves could easily violate. The massive double portals could be secured at night or against danger with a timber crossbar. Swinging half-doors nestled inside the door frame, which included a ledge that was supposed to trip up evil spirits trying to enter. A wrought-iron gate was installed at the entrance to the courtyard. All that remained to be done to the outside of the house was for stonemasons to carve the decorative fauna, birds and flowers in the half-moons above the windows and in the lintels above the doorways, and to plaster chalk-blue lime on the front wall.

When Chan Sam learned Huangbo was with child, the two of them poured tea for each other, letting the cups overflow to show their happiness had increased ten-thousand-fold.

Chan Sam arranged the sale of the old house to a relative and decided to move his pregnant wife and family into the new one while work proceeded on finishing the interior. Perhaps he chose a dishonest relative for a buyer, or one who was simply jealous of his wealth, or one who subsequently fell on hard times. Whatever, no money was to come of the sale.

Living in the unfinished house and among the workmen was especially trying for Huangbo as her pregnancy swelled. The sound of hammering and sawing was constant. Lime dust filled the air. The acrid lime wash used to whiten the walls stung everybody's nose and throat passages. Dust and sand got into the food. Huangbo, constantly pouring tea for newly arriving painters, carpenters, artists and calligraphers, worried that the children would step on a nail, trip on timber left around, bump over a ladder.

In the last weeks of her pregnancy, calm at last prevailed. The noise ceased as the finishing decorative touches were put on the interior. Craftsmen from Shekki painted the carved branches above the door frames in gold leaf, the leaves in red. A different oriental design was stenciled on the face of each step of the stairs. Wood panels divided the sleeping quarters from the reception rooms downstairs and enclosed a room to entertain guests upstairs. Each room's panels were decorated differently, some inlaid with diamond shapes of stained glass, others carved with delicate birds perched on flowering branches. Atop each panel were inlaid oval porcelain paintings. The storks symbolized immortality, the mythical dragon and phoenix, traditionally the symbols of the emperor and the empress, in the home symbolized husband and wife, father and mother. Chan Sam and Huangbo themselves sat for a portrait artist. The double portrait was hung opposite the much larger painting of his parents in the main reception room.

Lastly, Chan Sam hired artists to adorn his house with mural scenes. All but the very poorest of peasants hired traveling mural artists, who could offer conventional scenes of historical incidents or famous figures in local folklore. What distinguished murals from one house to another was usually how many there were. The more pretentious the house, the larger and higher they were, embellishing every recess of every entranceway, doorpost, lintel, window frame, every gable end and roof beam. Chan Sam showed restraint, reserving the lintels above the inner doorways for traditional Chinese landscapes. Where he surprised the artists was in commissioning special murals in each of the two reception rooms. He wanted something to reflect the experiences of his father and himself of going abroad, and of striving to raise themselves above the class of the average uneducated peasant. Relying on Chan Sam's descriptions, the artists painted three scenes in the main reception room. Two were the sojourner's first sights upon his arrival in Gold Mountain: one was San Francisco's Golden Gate Bridge, the other was a Vancouver landscape of sea, mountain and towering Douglas firs. The third scene hinted at the life of luxury in Gold Mountain: a couple in a roadster, its top folded down, motored by a coral-colored mansion on a wide, winding boulevard lined with palm trees. In the second reception room was a mural of fruit and of potted chrysanthemums and orchids, the symbols of a gentleman. There were accompanying sayings: "Books on my giant desk pile up to my eyebrows" and "My well-educated family fosters officials with a good salary." And in deference to his family being tied to the land: "My well-cultivated *mau tin* produces crops like precious gold."

The furniture was moved indoors from the courtyard, where it had been stored until the house was completed. There was only enough to partially fill the many rooms, but at least all of Chan Sam's overseas riches could be put on full display. The three large wall mirrors were mounted in the reception rooms, where the clocks ticked loudly. The two mahogany dressers were moved into separate rooms. Platform beds were built, on which were stacked overseas comforters and wool blankets. And in readiness for the imminent arrival of the new baby, Chan Sam cleaned up the old crib and pram and moved them into the back bedroom.

When Huangbo felt the first pangs of labor, a village midwife was summoned. The head presented itself; a few pushes later and the midwife caught the baby in her hands. "You have given your husband a son," she announced to the baby's mother.

The look of horror on the midwife's face, frozen in a moment of hesitation before she handed the newborn boy into his mother's arms, said it all. When Huangbo saw how her son's feet were bent backwards, she wailed with remorse.

"I blame myself," she told Chan Sam. She was convinced that she herself had brought a bad omen upon the baby in the womb. During the pregnancy, she had slaughtered a chicken. She was hurrying and had other thoughts on her mind. The pot was too small for the chicken, and she had bent the chicken's feet and legs backwards to make it fit. She felt the snap of the bones as the feet broke in her hands. That was how baby Yuen's feet looked, snapped tightly backwards. Huangbo was anguished that instead of a gift of a son who would take care of his aging parents, who would be able to cultivate the *mau tin,* she had given her family a son with a deformity who was as much a liability as a daughter.

Against her husband's wishes, Huangbo put an altar table inside the central entrance, where she made offerings to seek contrition from the gods for her son's deformity. Chan Sam refused to believe in superstition. He voiced only regret at having moved his family into the unfinished house; perhaps the chaos had affected the pregnancy. But the altar was the only way Huangbo could be consoled.

Chan Sam was not going to be deterred from the joy of having a firstborn son, crippled or not. He insisted that there would be the traditional Full Month celebration of the birth, together with a celebration to mark the completion of the house, and that most of the village would be invited. Another father with a deformed child, considered a blight on a man's virility, might have kept the child hidden away. Not Chan Sam. He lectured his daughters Ping and Nan that they were not to be embarrassed by Yuen's crippled feet. He told Huangbo he would do his utmost to see that his son would not be just another mouth to feed, but that he would have an education so that one day he might support himself and his own wife and family.

On the day of the celebration, more than two hundred men, women and children from the village came streaming to Chan Sam's new house to celebrate the double happiness of the house and the birth of a son. They took their places at a thirty-table banquet that spilled from the reception rooms into the courtyard. When the food was gone, Chan Sam's closest men friends retired upstairs to his guest room, to enjoy a glass of whiskey and settle in for a night of mah-jongg.

The next morning, Chan Sam told Huangbo he would leave for Gold Mountain within weeks. She had been expecting the news. It was not what Chan Sam's heart wanted, but there were two equally compelling reasons—one beyond his control, one within his control—that made him decide to leave then.

The first was the menace of war, which might close the country's ports. Japan, a modern, powerful and ambitious state with an expansionist foreign policy, had set its sights on crushing China. In 1931 it had occupied Manchuria, and from then until 1937 it had engaged in a series of military maneuvers to carve out northeast China for itself. In 1936, Manchurian soldiers kidnapped Chiang Kai-shek for not fighting for their land. When the Communists, with whom his Nationalist government had been engaged in a debilitating ten-year civil war since 1927, negotiated his release, they demanded that he halt the civil war to unite the country in order to resist the Japanese. In the summer of 1937, one month after Yuen was born, the Japanese advanced on Peking, which fell without a shot being fired. In August, their bombers and warships converged on Shanghai, and real fighting would begin as the Chinese began a valiant but hopeless resistance effort.

Chan Sam decided he could no longer linger at home. If the war came to the south, or if ships were commandeered to move troops, he could be trapped in China. He also feared that he would have no way of finding out should the Canadian government suddenly decide to change the rules of the certificates for returning Chinese. He did not want to jeopardize his chances of reentry by staying away any longer than he had to.

The other urgent reason to return to Canada was to see to his responsibilities for the other half of the family there, the concubine and the third daughter. With the threat of all-out war and economic chaos in China, his best prospects remained in Canada. May-ying, the only wage-earner in the family, was a resource. Like the *mau tin* at home, she had to be husbanded. Chan Sam was uneasy about what his absence might have done to encourage her strong personality and rebellious nature. He also wanted to see his youngest daughter, Hing, to make sure that she began her studies in Chinese.

One day in the autumn of 1937, he went upstairs and stood on the balcony that swept around the upper floor of his house. He took a long last look at the view it commanded of the fields beyond. He cradled baby Yuen in his arms for the last time and called Ping and Nan before him to issue last-minute instructions.

"Keep clean. Keep your clothes folded away," he told them. "Don't wear too much black, black is for people who have no home." And lastly, "Study hard; if you don't, you will be nothing more than peasants chasing crabs by the canal and toads in the field."

He had a last word for Huangbo. If he did not die in the village, he said, he would not die happy. And then he was gone, the hired motorcar coughing and sputtering to take him away.

# CHAPTER SIX

WHEN CHAN SAM was away in China, May-ying took to dressing her youngest daughter in short pants and suspenders. "You get so dirty when you play; you're going to wear pants. I'm going to change you into a boy!" she told her. The child thought her mother meant it the day she took her by the hand to the barber. In Nanaimo's Chinatown, Dai-Dao Sing's chair was the only place to get a haircut; any woman looking for a hairdresser had to go to one in a larger Chinatown. Hing was terrified. Usually, her mother cut her hair by simply tracing a pair of scissors around a dried coconut half-shell placed atop her head. She had to be dragged across the street. "Cut her hair like a boy's," May-ying told the barber.

To have the pleasure of being able to look at a son whenever she wanted, on the next outing to Vancouver, she took Hing, in boy's dress and a boy's haircut, to Yucho Chow's studio. Mother and daughter posed together. May-ying, her hair waved by the hairdresser Emiline Yip in Vancouver, was dressed in an elegant calf-length dress with a ruffled and pleated bib. Hing stood beside her, a sad scowl on her face. Whenever she was to look at that photograph, she saw it as proof of her mother's disappointment that she was not born a boy. The image, the first ever taken of the concubine's third daughter, foreshadowed a childhood filled with fear and confusion.

⊰⊱

On her own with her mother, Hing did not miss her father. She had discovered playmates her age. There was Nellie from the Wong family, Violet, the youngest of the Chang family (who owned a pig farm and general store), and Doreen Jang and Elsie Joh, daughters of other waitresses. They played out of the way on the balcony of the Canton, where May-ying could keep a watchful eye on young Hing even while she worked. The girls spent hours playing underneath a table put outside for them, having pretend parties with snack-sized cans of pork and beans and rolls of Gold Coin egg biscuits. When they graduated to playing outside on their own, May-ying still insisted they stay within sight of the Canton. They played their games of hopscotch, marbles (using ball bearings) and jump rope on the dirt street or the plank sidewalk below.

In the afternoons, when the tea houses were closed between the lunch and dinner hours, May-ying, with Hing in tow, went to play *fan tan* in one of the gambling dens. When she came back on shift, Hing did too. After taking the evening meal with the staff, Hing would sit in a booth by herself, waiting for her mother to finish. At midnight, or often later, she followed her mother back to the *fan tan* tables. No one there thought May-ying a negligent parent. In fact, men complimented her child-raising: "Hing is so smart, so well-behaved." The child impressed adult company with her good manners: she was obedient, she said "please" and "thank you," and most important, she greeted every adult she met with the correct title. She remembered what May-ying had told her about using *Sook* for a man younger than her father and *Bak* for a man older than her father. (There were corresponding terms for women—*Sim* for one younger than her mother and *Moo* for one older—but rarely was there occasion to use them. Waitress friends were all addressed as "Auntie.")

With the first September of Chan Sam's absence came time for Hing to start kindergarten. Though she bought her daughter two new dresses to wear, May-ying did not care enough about Hing's first English schooling even to rouse herself to send her off on the first day. Hing, feverish with excitement, woke before dawn. She watched the hands on the Big Ben alarm clock on the dresser move slowly towards eight o'clock. At the top of the hour, she climbed over her sleeping mother, put on one of her new dresses and went outside to sit on the plank sidewalk. There, she waited for the rest of Chinatown's children to start down the hill towards town.

In the line to register were white children, accompanied by their mothers or driven to school by their fathers. When Hing gave her name, the teacher refused to write it down. "Ask your mother to give you an English name," she said.

Like most Chinese parents, May-ying did not speak English, and did not want to. So after school, Hing and her friend Elsie sat on a bench outside Tong Yick store and put their minds to a name. Elsie had got hers from Mrs. Mossap, the Sunday school teacher at the United Church, where her mother, a convert, had enrolled her. From following their mothers on the waitress circuit in Victoria and Vancouver, the girls knew a Rosie, a Jean and two Winnies. Hing liked best the girls named Winnie. And so, outside Chinatown, Hing became Winnie Chin (the Chinese character for her surname was anglicized as Chin, Chan or Chen, which were considered equivalent).

The winter of 1935-36 brought snow, which was unusual for Nanaimo's temperate climate. To May-ying, it was more important that Hing, who didn't own a winter coat or boots, stay out of the cold than stay in school. "Tell your teacher you are going to China," she told her daughter. When the snow melted and Hing returned to class, the teacher asked her to tell the class about China. Hing, who knew nothing of her parents' birthplace except that there was another mother and two sisters there and that her father had gone there to build a house, made up a story as best she could.

May-ying did not tell, and Hing did not ask, about the other half of the family in China. The relationship between May-ying and her daughter was typical of Chinese families: parents were a source of discipline and instruction; children were silent unless spoken to. Even asking questions was rude. Mention of the absent family came up only when May-ying sought help from one of the men at Tong Yick store to write a letter to China. She would also have him write out a sentence or two of respect for Hing to copy out, to close the letter.

Though May-ying did not speak to Hing of her father, she also did nothing to conceal from her the gossip about him that spilled at the waitresses' confessional get-togethers. The stories that Hing overheard in Nanaimo, when her sleep was disturbed by these noctural sessions, she heard repeated on trips to Vancouver and Victoria, when she sat silently in a corner waiting for her mother. May-ying's complaints affected Hing's view of her father. They also brought into focus one of her earliest memories. In her mind, she saw her father grabbing her mother's dress, and heard her own voice crying out in fear, "*Baba,* don't do it. Don't do it." And yet, another memory of her father portrayed a different man altogether. They were alone together and he was cooking dinner for them. When he called her to "*sic fan,*" and she came to the table to take up her chopsticks, she saw that the dish presented was not her favorite. She wanted stir-fried cauliflower and dried shrimp. Refusing to eat, she got down on all fours and rubbed her knees and palms black on the linoleum under the table. Her father laughed, removed the dish and prepared her favorite instead.

For Hing, the passage of time while her father was away was marked by the letters her mother received from him. She watched her mother open them in bemusement and derision. It got so that when another came, she too could guess its contents—*Baba* had run out of money again and needed *Mama* to send more so he could finish building the house. Her father's uncompleted project was evidently on Hing's mind because she decided she wanted building blocks herself. Six-year-old Hing, now in the first-grade, and her friend Violet took a detour on their way home from school to look at the colored Christmas lights and the festive shop windows on Commercial Street. On display in a toy shop window was a Chinese home in miniature, built of bright red, blue, yellow and green blocks. Behind high walls was a house of many doors, with gold-trimmed pagoda roof ends, and behind the house, a garden with curved bridges. The only thing Hing had ever taken home from Commercial Street were some wallpaper samples that she and her young friends had once persuaded a hardware store clerk to give them.

"How much?" she asked the shopkeeper, pointing to the model home.

On the way home, Hing conspired with Violet: "I'll get twenty-five cents from my mother. If you get the other fifteen cents from your mother, I'll let you keep the blocks half the time." Hing knew there was always change in her mother's apron which hung on a hanger on a nail above the bed. She didn't think a twenty-five-cent piece would be missed; her mother sometimes gave her that much to play the lottery.

When she brought the new blocks home, she felt compelled to explain their appearance. The "white people's Santa Claus" gave them to her, she said, to her mother's amusement.

<hr/>

For Hing, the first lessons of serving her mother well involved having to tend to May-ying's aches and pains. May-ying had developed an ulcer and suffered from back pain. A line of pickle jars on her dresser was her medicine cabinet. To treat various ailments were rarities such as deer's tail, deer tendon, bear claw, sometimes skunk's gall bladder and lady slipper bulbs. These were preserved in spirits, supplied from the bottles of gin and whiskey standing alongside. For everyday use, to promote circulation, energy and vitality, were more common dried herbs, including *yuk choy, dong guai, ginseng* and various grasses and tree barks. May-ying would also send Hing out to the herbalist to buy the ingredients to make nourishing teas or soups, for which Hing had to memorize various combinations and measures of herbs.

Before school, Hing's daily chore was to empty the chamber pot. May-ying preferred the chamber pot to the communal toilets; she allowed Hing to use them but with strict guidance about avoiding contact with the board. Hing carried out this chore, and others, like washing her own hankies, socks and underwear, diligently and without complaint. "A person cannot be lazy," May-ying said. Some mornings the sound and stench of vomiting woke Hing. When she went to clean the chamber pot of her mother's vomit, her only thought was that her mother's frail body was giving her stomach troubles again. She was too young to know it sometimes had to do with having too much to drink the night before, too many sips of whiskey with patrons at the tea house or at the gambling dens when off shift.

After school one day, Hing herself had an attack of stomach cramps and went looking for her mother for something to relieve the pain. The tea house closed at half-past two, and as it was after three she should have been off shift, but she was not in their room. Hing decided to try the tea room. She found it empty and quiet. Her cramps worsening, she went to lie across the seat of a chair to press her stomach against a hard surface. She froze when she realized she was not alone. There was somebody in one of the booths. Crouching to see beneath the drawn half-curtains, Hing saw the good-looking man, Pang *Sook*. He was from the house of Poon-ye men, a fireman at the coal mine who had once taken Hing and her mother on a tour there. A woman was sitting on his lap; it was her mother.

Hing didn't know what to make of what she had seen. Other than her mother holding her by the hand when crossing the street, or posing for a photograph, she was never demonstrative about her affections—but neither were other Chinese parents with their children. Hing, thinking it best to pretend that she hadn't seen anything, left without a sound, hoping they hadn't seen her.

⋯

When Chan Sam returned to his Canadian family in 1937 after more than two years' absence, his first act of authority was to move the family to Vancouver. There were pragmatic reasons to choose Vancouver over Nanaimo, which supported his own prejudice that Nanaimo's one-street Chinatown was more May-ying's territory than his. Nanaimo's Chinatown was a poorhouse during the Depression, a waiting room for unemployed Chinese men until there were jobs again in the sawmills, the mines or the logging camps. But in Vancouver, by the late 1930s, the Depression had driven enough men back to China for good that jobs were again available for the Chinese who stayed. The economy was beginning to pick up and Chan Sam expected to be able to find at least temporary work, washing dishes perhaps, until a sawmill job became available.

May-ying did not mind leaving Nanaimo; she did not lack for a job or friends in any Chinatown. But the last of the tea houses in Vancouver, where guests were entertained above the noise and commotion of the street, had long ago closed down. The new order was the café at street level, with a coffee counter, the better to serve customers in a hurry. The cafés served only western food, which their Chinese customers enjoyed because they rarely, if ever, cooked it at home. Lacking for Chinese waitresses, the owners of the many cafés along Pender had turned to white help. However, in 1937, the year Chan Sam returned from China, city council ruled against the employment of white women by Chinese bosses. Forced to dismiss some thirty white waitresses, the owners suddenly had a labor crisis, and May-ying had a job.

Chan Sam, May-ying and their youngest daughter went to live at the Royal Hotel, around the corner from the Kuomintang building. The Royal, above a book shop and a printing business, was a rabbit warren of a rooming house, with two wings of single rooms on each of its three floors. The family took two rooms; May-ying and Hing had one, Chan Sam was one floor up in the opposite wing.

The bad news from China united the politically fractious Chinatown. Since the late summer of 1937, headlines around the world had blared news of the ferocity of Japan's attack on China, the first big international conflict since the First World War. In

Chinatowns abroad, the feeling of wartime was heavy in the air. No one needed to be able to read a newspaper to know the toll of the war in its horrific detail. The Japanese, intoxicated by the ease with which they had inflicted casualties on the badly equipped Chinese army, had turned their brutality on civilians, and city after city in north and central China had fallen.

Even before Chan Sam returned to Canada, war was the only topic of daily conversation in the cafés, in the gambling dens and at home. Other than news of the family, May-ying wanted to hear from Chan Sam only what he knew about the war in China. The two of them papered over their own differences, uniting in their fear for the future of the motherland and hatred for the enemy Japanese.

When it appeared inevitable that war would spread to the south of China, overseas Chinese worried about their property and relatives at home. Stories circulated about alleged Japanese atrocities; of war planes dumping ammunition by swooping low to machine-gun villages; of soldiers torturing the Chinese by pulling out fingernails, forcing them to walk on glass, making them dig their own graves before shooting them in the back.

Chan Sam did the only thing possible from his end: he sent Huangbo money to be her cache against the exigencies of wartime. He wanted her to have the money to pay someone to take his Chinese family to safety if necessary, and to help pay for the inevitable shortages of food during wartime. He worried too that wartime would cut off overseas mail service and the services of the courier he used out of Hong Kong, which would interrupt his remittances to Huangbo, so when he could, he sent more than his usual remittance. May-ying saw the same necessity.

Chinatown initially organized a boycott against commerce with Japan and Japanese-Canadians. As the war accelerated, the local Chinese population clamored to do more to help those at home resist the Japanese. Upon Chiang Kai-shek's urgent appeals to overseas Chinese for funds for his war chest, Chan Sam busied himself attending meetings to organize fund-raising drives. The money went towards the purchase of guns and winter jackets for

Chinese soldiers, or to aircraft, ambulances and medical supplies. Other drives were to provide aid for war orphans.

Chan Sam and May-ying took each other and Hing to their respective clan fund-raising banquets. Like other Chinese children, Hing too had a sense of the enemy. She handed out tags saying "Help our country" when she collected money in tin cans handed out by her Chinese school. At school, she sang "Fight the Japanese" to the tune of "*Frère Jacques*." She and her mother sat through repeat performances of Chinese opera benefits, inspired by the words in the program: "In entertainment, we must not forget saving the country." In everybody's head echoed the same anti-Japanese marching song, which was played over a loudspeaker at every fund-raising meeting, clan meeting, school assembly or opera benefit:

Stand up all the people, we will not be slaves
Join our flesh and blood together to become the new Great Wall
We the Chinese people live in such dangerous times
We are united in one heart to resist the cannonfire of the enemy
Forward we march! Forward we march!

The contributions from overseas provided one-quarter of China's military expenses in the first year of the war. There was also a dramatic rise in remittances, which provided enough foreign exchange to maintain China's balance of payments until the end of the second year of war. Chiang's war effort might well have collapsed were it not for the pull of the strings to the motherland, and the sense of obligations to relatives revived anew. On that front, Chan Sam and May-ying stood unwavering and in solidarity.

In the Confucian family, the relationship between husband and concubine ranked below the relationship of father and child. While Chan Sam's return to Canada was motivated by his desire to reassert control over May-ying, he was equally conscious of his duty to his youngest daughter. Upon the move to Vancouver, he immediately enrolled Hing in the private Mon Keong School.

Sponsored by the large Wong clan association, it was the best of Vancouver's three main Chinese schools. A block down Pender Street from the Royal Hotel, it occupied the third and fourth floors of the clan's building and offered six grades of instruction. Classes were held weekdays from four to six in the afternoon, and for higher grades, from seven until nine in the evening, with a general "speech day" held every Saturday morning.

Whenever a letter came from the family in China, Chan Sam told May-ying any news and reminded Hing that he would expect her in his room later to write a reply to her family in China. Hing was enthusiastic. She would race up the three flights of the Royal, swinging herself round each landing by grabbing hold of the oak banister, and skip down the dark hall to her father's room.

Each letter was virtually the same; the salutation and sign-off she had to copy out were invariably longer than anything else she wrote:

Honorable Mother, I kneel before you with my head bowed and my hands clasped. How are you. I am a good girl. I listen to my mother. I hope my two sisters listen to you. May you be blessed with health and contentment, your humble daughter, Hing.

Chan Sam found Hing to be a more attentive student than her sisters; she reveled in his explanations of the balance and rhythm of Chinese characters. She copied how he held the brush, lifting it with assurance from the paper to take each stroke to infinity. To her, these sessions were pleasant and enjoyable, and she looked forward to them every time.

Hing wrote less often to Ping and Nan, but she did, upon her father's return, see for the first time what they looked like. "Here are your sisters," he said, producing a black-and-white photograph taken in China. When she saw the image, Hing felt the reality of siblings for the first time, and she wondered when she would meet them. She imagined herself holding their hands, as they did each other's in the photograph. May-ying put that photograph on her dresser top, beside the one of herself posing with

Hing. As in real life, two daughters stood on Chinese soil; one on Canadian. Also as in real life, the eldest two, in matching print dresses, were the picture of little girls; the youngest, in short pants and suspenders, was the son denied.

It took but a few months before the renewed relationship between Chan Sam and May-ying, held together by duty and bolstered by patriotism, came undone. May-ying was genuinely happy about the birth of Yuen to Huangbo, for the continuation of the lineage ensured her own afterlife as long as she was part of Chan Sam's household. In some ways it was also a relief to her, for it confirmed that she and Chan Sam had left behind any physical relationship. At the same time, it undermined her importance in the family compared to Huangbo.

In the times May-ying and her husband did share—mainly over the dinner table—their differences began to choke each other like weeds. May-ying was less inclined to hold her tongue about what irritated her about Chan Sam, while he held an ever higher regard for his moral authority over her. She was more quick-tempered with him than before; he became more moody and temperamental with her. They took issue with each other over everything and over nothing. She objected to him buying more than fifty Hong Kong dollars' worth (about sixteen dollars Canadian) of War bonds for Chiang Kai-shek—which was the mimimum purchase the Vancouver Chinese community required of every adult male—saying it was better to send the money home to the family. He noticed May-ying was smoking more than ever. He repeated back what he had heard about her, that she was *lan doh* and *lan yum,* one who would gamble and drink until she was broken to pieces. He cared less about whose company she was keeping, but he was disgusted that she could drink until she was dizzy and staggering. She was disgusted by what he thought was a meal, rice with ketchup or jam on top.

It was true that May-ying had not tried to moderate her gambling and drinking ways. And that was not the only way she showed that she would neither live by Chan Sam's rules nor as if she belonged to him. She began an intimate relationship with the one close friend they shared, Jang Noong. This was her first affair of the heart, although eventually his love for her was returned only in a lifelong friendship.

Inevitably, word came back to Chan Sam that May-ying was no longer acting as if she was his. One day he summoned Hing, saying he needed her to accompany him on an errand. They walked down Pender and he stopped at the bottom of the staircase to the Asia Hotel. He sent Hing up while he stayed outside. She knew which door was Jang Noong's, having come calling on him with her mother on outings to Vancouver from Nanaimo, when Chan Sam was away in China.

There was no light from the window above his door. She knocked. "*Mama?*" There was no answer. "*Baba* wants you to come home," she said, hesitantly.

The voice that answered was her mother's. "You go on home. I'll see you there."

There was no point in Chan Sam or May-ying saying anything more. The incident in front of Jang Noong's door, in exposing the charade of the Canadian half of Chan Sam's family, had said it all. May-ying simply announced her refusal to live with Chan Sam. Living in the same Chinatown was too close for her liking, so she decided if he was staying in Vancouver, she was moving back to Nanaimo and taking Hing with her. Chan Sam agreed that they should separate, but he made no mention of "outing" May-ying from his household. As far as he was concerned, she was still his concubine; the only difference was that they were living apart. She packed up her belongings in her one metal trunk, and she and her youngest daughter left for the ferry.

⌐⊷⊶⊷⌐

By 1938, Nanaimo's Chinatown, looking ever more dilapidated, was not the haven it had once been. Japan's invasion of China had unsettled life in Chinatowns abroad, enough in this small community to throw its fragile economy off balance. Ocean freighters that once carried Chinese foods to buyers in America were commandeered into wartime service. When supplies dwindled, including rice, prices rose sharply—ginger root by as much as 300 percent, soya sauce by 1000 percent. In Nanaimo, Chinese shopkeepers were hauling out dry goods which hadn't moved in years and looking for ways to stretch supplies on hand, even tampering with soya sauce by diluting it with water. The three tea houses suffered most; the growing scarcity and high price of Chinese ingredients essential to *dim sum* delicacies—bamboo shoots, Chinese mushrooms, dried shrimps, salted turnips, rice flour, bean sauce, *hoi sin* sauce and oyster sauce—were to foreshadow the end of a tradition.

But Nanaimo's Chinese population, in decline because Depression had forced many back to China, had seen tough times before. The spirit up and down the dirt stretch remained buoyant, helped by the appearance of Mr. Wong's brand-new 1937 Plymouth, Chinatown's first car. May-ying, by the grace of the owners of three tea houses, became a shared asset as she bounced between them, each helping her out so that she was not without work. Hing, upon their return to Nanaimo, took it upon herself to enroll again in the first grade. She was seven, almost eight, and should have been in the second grade. But thinking there must be more to learn in the first year of English school, she had reenrolled herself. She vowed to be more thorough the second time around.

The move back to Nanaimo gave both May-ying and Hing a taste of freedom. There was enough space to roam to give a child a sense of territory off limits to adults. In the company of other children, Hing would do what no adult dared—brave the ghosts of the bone-house, the garage beside the Chins' house. The children peered through the cracks in the wall at the apparently forgotten piles of gunnysacks holding bones of the dead awaiting crating and shipment to China for final burial. When they were up to mischief, they would spy on the comings and goings from the room of the waitress nicknamed "Wild-Snake Jun." They'd fetch each other to look through the keyhole whenever there was a man with her, with nobody quite sure what it was they were up to inside.

Hing's best friend was Elsie. She would come by on her bike and Hing would hop on the back. The two liked to ride down back lanes, often stopping at a pig farm, watching squeamishly as men scalded live pigs hanging from hooks. Sometimes they went to the bluff at the end of Pine and climbed down through the brambles to the stream below to pick watercress to take home to their mothers for soup. Other times they wandered through backyards to steal apples and cherries. When they went downtown to the "white man's town," they took a shortcut by following the railway tracks. Sometimes they went further, down to the docks to dangle a string off a stick and try to catch fish like the Indians did.

Having just taken her leave of Chan Sam, May-ying was not about to relinquish her restored freedom by falling into the arms of another man. But, because she had arrived back on Pine Street a woman separated from her husband, like it or not, she was considered even more "available" than when Chan Sam had merely been absent and away in China.

Nobody fell harder for her than young Wally Chang. Because he was only twenty and she was already a woman of thirty, Wally's infatuation for May-ying caused a ripple of teasing among the men up and down Pine Street. They knew, from Wally himself, how he ached for any sign of notice by the woman with so many male admirers. Then came the first day she addressed him by his familiar Chinese name. Another day, her pink and white embroidered silk handkerchief fell within his reach and he thought he was hers. When Wally bought a car, Chinatown's second, he and May-ying would go for a ride, with Wally's black cocker spaniel between them on the front seat and Wally's twelve-year-old kid brother George in the back.

It was May-ying who brought an end to their flirting. There was no future in it for Wally; his mother, the wife of the owner of the Chang store and pig farm, would have disapproved had she known her son was seeing a lowly *kay-toi-neu* working the tea house circuit.

If May-ying ever tried to forget that a higher social standing was not within her grasp, she was reminded once a month, every payday. On that day, the appearance in Nanaimo of the familiar, tall, thin figure from years before surprised no one. "Chan Sam's here because he needs money and he needs her to get it for him," people said. But May-ying handed over willingly whatever amount of her pay had been agreed upon to keep the peace between them, money which he always said he needed to send to China.

After pleasantries rarely exchanged when they last lived together, May-ying asked Chan Sam what news there was of the family in China. When the war came to the south of China, all she wanted to know was whether he had word that Ping and Nan were still alive. He asked after Hing, and then he left town. Hing never saw her father on these occasions; she did not even know he came into town.

When Nanaimo's tea houses became another casualty of the distant war in China, what was once May-ying's fortune—her beauty and wit—became a luxury the tea house owners could no longer afford. To forestall closure, they cut back on staff and hours and the menu. Each cutback dismantled further the idea of the tea house. The Depression had only given a dying tradition and a dying profession a brief reprieve. May-ying finally had to settle for a waitressing job at Ho Yuen, a ground-floor restaurant with four booths and four tables of open seating in a ramshackle house. The house specialty was fresh rice noodles.

The owner lived in the attic, his window overlooking the woodpile. In the back garden just shy of the outhouse was a shed with three small rooms. One room was empty; no one wanted to live in it because a man had died there years before. May-ying and Hing moved into the other two.

People liked to say that tea house waitresses did not make good mothers. Hing herself had little experience of any other home life except on her own with her waitressing mother, or of any home except in a restaurant. She slept, ate and played wherever her mother worked. Once she was of an age where she could be left alone, she was unafraid of the independence that came with it. If she ever needed her mother, she knew where to look for her. If she wasn't at work, she was in one of the gambling dens.

But Hing, like any child, looked for guidance in growing up. As a child does of a parent, she looked for consistency. She was to find it only in the knowledge that she would be disciplined, with or without provocation.

It had begun in the days before she started school, when, for a time, her dresses were exchanged for boy's clothing because she got dirty while playing. "Look at you! You can never keep yourself clean!" May-ying said at the inevitable reappearance of dirt. She held a chicken feather-duster by its end and brought its bamboo handle stinging across the back of Hing's legs. "Keep crying and I'll hit you that much harder!"

By the time Hing was seven or eight, her mother expected her to assume certain responsiblities. In particular, she was supposed to know when she had played enough. Too much play—how much was too much was never clear—was wrong. "*Ah* Hing! Come inside!" May-ying's voice interrupted her daughter's play and cast a pall over the gaiety of the other children. "You play too much. All you know how to do is play! Play so much your mind will turn wild," May-ying said, as she shut the door behind Hing and brought the feather-duster down on her legs.

Still, Hing always stayed out longer than her mother liked. She simply didn't know any better, as no other children were heading home. Once May-ying reached into a crowd of children to grab hold of Hing by the hair. "Where have you been?" she said. "I've been looking all over for you. Come home!" But the spanking Hing had been expecting didn't happen. Her mother, once back in their room, vomited, then fell asleep on the bed, leaving Hing to mop up the mess on the floor.

Another time, when Hing wandered back to the Ho Yuen from an afternoon of play, her mother was waiting for her. She stood at the front door of the house, which opened to the room where the restaurant was. As usual in any Chinese establishment, there were people about. Even if it wasn't mealtime at the Ho Yuen, there was always traffic in and out—people dropping by to chat and visit, to help themselves to a cup of tea.

May-ying took out a chair and sat in it, glaring at her daughter. "Stand in front of me!" she ordered. *Wham!* A stick, a piece of kindling, came whipping across the back of one of Hing's legs. *Wham!* across the other. On her third time across each leg, some of the men nearby started to plead with her.

"*Ah* May-ying," they said, "don't be so harsh."

Demonstrating authority to people beneath one was the old Chinese way. In China, a foreman wouldn't walk by his workers without yelling "Hurry up!" Never mind that they were already working diligently, they needed reminding who was the boss. Those were the old ways of teaching obedience and discipline. In the new world, where there were few children and their presence was sadly missed, the attitude of many parents had softened.

May-ying's had not. She was determined to prove that she was not afraid to stand by the traditional values of what made a good parent and what produced an obedient child. She turned on the men: "As long as you hit a child on the leg, you can't do permanent injury. The more you tell me, the harder I'll hit. She's my own flesh and blood. If you think what I'm doing is wrong, then take me to jail."

When she was done, May-ying ordered her daughter: "Kneel down!"

With her head bowed, Hing, meek and submissive, echoed her mother's words.

"I will be obedient. I admit I was naughty. I will be a good girl."

The spectacle over, Hing, in tears, practically limped away to sit on a nearby chair. Her mother brought her a bowl of rice noodles in broth. Feeling sorry for herself, and wanting to let her mother know, Hing kept gasping and choking for air. May-ying couldn't stand it. "Cry until you die—why don't you cry until you die!" she told her, and then she walked away. Forgotten, Hing wandered off, found a table to crawl under, shed a few silent tears and fell asleep.

After that incident, spankings became almost a daily ritual if

May-ying was around and not sick in bed when Hing came home. She wasted no breath on a lecture about play. There was just the ominous order: "*Ah* Hing! Fetch me *tew chai.*"

Hing knew what she had to do, but it only got harder each time. She would step out the door of their room onto the path and run back and forth between the woodpile at the kitchen side of the Ho Yuen, past the door to the outhouse at the other end. She was a child possessed, going closer to the woodpile and her appointment with her mother, then retreating. Finally, when she thought she could delay no longer, and shaking with fear, she would select the stick with which her mother would beat her.

"Go inside and face her," she told herself as sternly as she could. Even before it was over, Hing was crying out to May-ying: "I will be obedient—I admit I was naughty—I will be a good girl."

The tears that were choked off would later fall so hard into her bowl that her rice would taste of salt, and would soak into her pillow so often that she got used to falling asleep on its dampness night after night.

No matter how May-ying prided herself on her strictness as a mother, she was not able to stop unflattering gossip about herself reaching her daughter's ears. More than once in the shops, when Hing had been sent on an errand, she overheard others refer to her mother as "*Jui-Mow Ying.*" Wondering what it meant to be called a "drunkard," Hing selected a bottle from among those displayed on the dresser back in their room. "Cream-coco" was what her mother called the Creme de Cacao liqueur. Hing licked the cork and found it a better version of Horlick's Malt, one of the foreign foods always on hand. The next day she licked more. After several more days, the level in the bottle was down a couple inches.

"The cream-coco is so good!" she told her mother.

"Are you drinking it?"

"No, every day I just lick a little bit."

"Well, that is alcohol. It's not for children. No wonder you were saying that you were dizzy and couldn't walk straight!" May-ying said, laughing.

Hing's lessons about the men in her mother's life had been inadvertent and had started in the tea house days long before she could comprehend them. There was the gossip she overheard in a communal bathroom. Some ladies were washing out their laundry in the basin, and one said that May-ying had "holes cut out of her bloomers." Hing, hurt and angry at the women for talking about her mother, did not understand why her mother would wear such underwear or why they should care if she did. She checked a pair hanging up to dry on the makeshift laundry line in their room. What those ladies said is not true, she told herself. But Hing would come to see what it was they really meant.

After school one day, she was returning to their room and went to push the door open. Immediately, she tried to ease it shut again. Her mother was with a man, and the two of them, fully clothed, were standing with their arms around each other, bodies pressed together. It was Lam *Bak*, one of the men who worked in a logging camp. Hing crept away. Beginning to decipher the code of May-ying's conduct, she now understood the discreet winks her mother exchanged in the midst of a tea house crowd. She also understood why Pang *Sook*, the man she once found with her mother in his lap, was always among the last of the crowd, hanging around as if he were waiting for everyone else to leave.

That was revelation enough, yet there was worse to come after they moved to the Ho Yuen. One night Hing, who no longer followed her mother around as she did when she was younger, put herself to bed as usual.

A man's voice woke her. "Is she asleep?" Hing recognized it to be the voice of Sam *Bak*, the carpenter. She had always liked him because of his mild manner, and because he always took time to talk with her. She had a sickening feeling that he was yet another of her mother's secret friends.

"Sh-sh!" It was her mother, hushing him. "She's asleep, she's asleep. Don't worry."

Hing made sure she was absolutely still. But the next thing she knew they had climbed into bed beside her, and he was on top of her mother. Hing's arm was pinned under them. "I wish they'd hurry up," she kept thinking to herself, so that the weight would be gone from her arm. It seemed like an eternity that she was in agony, but she was too terrified to try to free herself. It came to her that her mother was no better than the waitress "Wild-Snake Jun." Afterwards, May-ying and Sam *Bak* whispered something to each other, and then he left.

If Hing didn't know right from wrong of what she saw of her mother's encounters with men, her gambling and drinking ways, she did know she didn't like it. The pain of such knowledge revealed itself in her own ailments. She developed recurring stomach cramps, she'd get hiccups often, and she suffered from daily nose bleeds, sometimes severe enough to stain her dress front. Her hair started to thin. But the worse was the eczema on her legs, which she scratched until they were raw and infected.

Her mother was not uncaring. May-ying dutifully and expertly ministered to all these symptoms. She brewed herbal teas to ease the cramps. She prepared soup to stop the nose bleeds by steaming a pig's head for hours in a covered earthenware pot inside a bigger enamel pot. She massaged a herbal tonic into Hing's scalp. She washed Hing's legs in day-old tea, and she herself carried bucketfuls of seawater up the hill for her to soak her legs in. When the eczema persisted, she bottled water on the seventh day of the seventh month—when water was believed to have special healing powers—to mix a bovine powder into paste to smear on Hing's legs.

Striving for some measure of self-respect, Hing was keen about both her English and Chinese schools. In the classroom, she excelled. In the schoolyard, she was the challenger to beat at marbles, jacks and Double Dutch. She spent much of her spare time at Tong Yick store, because there she was indulged, praised and often the center of attention. The men from Poon-ye who hung around there taught her to read the characters in the headlines of the Chinese newspaper, then mostly the vocabulary of war and resistance. They teased her with Chinese riddles: "When does ten plus ten equal ten, and ten minus ten equal ten? When you put on a pair of gloves on your ten fingers and when you take them off again!" So quick-witted was she that their nickname for her was "*Jook Gee* Hing"—a girl named Hing fast enough to chase and catch pigs.

May-ying seemed to know what she herself had to run from. Whenever her drunken haze lifted, the reality of her situation must have stared at her. She continued to make her monthly trips to Victoria to visit the temple there. Only to the god-image in the warm, womb-like room, shrouded in red silk lanterns and tier upon tier of red and gold banners did she reveal what guidance or mercies she sought. As for Hing, she did as she was taught, clasped her hands, bowed three times. But she stood to the side when her mother kneeled in silence and shook the shaker of fortunes, with its one hundred and three bamboo sticks, until one rose above the rest. The temple keeper would read the corresponding numbered page from his book of ancient sayings, leaving May-ying to interpret its significance.

The only time May-ying would challenge fate was in gambling-table chatter. "When I win big," she used to boast, "I'm going to bring my two daughters over from China." Sometimes others reminded her of what she had said, especially when the fall of Canton to the Japanese in October 1938 sent shockwaves through the Chinese community.

When Hing heard mention of her absent sisters, she thought of that photograph on their dresser that her father had brought home from China. She thought of the two of them there, of herself alone in Canada, and of how they could be the company she longed for. When she dared to hope too much, she had only to look around the room she shared with her mother and ask herself where her sisters would sleep to realize that it was nothing but empty talk and wishful thinking.

# CHAPTER SEVEN

WITHIN A YEAR of her return to Nanaimo, the declining fortunes along Pine Street forced May-ying back to the ever-smaller waitressing circuit in search of work. With Hing in tow, and using Nanaimo as a base, she took to the road—a month here, a month there—bouncing between temporary jobs in Victoria and Vancouver. Mostly it was lower-paying waitressing in cafés in Vancouver, where the tips were paltry. With every prospective employer, May-ying would try to bargain her daughter's meals into her contract. "What about my daughter?" she'd invariably have to ask again. "She doesn't eat much." The times Hing wasn't included, May-ying left her behind in Nanaimo with other women who rented rooms at the tea houses there.

Although Hing did not miss her mother, she also did not like the experience of being looked after by someone else. One lady she thought unreasonable, the other badgering. The first made Hing hand-wash laundry and left her to struggle with wringing out items too large for her to manage, including a heavy flannel dress; the other lady slapped her wrist whenever she found Hing using her left hand instead of her right.

One of May-ying's temporary employers was the B.C. Royal Café in Vancouver. The café was famous in Chinatown for its pastry; egg tarts, apple tarts, butterhorns, ladyfingers, Boston cream pies, strawberry shortcakes and pound cakes were baked fresh daily. There was always fresh coffee, made by breaking an entire egg, shells and all, in with the grounds in the urn. The meals on offer depended on the day of the week: Thursday was popular because it was roast beef day, other days there was roast pork, oxtail and beef tongue or stew.

One afternoon in 1939, at half-past two, a man walked into the B.C. Royal and, noticing May-ying behind the counter, sat on one of the red vinyl-and-chrome stools there. She was wearing the standard-issue café uniform, pale green with a white detachable collar and clip-on buttons. He was stern-looking and of average height, and perhaps ten years older than May-ying's thirty-two. He was wearing an impeccably tailored suit with the sheen of silk and wool. He sat himself down and ordered from May-ying a cup of coffee and a butterhorn.

He came in the next day at the same time and ordered the same thing. He repeated this pattern whenever May-ying was on shift. Believing that she was beautiful enough to have her choice of men, he worked hard to catch her attention and persisted until she took enough notice to strike up a friendly conversation. His name was Chow Guen, a name known to every big-time gambling club owner in Chinatowns across Canada. A professional gambler and an educated man, whose Chinese penmanship was much admired, Guen was in demand as the hired head man, the banker of the operation and the croupier running the tables. He had arrived in Vancouver to take up an assignment running a gambling club. The club, across the street from the B.C. Royal, opened at three in the afternoon.

The courtship that began over the counter between Guen and May-ying continued when she was off shift. His loud, aggressive and authoritative manner was not off-putting to her and he liked how self-assured she was. Conversation flowed between them. He smoked, so did she, though not as heavily. He enjoyed his whiskey with every meal but, unlike the rowdy patrons she used to serve at the tea house, did not insist that she join him in one. Her weakness was in drinking with friends; she did not drink alone. But the real glue in their attraction for each other was their gambling kinship, the unspoken trust and honesty and a quickness of wit. To May-ying, Guen must have seemed everything that Chan Sam was not: where Chan Sam was ham-fisted, the other was shrewd; Chan Sam had to look for work, employers came looking for Guen; the respect that her husband wanted so much, Guen already had.

When May-ying returned to Nanaimo, Guen traveled back and forth from Vancouver to spend his days off with her. Often he stayed overnight. On those occasions, he rented another room from the tea house, if that was where May-ying was staying, or if she was at the Ho Yuen restaurant, he stayed in the second room of her quarters in the back garden. At every meal, taken in the tea house or café, Guen, May-ying and Hing sat and ate together.

As Guen moved naturally into her mother's life, Hing found herself resenting his presence. Whereas she had to pretend that she had seen nothing and knew nothing of her mother's fleeting encounters with other men, there was no denying the coziness with Guen. In fact, his arrival coincided with the passage of those other men from May-ying's life, and the end of the seamier side of her life. But all Hing could think every time she saw him was: "Guen *Sook* is NOT my father." To make things worse, he had hardly arrived on the scene when he began to support May-ying's sternness in disciplining Hing. "You love a child with your heart," he said, "not with words from your mouth." Hing thought to herself, "I can honestly say I hate him."

Hing came to feel that she was the odd one out in this new family, and that Guen had stolen her mother's loyalty. On one of Guen's visits to see her mother in Nanaimo, he paid for two rooms at a hotel downtown, instead of the three of them staying in Chinatown. Rather than doing something together, as Hing had expected, she was sent on an errand to Chinatown to buy barbecued pork for the three of them. Hing could see through the ruse. It was an hour's walk there and back; Guen and her mother didn't want barbecued pork so much as they wanted her out of the way.

One of Guen's visits was on the same night that a famous ice skating troupe was putting on a show at an arena downtown. Her mother enjoyed such special events as much as Hing, and she had promised that she and Guen would take her. That day, Hing got special permission to leave Chinese school half an hour early to make the eight o'clock show. She ran home to Ho Yuen, through the restaurant and out into the back to their two rooms.

"*Mama*, are we going now?" she called out. The door to the bedroom was closed. Hing opened it. In the darkness, she saw her mother in bed with Guen.

"We'll go another time." It was Guen who answered.

"But you said we were going to go tonight, *Mama*," Hing said, the annoyance in her voice aimed at Guen for interfering.

"*Ah* Hing, we're not going," her mother replied.

Hing persisted. "But I came home early especially."

"If you say any more, I'm going to silence your mouth!" her mother said.

Hing sat on the floor on the other side of the door, feeling more sorry for herself as the show went on without her.

Hing found ways to make it hard for her mother in front of Guen. At one meal, she reached for a toothpick, and like everyone did at the end of a Chinese meal, she put it in her mouth. When her mother's back was turned, she pretended that Guen had bumped her, ramming the toothpick into her cheek. Seeing through the trick, May-ying slapped her across the face, the only time Hing could remember her mother doing so. It was Guen who restrained Hing's mother: "Don't mind Hing," he said, "she's young."

Few people in Chinatown carried bills in their pockets, most had only coins. Not Chow Guen. He always carried a thick wad of paper money, stacked and bound with a wide rubber band. The denominations were sorted from one hundred dollar bills on

The photograph May-ying affixed to the false papers she used to enter Canada in 1924.

May-ying and newborn Ping. Printed on the back is: "Made in Canada."

Vancouver's Chinatown, Pender Street, 1929 (courtesy Vancouver City Archives) where Chan Sam's mah jongg parlour was and where May-ying worked at a tea house.

Chan Sam and May-ying in 1928, before they brought their two daughters from Canada to China.

Opposite page: The concubine's eldest daughters, Ping and Nan, on Chinese soil (left), the photograph which stood on May-ying's dresser alongside the one of her youngest, Hing (right), taken in a Vancouver studio. So taken was May-ying with dressing her as a boy that she commissioned a portrait; in the original, mother and daughter stood hand in hand.

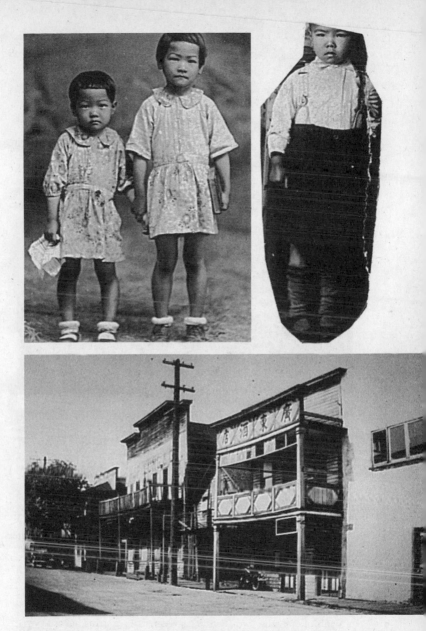

The Canton House in Nanaimo's Chinatown years after May-ying worked there. (Courtesy British Columbia Archives and Resource Services [cat. 83200], c. 1950s)

Above, half of the image of May-ying with Chow Guen. In the original, they were posed as man and wife; he stood behind her chair.

May-ying's 'family' portrait with Hing and newly-procured Gok-leng, the son she always wanted.

A Vancouver sidewalk photographer captures Hing and Gok-leng. She wears the brown knit coat which Ping and Yuen would return to her in China more than four decades later.

Below, the photograph Hing commissioned upon graduation from Strathcona School.

Ping's photographs taken to accompany her papers to leave China for Canada. She would change her mind, unable to leave her two-year-old son.

Ping and her son. She would have three more children, before her husband (inset) fled to join his mistress in Hong Kong.

Winnie, a student nurse at Essondale. (Inset) Leaving the grounds, she trades her nursing shoes for her street shoes for the last time, having quit nursing to marry John Chong.

Winnie and her father leave for the church. (Inset) Winnie and her mother.

Winnie and John Chong, September, 1950.

The Gladstone Street house, taken some years after we lived there.

My sister, Louise, and I (inset) cooling ourselves off in the back yard, and on the sidewalk in front of the Gladstone Street house.

Our house on Prince George Airport where we moved in 1958.

My sister and I with our two brothers recreate our parents' wedding. (Inset) My grandmother and Wayne, the youngest, two years before her death in 1967.

Huangbo, with Yuen, his wife and children in front of my grandfather's house in Chang Gar Bin. Huangbo died two years later in 1968.

In 1987, Mother and I are in Hong Kong, celebrating her fifty-seventh birthday as we await word about travel arrangements to Chang Gar Bin.

Mother and Yuen meet for the first time at the Overseas Chinese Office in Chang Gar Bin.

Ping and Mother, having just met, walk to Yuen's house. (Inset) In front
of the main doorway.

Ping stands where once stood my grandfather's old house, where Mother was conceived. (Inset) Yuen sits on a wall there.

A drawing of Huangbo and Chan Sam (above) that hangs in the reception room of Yuen's house (below), the house my grandfather built and my grandmother paid for.

down. Such big sums did not leave Guen casual about money, however. He was as meticulous with his personal expenses as he was about the money belonging to his gambling business. Every day, he took up his brush and recorded every cent that came in and and went out, down to a streetcar fare, even a cup of coffee. In that account were also the few dollars here and there that he lent May-ying. He was happy to give her what she asked for, though he had to know what it was needed for beforehand. "I'm not here to bail you out of your debts," he told her, which wasn't necessary, because May-ying had no intention of taking advantage.

What May-ying wanted most, what she sought Guen's help to get, was security. She had a measure of security in her jade and gold—the dangling earrings, the jade pendant and other small pieces that she had been able to afford here and there, like a jade monkey holding a coconut, which she kept for Hing to wear on special occasions. The Chinese were always buying and selling jewelry among themselves, and if she ever needed her next meal, she could always sell a piece. But her hunger for security went deeper. Her separation from Chan Sam and the ongoing war in China had left her future in Canada indefinite and uncertain. "I'm concerned about my old age," she told Guen one day. "I'm concerned that there will be no one to look after me."

He understood; she was talking about sons. His own days of bringing forth sons were behind him. He and his wife in China had two, one of whom was a schoolteacher. Both lived at home with their mother; both were married, both had children. Guen already knew what May-ying was going to say next, that she would like to find a baby boy whose mother wanted to "adopt out."

"But," May-ying added, "I wouldn't have the money to go through with it."

In Chinese communities abroad, the going price for a baby boy was ten times that of a girl. If May-ying had been looking for a girl, she would not have used the term "adopt out," for girls were "given away." In China, families without sons typically went to relatives with sons to spare. But here in the new world such family connections were few, and both boys and girls were scarce because there were so few women to bear children. The ratio of males to females in Vancouver's Chinese community—ten to one when May-ying first arrived in Canada—had only improved to five to one. Children or babies available for adoption came from unmarried girls with unwanted pregnancies, mothers in dire straits, or those who, for some reason, couldn't care for their children.

Guen promised to give May-ying whatever it cost to procure a boy. She then contacted a woman known in Vancouver as Granny Yip. Nellie Yip, a white woman, was a former midwife. Having once worked in China, she was fluent in five Chinese dialects. She lived with Yip Gong, a prominent jeweler, now retired. Chinatown's first mixed couple, they had met in New York and he had brought her to live in his family's building. Nellie had made a name for herself inside and outside Chinatown working on behalf of the Chinese. It was she who got the Vancouver General Hospital to overturn the rule that confined Chinese patients to the basement. Though retired, she still had the necessary connections with white doctors and nurses (since nobody outside Chinatown hired Chinese medical graduates, they almost always left North America for China) whose cooperation was essential for her to be a go-between for people like May-ying.

May-ying was not Granny Yip's typical client. Usually childless couples, or couples longing for more children, came to her. Some had daughters but no sons, others had one child and wanted more. Often, by the time wives joined their husbands in North America, they were too old to have children. In Chinatown, putting children up for adoption was an accepted family practice, and these children were simply referred to as children "brought up by someone else" or children "using another family's surname."

"You're going to have a baby brother," May-ying told Hing.

When word came, the two of them went from their home in Nanaimo to Vancouver. Hing's thought was that she was at last going to have the company she longed for; May-ying's that she was at last to have the pleasure of looking upon a son, who would be her future security.

They went to World Rooms, a rooming house above a fish-monger and a butcher shop on Pender, and waited. Granny Yip knocked at the door, came in and laid a ten-day-old boy down on the bed. May-ying liked what she saw. The next day, she went to Granny Yip's house and paid her three hundred dollars, and Granny Yip handed over the baby and a birth certificate. It said the baby was born in Vancouver on July 25, 1939. The name of his mother matched the name on the false birth certificate that had got May-ying into Canada; Chan Sam was named as his father. The baby was registered as Leonard Chan, Leonard being Granny Yip's doing. May-ying called him Gok-leng, a Chinese name Guen had chosen.

Only mother, daughter and son appeared in the family portrait taken at Yucho Chow's on the day of Gok-leng's Full Month. It was a photograph that captured a mother's pride. May-ying's *cheong sam* was a cascade of shimmering stars on pale silk; her son, in a white bonnet and leggings, sat on her lap, and standing at her side was her nine-year-old daughter, looking girlish this time with a satin ribbon encircling the waist of her skirt and another tying back her hair. Like their mother, both children were adorned with a flash of gold and jade. Around Hing's neck hung the jade pendant of the monkey holding a coconut; around Gok-leng's tiny wrist was a pale jade bangle.

When the three of them returned to Nanaimo, the carpenter Sam *Bak*, the same man who had climbed into bed with her mother when Hing was supposedly sleeping, had built the baby a crib. He was to be disappointed when this gesture of his affection did not win May-ying back.

The crib was moved into the Wongs' living quarters behind the kitchen of the Canton. May-ying had arranged to board Gok-leng there in the care of the eldest daughter, Mamie. There was no way that May-ying, a single mother, could care for a baby and work at the same time. But hardly had Mamie taken Gok-leng in when Mr. Wong fell gravely ill. When the blinds of the Canton were pulled down to announce his death, the family decided to give the baby back.

Until May-ying could make other arrangements, Gok-leng's care fell mostly to Hing. Often Hing had to go in search of her mother at work, or if it was after hours, in the gambling dens, when the crying baby couldn't be consoled.

That autumn, in September 1939, Canada entered the Second World War. The government announced that construction would begin the next year on a military camp in Nanaimo to train as many as twenty thousand soldiers to defend Canada's west coast. But for this news, the tea houses would have closed. As it was, they had to cling to life for yet another year. It wasn't until 1941, when war spread to the Pacific with Japan's attack on Pearl Harbor, that the soldiers moved in. Their arrival would keep the tea house owners in business but consign the tradition of the tea house to history. Down would come the booths and curtains of privacy, out would go the spittoons, and *dim sum* would be replaced by chop suey.

But May-ying didn't linger any longer in Nanaimo. The B.C. Royal Café had offered her a steady job. She packed her metal trunk and took Hing and four-month-old Gok-leng to settle in Vancouver. She boarded him with Granny Yip and her elderly husband, who lived several blocks east of Chinatown on Keefer Street, where they had bought a house. May-ying took a room for herself and Hing at the Royal Hotel—the same place that Chan Sam and May-ying had lived as a family after his return from China, before they went their separate ways. The compelling reason May-ying moved to Vancouver was her lover, Guen. He lived a block away from the hotel in some bachelor rooms on Market Alley.

Shortly after they were settled in Vancouver, it was Hing who caught sight of a familiar tall, thin figure. She and May-ying were crossing Pender.

"Oh! *Baba!*" She pulled on her mother's sleeve, gesturing excitedly at her father coming towards them.

Every Chinese on Canada's west coast passed through Vancouver's Chinatown at one time or another, so it was inevitable that even though Chan Sam had work outside Vancouver at that time, he and his estranged family would pass by chance on the street.

"Don't call him *Baba!*" May-ying snapped. "He's not your father." She forced Hing to turn her head. She heard her father say, "Oh, *Ah* Hing..." but they passed him by as if he were but a cardboard figure in their lives.

Though Hing was confused about this deliberate show of disrespect, she was accustomed to the children of waitresses not knowing where their fathers were, or even who they were. Doreen Jang, one of Hing's first playmates in Nanaimo, was now living in Vancouver, and upon Hing's arrival, the two became best friends. Once, on their way to school, they came upon a man writing Chinese characters on a shop window. In Chinatown, there were only two artists who did such calligraphy for shops, and who painted interior wall murals and scenery backdrops for opera performances. "Doreen, there's your *Baba,*" one of the men standing around called out. "Go ask him for some candy," said another. Doreen, who addressed the man her mother lived with as "Uncle," told Hing that her mother had told her that her father was dead. Whenever Doreen came upon that artist again, she never addressed him as *Baba,* but he stopped what he was doing and gave her candy. Once, he gave her a ballpoint pen, another time a dollar bill.

The truth was that Chan Sam had disappeared from Hing's sight, but not from the ledger of her life. Chan Sam himself went to Mon Keong Chinese school once a month to pay the three-dollar monthly tuition for his daughter. However, he had stopped coming to collect what he regarded as the family's share of May-ying's wages. For one thing, she was no longer earning the high wages of a tea house waitress, and in any event the war had interrupted Chan Sam's remittances to China. To pass on news from the family in China was the only reason he sought out May-ying, and on that score, he was faithful. But letters from war-torn China came, at best, sporadically.

Hing missed Nanaimo terribly. It wasn't just the progress of pave-ment and buildings, or the stoplight in the intersection in the middle of Vancouver's Chinatown that hemmed in play; it was life at the bottom of the larger, class-conscious community. In Nanaimo, Hing could join any children playing in the middle of Pine Street, but in Vancouver, mothers wanted to know another child's mother before allowing their children to play together. Hing was not a child other mothers wanted their own to befriend. So she received no invitations to the family apartments above the businesses that their fathers ran. Nor did she invite anybody to the rooming house she lived in. Rooming houses, filled mostly with single men, were not proper homes in anybody's eyes; no child ventured into one except those who lived there.

Hing's life became more solitary as friends and family evapo-rated from her life. Only sometimes did May-ying take her along to Granny Yip's—which was a twenty-minute walk away—when she went, twice or three times a week, to see Gok-leng. By day, mother and daughter were like two figures in a cuckoo clock, coming and going separately from their room at the Royal Hotel. By the time Hing returned from public school and then two hours of Chinese instruction at Mon Keong School, May-ying had gone on shift at the B.C. Royal. Occasionally Hing took sup-per there. Sometimes she was indulged with dessert, a glass of milk and a slice of pound cake. But more typically Hing cooked for herself at the rooming house, preparing rice and stir-frying green beans in soya bean cake sauce over the gas burner at the communal kitchen.

On nights when Hing had no homework, she went off after supper on her own to catch the seven o'clock performance of Chinese opera at one of Chinatown's two theaters. The theaters were both cavernous, with seating for several hundred. During the week, she and mostly older men filed past the doorman. She, like the old *Bak*s, had no other entertainment. Other children had friends, school clubs and sports, but May-ying would not allow Hing to have anything to do with something she did not know well or understand. She approved of opera because she had seen many of the same classics when she was a girl. As the shows didn't finish until midnight or later, well past a child's bedtime on a school night, most other parents permitted their children to go only on weekends. But May-ying bought her daughter a season's pass. She preferred to know exactly where her daughter was each evening, and to have confirmation, from the doorman.

Luckily Hing loved the world of the opera. She had her favorite wooden bench in an upper balcony; she knew the faces in the orchestra, the stage nicknames of the stars. She understood the symbolism of the costumes and makeup. The emperor wore yellow, honest men wore black and good persons wore red; faces painted red or purple were persons of strong moral character, while faces painted predominantly white were of bad character. She identified with making something out of nothing: a table was a table in one scene, in another it became a cave, a bed, even a mountain. If a general was going on a journey, he pretended to mount a horse while a soldier cracked a whip and ran across the stage to announce his arrival. She identified with the masking of emotion, recognized fear in a trembling arm, weeping in a palm slowly raised in front of a face. In the dark, Hing's tears of laughter or sorrow ran freely. She chose which opera to see according to the handbills posted in shop windows, and whether she was in the mood for a tragedy or a comedy. The choice would be between something like *Pity the Girl*, about a widowed mother looking for her son, which promised to "make your tears red all evening long," and *Robber's Love Nest*, which promised laughs so hard "the oil in your ears will run." Hing sat through so many repeat performances that she would knit in the dark; in the third grade, she knit 112 cotton washcloths for the Red Cross to send to Canadian soldiers fighting in the Second World War, enough to win the competition at her public school.

When the final curtain was lowered, Hing returned to reality. She wandered by either the White Lamb book shop or Sing Kee Confectionery, knowing she would find her mother in either of their back rooms playing mah-jongg. When May-ying saw Hing come in, she asked Guen, if he was there and not at his club, or else one of the *Bak*s she knew well, to escort her daughter home. Otherwise Hing sat silently by her mother's side. Around two in the morning, the two of them would head home. Eventually, Hing was trusted to go directly home from the opera herself, and was asleep by the time her mother came in.

Hing knew that during the week her mother saw Guen in his rooms, which had the privacy the rooming house did not. On Sundays her mother took her along. The three of them would pass an afternoon and evening, with Guen singing and accompanying himself on a harp-like Chinese musical instrument. He was always the one who would cook supper. Once the dishes were done, he and May-ying would each roll their week's supply of cigarettes, and then May-ying and Hing would go back to the Royal Hotel.

While Hing remained determined not to warm to Guen, she melted in the presence of two other male friends of her mother's. There was the ever faithful Jang Noong. Sometimes Hing and her mother dropped by the Eagle Café on Hastings, where he was a chef. He'd make them a Spanish omelette and serve them his lemon meringue pie for dessert. The other friend was someone else from the early days of the mah-jongg parlor, a man known affectionately in Chinatown as "*Fee Bak*," "the fat man." Then a cook on the coastal tugs, he took Hing on an outing whenever he came in from ten days at sea. He'd take her to Woodward's to buy candy; once he bought her a hat there. In his absence, Hing would pray nightly that his boat wouldn't capsize or that a storm wouldn't sweep him overboard. "*Fee Bak* is like a father to me," Hing told the celestial powers, as she began to miss the real one she wasn't allowed to have.

⬅━━━➡

As important as Guen's rice bowl and his chopsticks at his place setting was his scotch whiskey. In his room, the bottle of Johnny Walker Black Label sat on the table. At a restaurant, he poured the supply he brought into a teapot. Guen would refill his glass or porcelain teacup three or four times with each meal, savoring each taste with a noisy smack of his lips. He had quite a capacity for alcohol, without any appearance of drunkenness. May-ying didn't always partake with him. When she did, she restricted herself to one glass.

May-ying was curbing her bad habits and sharpening her image in other ways. Her fashions showed a return to the stylish city image. When not in her work uniform, she went about in printed dresses nipped in at the waist and shoes with modest heels. Her legs had the sheen of nylon stockings, which were held up by the elastics she hand-sewed around the tops. The top drawer of her dresser mirrored her meticulous attention to grooming; it held a neatly arranged treasure trove of hair clips, combs and embroidered silk handkerchiefs, lacquered boxes of dusting powders, bottles of fragrant waters and stacks of accordion paper to stain her lips and cheeks red.

At the same time, influenced perhaps by Guen's image as a professional gambler, she added a masculine touch to her wardrobe. Luck at the gambling table was a big part of the business at Modernize Tailors, Gung Lai Wong's family business. Their customers were men, though on occasion it was a wife who marched in to sew up a husband's gambling wins from the night before into a custom-tailored three-piece suit. May-ying came in one day to order one for herself. She selected one of the styles from a poster of illustrations of "American Gentlemen Fashions," from a fashion tailor on Broadway in New York. She picked out a fine worsted wool imported from England and buttons from the jars of oddments, sorted by color, behind the cutter's table. At the fitting, she tested the extra inside jacket pockets she'd ordered by emptying the contents of her handbag into them. She worried about carrying a handbag so openly going to and from the gambling dens after once having it snatched; there was a lot of such petty crime on the streets. At her last fitting, she liked the finished look so much that she went out and bought a man's tie and cap to match.

When May-ying was seen dressed in this way in the gambling dens and around Chinatown, it was as though she was making the statement that she was taking her rightful place in a man's world; that a woman who made her own living, who didn't depend on a man for support, should be respected. Perhaps more than anything, her masculine dress was a statement that a woman could do as she pleased with her life. As if to prove some solidarity, she convinced two other women friends to do the same, to wear men's suits and matching caps. They called themselves "The Three Sisters." A photograph of the trio taken at Yucho Chow's stood on May-ying's dresser, alongside those of her three daughters, the three real sisters.

Gossip was the currency of Chinatown, and it came to Chan Sam's attention that May-ying was Chow Guen's "lady friend." Chan Sam turned fifty-three in 1940. He'd been a loner since he and May-ying separated. Men his age living abroad had little choice; there were very few women available for any aged bachelor. Such continuing exile for Chan Sam only romanticized his dreams of what he was missing at home; when he went to sleep at night, he had thoughts only for Huangbo in China, and there was not a letter that he sent to his wife in which he did not tell her so. But he could not ignore the news of May-ying. To him, it was a loss of face; she was still his concubine and not free to act without his consent.

Divorce was his privilege to invoke, and though at least two of the seven traditional "outs" applied to May-ying—"wanton conduct" and "garrulousness"—he had chosen not to "out" her from his household. Were he to do so, and May-ying wanted to protest, she could have invoked one of a wife's three "not-outs," that of "not having a home to return to." But while these were the customs of marriage in China, in the new world they had lost all meaning. Almost two decades of exclusion had warped the male-female ratio. As a consequence, the older Chinese community had become less censorious about unmarried relationships. Those like May-ying and Chow Guen's, where a woman took up with a man whose wife was in China, were accepted and even condoned. Such women were typically former waitresses, and nobody could blame them if they found a man to give them a house and to provide for them and the children they'd had along the way.

Chan Sam, not one to let reality overtake tradition, came to

May-ying's room and confronted her.

"I'm the one who brought you here from China," he told her angrily. "Chow Guen should come to me. By right, he should be asking me for permission to have anything to do with you."

Disgust coated May-ying's voice. "I don't have a wedding ring on my finger," she said. "You do, but it's not because of me." It was true. Chan Sam wore a gold wedding band. It was one he'd worn for almost thirty years, since he'd first arrived in Canada a married man, having left behind in China the wife he'd wed before Huangbo.

"If you want to go live with him, go then," Chan Sam said. "I won't stop you, on one condition. Chow Guen has to pay me three thousand dollars." He was proposing to do what he would have done had he been in China, sell her to another man. The amount he named was more than most Chinese saved during a lifetime in Canada.

May-ying practically spit her words out. "I am not for sale. You are such a greedy man. How could you?! He'll never pay you, and I'll do exactly what I want to do."

She was right; Chow Guen never paid Chan Sam, and May-ying set a course independent of either man. As long as she and Hing lived in Vancouver's Chinatown, she would live apart from Guen. Fiercely proud, she was determined to prove to herself, if nobody else, that she was not after Guen for his money. Thereafter, she decided if she ever needed money she'd ask others before she'd ask him, or else she'd go to the pawnshop or go hungry.

Neither Guen nor May-ying considered marriage. Yet despite what she had told Chan Sam, she was to end up with a ring on her finger. It was quite acceptable among the Chinese as a point of conversation to look at and comment on each other's jewelry, and to inquire if a piece might be for sale. May-ying had remarked to Guen, "Your diamond ring is so handsome—I'd like to have one like that for myself." The diamond was uncut, straight from the mine. "You like it, you can have it," he said.

She must have attached some sentimentality and importance to Guen's diamond, for she had it reset in gold and wore it on her left-hand ring finger. And she also told Guen she'd like to have a photograph of them together. Yucho Chow posed them in the image of man and wife, May-ying in a chair, Guen standing behind. He wore a suit, with a vest that she had knit; she wore her favourite *cheong sam,* a rich, cut-velvet silk in dark brown which had been wrapped in tissue at the bottom of her trunk. Her hair was done as she had worn it only once before, twisted into chignons above the ears. The photograph was to have an honored place on her dresser for as long as she lived.

⁓

While her mother made some truce with her fate, Hing, as she grew older, became more aware, and consequently resentful, of her own. In Vancouver's Chinatown, she saw that her life was not normal, that how she lived was not how most other children lived. Hing was still the obedient and respectful daughter, but a glum, serious expression came to live in her face. Her cheeks were quick to flush in embarrassment. People noticed. "Why is it that May-ying is so pretty, and yet she bore such a bad-looking daughter?" they asked each other.

Especially at school, Hing became acutely self-conscious about her appearance and her mother's poverty. May-ying made certain her daughter was always clean and well-groomed; she regularly plucked Hing's eyebrows and drew a fine cotton thread above her upper lip to remove any beginning hair growth. But her efforts to meet Hing's request for new clothes fell short in Hing's eyes. To get more wear for what she spent, her mother bought everything oversized—the three-inch hems of Hing's new dresses had to be doubled, new shoes had to be stuffed at the toes with paper napkins. As if the clothes weren't awkward enough, Hing deliberately hunched her shoulders to compensate for the height she had on her classmates, as a result of having enrolled twice in the first grade. Later, she would stitch her brassieres down to flatten her maturing chest. But what embarrassed her more than anything else, especially when bobby sox and saddle shoes came into fashion a few years later, were the scars on her legs caused by eczema.

Every time she and her classmates walked home from school back to Chinatown, Hing's cheeks flushed when she had to part company with them. They said goodbye to her and went home through tiled entranceways with graceful moon doorways; she was the only one who turned at the sign of a rooming house, who went up a doorless, dark, dingy staircase. Everyone knew where such-and-such a family lived. But no one could keep track of where Hing lived, because whenever her mother found a place with lower rent, they moved again.

Hing's envy of her classmates added to her resentment of her mother within their four walls at home. She now saw unreasonableness in the servitude her mother expected. "*Mama* thinks nothing of waking me up in the middle of the night," she muttered to herself as she turned the light on in the communal kitchen and lit the gas stove to warm coarse salt and ginger root in a frying pan, before wrapping it in a towel to rub her mother's aching back. She found the long-windedness of her mother's lectures, which had replaced the spankings, harder and harder to accept. They always began over something trivial—Hing might have broken a dish, as she often did. The complaint over her clumsiness dissolved as usual into her mother's own lament: "I'm raising you myself; it's so laborious to do it singlehandedly." It left Hing feeling somehow guilty for her mother's predicament. "Oh, there's that bitter, sad expression on your face again," her mother would say, like a mirror talking back. Then, as usual, she'd blame her daughter for more: "No wonder when I gamble I don't win. You don't bring me good luck."

Also there was Guen to compete for her mother's attention. Hing had already been peeved at his arrival on the scene, and she was glad when he took a temporary three-month assignment in Calgary. But her mother suddenly decided she would follow, and Hing was left behind in Victoria, in the care of Yoong Fong, her godmother. Fong's parting words for May-ying left a lasting impression on the daughter: "Why are you so foolish to follow that man, of all people? He talks so loud, he drinks and he looks as if he has a bad temper. He won't provide for you; he won't give you the comfort of a house." When her mother turned her back and boarded the ferry, her godmother snorted, "Humph! May-ying doesn't even have a tear of goodbye for her own daughter!"

When Hing was about eleven, she became convinced she was trapped on a treadmill of her mother's making.

May-ying called her and said they were going out. They walked along Columbia to Hastings, outside Chinatown, and Hing assumed they were going to Woodward's, where her mother sometimes needed her to translate for her. They stopped a block short, and went through a doorway under a two-story-high revolving sign: "B.C. Collateral Sells Everything" ran across one side, "Loans on Anything" across the other.

Inside the pawnbroker's, there were four tellers, each behind a wire cage. May-ying pushed open the swinging half-doors to one. She opened her handbag and unwrapped a paper napkin. She put it on the counter and pushed it towards the man.

"How muchee?" May-ying asked the man, using what pidgin English she knew.

He looked at what was there, the dangling earrings and the jade pendant. "How much do you need?" the man asked.

May-ying waited for Hing to translate. Hing didn't understand that her mother was asking for a loan and looked confused.

"How much money does she want?" the man said to Hing, when he saw her hesitate. She asked her mother.

"I likee toondee-fie dollah," May-ying told the man. The rent alone at the rooming house was eighteen dollars a month, and Gok-leng's room and board another fifteen.

"How long does she want it for? Thirty days? How long?" the man asked. He went on to explain the terms of repayment. "The outside limit is ninety days, but the sooner she comes back to claim this, the less interest she has to pay."

Hing didn't understand what "interest" meant, in English or in Chinese. She started to translate, then got mixed up and fell silent. She was too shy to ask the man to explain himself.

"What is he saying?" her mother demanded to know. "When I ask you a question, you answer!"

"Speak up, girl!" the man said, in sympathy.

By now Hing was too agitated to even think. "I don't know what he is saying," she said.

"What do you go to school for?" her mother snapped.

I'm only a child, Hing thought to herself, and the tears started to roll down her cheeks.

On the way home, when she couldn't stop crying, her mother only made it worse: "If your life is so miserable, why don't you just go and die!"

Of course, May-ying only ever got a fraction of the value of her jewelry, because the pawnbrokers had to have room for a profit if it wasn't reclaimed and they had to sell it. Hing learned the routine of bringing her mother's jewelry home again when they went back with the claim receipt and the money in hand to repay the loan with interest. Her mother always went back within the time limit, sometimes within days if she'd won enough at the gambling tables. Hing came to dread the sight of the jewelry going back and forth, each time feeling a sense of desperation.

Hing's escape from the misery of her life was school. At Chinese school, she skipped a grade. At English school, she was always in her grade's first division, among the honor students, and the first desk in the first row, reserved for the top student, was usually hers. In both Chinese and English, her main rival was Norman Wong, whose family owned the large Ming Woh cookware store in Chinatown. His incentive to work hard was the slap he got at home for coming second.

Hing, having only her teachers to commend her, threw herself more and more into what school had to offer. She turned what she'd seen in Chinese opera to advantage; she was regularly chosen to perform in Chinese school plays. Hing's sixth grade science teacher gave Hing her classmates' tests to take home to mark for him. Before long she had enough certificates of achievement and recognition to wallpaper the wall on her side of the bed at the rooming house.

⟨⟩

One day, a knock came at their door, and when May-ying

answered it, Chan Sam stood there. However surprised Hing was to see her *Baba*, his long face and the way his feet seemed to drag as he came into the room clearly indicated something was very wrong.

"*Ah* Ying, I have a letter from home," he said. "I have some not very good news to tell you. Let me sit down and I will read it to you."

May-ying was already impatient. "Well, what is it?"

Chan Sam would not be rushed. In a slow, deliberate voice, he read the letter from the beginning: "My beloved husband..." The letter was not long. It said that Nan's health was never that good, that she had been sick for almost one month and had not recovered. It gave the date she died, and said that she was buried in the family plot. The letter addressed May-ying at that point: "As a mother, I know how you feel and how heavy your heart is about your daughter—"

May-ying interrupted him. "Don't read any more. My heart aches too much."

Though he so often said the wrong thing, Chan Sam found the proper words to comfort May-ying, whose eyes were wet. "Don't let your heart hurt so much, *Ah* Ying," he said softly. "You live or you die, you have no control over it."

He kept talking to fill the silence. "It is a pity, Nan was so young and so pretty. She was so clever in school, not like Ping. No matter how much Ping studies, nothing will go into her head. Nan was the opposite." He kept talking about Nan and Ping, and as Hing listened, it was as if there were only two daughters, not three, in the family.

Not ever having met either of her sisters, and not knowing the feeling of having a sister, or any sibling for that matter, Hing felt no sense of loss. But what struck her most about the news of Nan's death was that she expected her mother to break down and cry and cry, but she kept her composure.

As is the Chinese custom upon a death in the family, May-ying sent a note of condolence along with money in a small white envelope—white was the color of mourning—to the wife in

China. She enclosed a separate note to her eldest daughter: "*Ah Ping, all I want as your mother is for you to look after yourself. The most important thing is to look after your health. Do not write to me any more. I am too heartbroken.*" In those few lines, May-ying's grief and anger were rolled into one, releasing words of bitterness that said she couldn't bear to have to say another goodbye.

# CHAPTER EIGHT

AS FAR AS China was concerned, what would eventually become the Second World War started in the summer of 1937, when the Japanese launched an all-out invasion. No foreign power came to China's aid. In the opening battles, Chiang Kai-shek's best units put up a fierce resistance and for three months managed to stall the Japanese, who since 1931 had occupied Manchuria and much of the northeast hinterland, behind a defensive perimeter inland from Shanghai. When Shanghai fell, the Chinese retreat westward turned into a rout. The fall of Nanking, the capital of Chiang's Nationalist government, forced Chiang to withdraw further up the Yangtse River to the industrial city of Wuhan, which left the Japanese in control of much of eastern China. Late in 1938, as Wuhan and other Chinese cities fell, Chiang, expecting a long war of attrition, moved his base and his war arsenal, relocating even steel mills and airplane-assembly plants, further up the Yangtse to Chungking in the remote, mountainous interior in the west.

Early foreign news reports told of the horrific brutality of the Japanese. In what would become known as the "Rape of

Nanking," civilians were massacred by the hundreds of thousands—in full view of foreigners, who reported that Chinese were being "hunted and shot down like rabbits" and "herded to execution grounds." Such reports didn't circulate within China until after the war.

It was the swiftness of the Japanese offensive that caught Chinese civilians by surprise. The country had been at civil war in the preceding ten years but had not seen the likes of modern firepower and airpower. As Chinese faces turned in curiosity at the sight and sound of planes overhead, bombs rained down, bringing destruction and devastation on a scale never seen before. Even as Japanese soldiers were overrunning Nanking, Japanese bomber airplanes had already roamed as far south as the coastal province of Kwangtung. Rumors that the Japanese were mobilizing for an attack on its capital, Canton, sent thousands upon thousands fleeing into the already heavily bombed countryside.

In October 1938, Canton would fall, giving the vastly superior Japanese army control of the most fertile province in China. By the end of that year, the Japanese would occupy all of China's great cities and control much of the coastal regions and all main lines of communication and transportation, including the all-important network of canals and rivers.

<hr/>

The effect of wartime was immediate everywhere in the sudden and severe shortages and soaring prices, as the Japanese imposed rationing and removed basic goods like raw cotton and cloth and anything made of iron from the market. The brutality of war came to Chang Gar Bin early in 1938, only a few months after Chan Sam left for Canada. The drone of airplanes and anti-aircraft fire echoed in the skies over the village. Huangbo, like other frightened villagers, took to the surrounding hills, creeping back only at nightfall. As the bombing intensified, Huangbo decided to take the risk of trying to reach Macau, the closest frontier with China. The Portuguese colony, a peninsular trading port on the south coast some seventy kilometers away, was thought to be safe because Portugal's fascist government was aligned with Japan's.

Under cover of darkness, taking only the clothes on their backs, Huangbo set out with her three young charges. She bound the infant Yuen to her back. Eleven-year-old Ping took her sister Nan, nine, tightly by the hand. Together, they set off on foot, following the line of the hills whenever they could, stopping only to scoop water with their bare hands from streams along the way. In the dark, they tripped over dead and burned bodies. By day, they shrank from falling bombs and anti-aircraft fire. Huangbo held the children close, and held back all their fear by chanting over and over: "Don't be afraid, don't be afraid."

Once safely in Macau, they headed for the "Thousand Relatives' Wartime Care Place." The shelter, built with donations from overseas Chinese, was filled with other Chinese who had either enough money themselves or who, like Huangbo, had overseas relatives to support them until they could return home.

Huangbo's first business was to find someone to write a letter to Chan Sam, to tell him they were safe and to give him an address to send remittances. Staying in Macau was costly; there was virtually no farming on its seven square miles of rock outcrop. The usual supply of food from China was interrupted by war, and other imported food was expensive. Chan Sam's family did not dare return home until the Japanese had stopped bombing the south.

When Canton fell in the autumn of 1938, Huangbo and her children left the shelter and set out for home. As they approached Chang Gar Bin, they found the fields around the village burned. Several homes were shattered, and there were beggars in the village. Atop the flagpoles of the school and the watchtower, where once flew the Nationalists' white sun on a blue background, now flew the red sun of Japan.

When Huangbo saw the familiar rooftop of her home in the distance, with most of its green tiles still intact, she almost danced with joy. She was relieved to see that her husband's house still stood. In her gathering haste, she almost ran headlong into the Japanese sentry at the gate. There were more sentries; one stood at attention at each of the three doorways of the house. Huangbo had arrived at the local headquarters of a Japanese regiment, there to establish the occupation of Chang Gar Bin and surrounding villages. The imposing house had been chosen because it was the largest in the area and because of the lookout afforded by its second-floor balcony.

The Japanese sentry at the gate shooed Huangbo and her children away. When she refused to leave, he gestured threateningly with his bayonet. He was finally forced to call an interpreter. She was told to find some place else to live, but it was decided she could come into the house to collect some essential belongings. At the sight of enemy soldiers bedding down on straw upstairs and down, Huangbo had to catch her breath. Her chest ached, not so much for herself, but for her husband.

It was a few weeks before the regiment living in Chan Sam's house in Chang Gar Bin moved on. Until then, Huangbo and Yuen lived with one neighbor, Ping and Nan with another. When she finally came to reclaim her house and belongings, Huango saw that the departing soldiers had looted and ransacked. Torn letters and photographs littered the floor. The soldiers had taken everything of value—jade and gold—and anything they fancied—the pram and wagon, the phonograph, the overseas wool blankets. Even Huangbo's tin whistle was gone.

Despite Japan's blockade of China and battle after battle going against the Chinese, the war quickly reached a military stalemate. The Japanese were unable to conquer China and the Chinese were unable to throw the invaders out. Overseas mail service, unreliable at best, was often suspended altogether. Months would go by during which Huangbo could not get word to Chan Sam about how his family was faring under Japanese occupation. And ever since he had returned to Canada, war at home had prevented him from sending his remittances in the usual pattern of one every two months. Whatever money he had managed to get to Huangbo in Macau was, for a long while, all that she had to rely upon.

Though Huangbo understood the necessity of frugality, she could not help but feel the burden of the debt she felt she owed her son. She was willing to sacrifice the rice for herself if she had to. When she went to the market—held every three to five days before the war, but now less frequently—she rushed through the food stalls, buying what she needed and not even browsing. But she searched carefully up and down the lines of other stalls of people selling their services. Among the tool-sharpeners, tinkers, scribes, barbers and dentists, she looked for the herbalists and self-styled medical doctors. Somebody, she hoped, would have the miracle cure that would turn Yuen's feet the right way around.

The markets were always crowded with peasants who had trudged in from smaller neighboring villages. Others would air their medical complaints on the spot, but Huangbo had the so-called doctors examine Yuen in her home. They would lift up the extra-long dresses that she had sewn for him. There was not a one who did not gasp at the sight, who did not bring a hand over his eyes. Each foot was bent down and under, so that the front and the back of the soles were drawn in towards each other. His mis-shapen feet always evoked superstition, a suggestion of angered gods, a suspicion that this was a boy meant to be a girl. His feet looked like a girl's that were undergoing the painful process of being bound, where the application of tighter and tighter bandages to bind the feet in that shape would result in the toes (excepting the big toe, which was left unbandaged) atrophying and falling off. One "doctor" after another tried to reverse the direction of Yuen's foot growth. Some sold Huangbo miracle tonics, many tried to bind Yuen's feet with bandages. No one had any success.

Huangbo felt swindled, and she felt badly that she had drained the money meant to sustain the family during wartime. But she could not be blamed for her lack of foresight. She could not know that the war would bring years of suffering and despair unknown since the first decade of the twentieth century. Before all-out war broke out, there had been legitimate hope of an upturn in the economy. In 1935, the same year that the Nationalist government replaced the volatile silver-based currency with a managed currency, it seized control of assets of banks that held part of the government debt. These two sensible policies were undermined when it came to financing the war. The Nationalist government simply helped itself to paper money from those banks, against which it issued worthless securities. Inflation, also brought on by the new currency, spiraled out of control. The government tried to protect state-run industries by giving them favors in supplies of raw materials, in financing, cheap fuel and power. Consequently, modern private industry fell into ruin. At the same time, government officials, carrying on a tradition of corruption, filled their own pockets with the money printed at home and the monetary aid from overseas Chinese.

In occupied Kwangtung province, a Japanese governor-general ruled over puppet Nationalist officials. In 1941, the Japanese invaded the British colony of Hong Kong, and when that economy collapsed, Kwangtung's already devasted economy dissolved into complete chaos. Some Chinese peasants lost everything, as paper money became worthless. Every time a new currency was issued, Huangbo burned the worthless piles of yesterday's money as fuel to cook the dwindling portions of rice for the table. Eventually she didn't even have money to burn.

When Chan Sam's Chinese family was down to one meal a day, Huangbo had no choice but to take Ping and Nan out of school to work in the fields. Huangbo worked for the local grain dealer, ferrying rice on a split bamboo pole, going up and down the stairs of his house with fifty pounds on each side. Because she could not have Yuen with her, the four-year-old boy was strapped to his eldest sister's back, his wasted feet bound into Ping's body by four extra-wide tie sashes on the square cloth. He dipped and bent with her as she worked alongside her sister in another farmer's rice paddies.

❧

Despite the gossip about Yuen's deformity and the superstition of bad luck in the family, Ping and Nan were known in neighboring villages as marriageable daughters. Prospective mothers-in-law were always calculating what kind of dowry and how much land might come with the daughters living in a house built with overseas money. When the two were but children, many a family had sent a matchmaker to talk to Huangbo to reserve them as child-brides for their sons. She had rebuffed every proposal: "My girls are not going to get married here; they are going back to Canada to marry there." The matchmakers did not give up. They wore out the path to Huangbo's door, expecting her to relent as the war diminished everyone's prospects and families more readily gave up their daughters.

As the two girls became teenagers and drew closer to marrying age—usually sixteen to eighteen for girls—they attracted growing attention. Both were regarded as pretty. Nan was admired for her "*bak-jeng*" skin; the women of Chang Gar Bin said it was white-clean like her foreign mother's. Of the two sisters, Ping, with her sharp eyes, quick tongue and air of authority, was more outspoken. "Ping is her Gone-Outside Mother's daughter," Huangbo would say.

Like the mother who bore her, Ping could face down anyone, even the Japanese occupiers. She would bring Nan with her when walking by her father's house, where a soldier was standing guard. "Hey! Come here, pretty maiden!" he would call out, using what little Chinese he knew. Ping would shoot him a look to let him know that it was her choice to talk to him or to ignore him. One soldier once offered Ping a slice of barbecued fatty pork, a luxury in peacetime, never mind war. "It won't kill me if it hasn't killed them," was Ping's thought. Nan, quieter and more shy, was too afraid to go so close to the enemy.

One day in the fall of 1942, Ping and Nan, then sixteen and fourteen, were working as usual in the fields. Yuen had started school the year before, and Ping left early to stop by the school to carry him home on her back. Nan was later than usual returning home. At first, Huangbo raised no alarm. Often Nan dawdled on the way; she liked to catch toads and crabs in a bucket, just as she'd done since childhood when she and Ping were playing truant from school. Now, she liked to collect a bucketful to sell on market days.

When dusk came and there was still no sign of her second daughter, Huangbo knew something was dreadfully wrong. Her children knew to be home before dark; girls on their own, out after dark, were in danger of being raped. They had been warned: "Bad people come out when the day turns to blackness." Huangbo was speaking not only of bandits, ruffians and ghosts but, since the war, of Japanese soldiers. The entire delta area of Kwangtung province remained in the front line of the war. As well, the Japanese soldiers were on reconnaissance and patrol against Chinese guerrilla attacks in the countryside.

A couple of Huangbo's neighbors were sent to look for Nan. There was a commotion as the men returned. They had found her in the fields, her bucket of crabs spilled beside her. Her clothing and legs were bloodstained, her face as pale as if she had seen a ghost. There was some hushed discussion among the adults; somebody said that Nan must be "bleeding from the womb."

Nan was put in Huangbo's back bedroom behind the main reception hall. Ping and Yuen waited and watched fretfully over their sister from outside the mosquito netting as their mother tried to bring her daughter's strength back with herbal remedies. "Somebody frightened Nan in the field," was all Huangbo would tell them about what had happened. Her ominous tone silenced any more talk or inquiry, though it did nothing to stem the tears of those keeping vigil.

As Nan got weaker and weaker, Huangbo thought about sending a runner to Shekki to fetch a doctor. She considered hiring porters to ferry her daughter on a cart to a clinic there. She hesitated; such expensive attention was normally sought for sons, not daughters. She was also afraid of repeating the mistake she'd made with the doctors who'd claimed they could fix Yuen's feet.

One month after she was carried home from the field, Nan died without ever having left the bed.

After a death, the mourning and concern is for the family. Whatever the horror of Nan's violent death, that she had died unmarried was considered the greater tragedy. Such a wandering soul was without any lineage and in peril of becoming a ghost who would haunt the living. Huangbo found herself thinking about the infant she'd buried many years ago, her own daughter by Chan Sam. The superstition about those who died so young was that an evil spirit had come in the guise of the baby. That first daughter was buried in a shallow grave in wasteland, so that the evil spirit would eventually find its way into a scavenging animal. Huangbo chose a more honorable burial for Nan. She interred her in the family plot high up on the hillside, the one Chan Sam had prepared on his last visit home. Huangbo's intention was that Nan would rest there until she could think of a way to buy off or redeem her wandering soul.

⋙══⋘

When her second daughter died, something died in May-ying. She wanted to run, the same feeling she'd had after the birth of the third daughter. It just so happened that after that bad news came the insult and inconvenience of being evicted from where she was living. An opera actress, also on her own with a daughter, had sublet one room of her three-room apartment to May-ying and her daughter. Upon hearing May-ying's persistent cough, the woman, fearing tuberculosis, had reported her to a public health nurse. Although no blood appeared when May-ying spat into a paper bag, the nurse said she ought to keep her dishes separate and check her sputum regularly. That didn't satisfy the woman, who told May-ying to find another place to live.

Chow Guen was not in Vancouver, and May-ying missed him. She needed his loudness to drown out her feeling of loss over Nan. He had decided to open his own gambling club and was traveling from city to city to see where he could make a go of it. The issue of whether May-ying would follow him never entered into his decision and was hardly discussed. She had to decide if she wanted to be near him, and if so, if she could afford to pick up and move the way he did. If she did join him, she would pay her own keep, pay the rent on her own room and pay for her own expenses; that was what both understood and wanted. He made no promise or even offer of support to entice her, except that if she ever worked at his business with him, he would give her a share of the profits, just as he would any partner.

May-ying chose to run. Guen was in Winnipeg, but probably not for long; she'd have to hurry if she wanted to catch him there.

She decided to join him. She thought it best if she left Hing behind in Vancouver rather than disrupt her schooling. But she wanted to take her son with her. To her, it was a chance almost to "start over," to have three-year-old Gok-leng get to know his mother and to have Guen there as a father figure. She picked him up from Granny Yip's, packed her metal trunk and boarded the train to Winnipeg. When Guen met them there, May-ying nudged her son forward. "Call him *Baba*," she said.

Hing would not live with her mother again for almost three years. During that period, she would feel as if she had been left to raise herself and she would wonder what it would be like to have a real home life. She would never know where her mother was until a letter came, written in Guen's hand, with an address where May-ying and Guen could be reached. Each time one came, Hing replied, as expected, in the language of a good daughter: she wished her mother good health, told her not to worry and said she was studying hard.

What she did not tell May-ying was that she felt like left luggage, not knowing when her mother would come back to claim her. At first she was shunted around from month to month between elderly couples and woman acquaintances whom May-ying hardly knew herself. Interested only in the extra money to be made, they couldn't care less about what she did, or even if she had enough to eat. To add to the gloom of Hing's solitary life, the shadow of war lengthened. Canada had gone to war in 1939 focused on Europe as the battleground, but when the Japanese bombed Pearl Harbor in 1941, the west coast of North America was suddenly gripped with fear that the Japanese might land their warships and send their planes to drop bombs there. Fear brought discipline. On the other side of the ocean from her sisters, Hing lived with rationing, not of rice, but of sugar, butter, tea and coffee. She donned a gas mask for the air-raid drills at school. At nine o'clock every evening, a city-wide siren sounded a curfew for children to be off the streets. The requisite black blinds were drawn.

For a few brief months, Hing had a taste of what Canadian soldiers, including some enlisting Chinese, were going to war to protect: home and family. The old lady Lee Yen, the one who was to tell Hing the story of how she had fallen from her mother's arms at her Full Month, took her in. She and her husband lived in a sparse but homey four-room apartment above Ming Woh Cookware. Once three of their four children had left home, they were happy to fill the spare bed by boarding a child. So desirable and reputable was their place—a husband and wife who were always around, who were kind and soft-spoken, neither drank or gambled—that the waitresses were practically lining up to get their children in there.

Hing was sitting at the kitchen table there doing homework when Chan Sam walked in. She'd not seen him since he came to announce Nan's death. "*Baba!*" she said in surprise; without her mother to censor her, it came out naturally. In what must have been a rare collaboration between her parents, they had arranged her stay at the old lady's, and he was there to pay the room and board.

For the first time in her life, Hing won some parental recognition for her achievements at school. On her father's monthly visits, he always asked how Hing was doing in Chinese school. He could not conceal his pride when Hing showed him a report card. "Your daughter should become a doctor," said the old lady. "Keep studying hard," he told Hing.

This taste of home life and a father was tantalizingly held out, then snatched away. May-ying returned briefly to collect her and take her to another guardian, Mrs. Lo, who lived on Market Alley. For the next two years, Hing went back to live on the alley where she was born. To help meet the rent on her five-room apartment, Mrs. Lo sublet three rooms. A succession of transient Chinese opera actors and actresses and other waitress friends and their children came and went regularly. During the week, Mr. Lo was away at a sawmill outside Vancouver, where he was the Chinese foreman. Mrs. Lo herself didn't get home until after she'd closed up at the Pender Café, where she owned a half-share, and concluded whatever socializing she did after that in the gambling dens or playing mah-jongg. Mrs. Lo decided that her twelve-year-old daughter, Beatrice, could use some company. Though Hing was almost two years older than Beatrice, Mrs. Lo thought that Hing, who had a reputation for being studious and well-behaved, would also be a good influence. May-ying also thought it a good arrangement, not least because it was cheaper.

Instead of one lonely girl, now there were two. Hing couldn't stand the conditions on Market Alley. That end of the alley, which had the lowest rents in Chinatown, reeked of bean sprouts soaking in a grocer's tubs and was damp from the steam of a laundry (where, according to Guen, someone had once dumped a body into a vat of lye without leaving a trace). Inside the hollow apartment, the greasy wooden floorboards, where it wasn't covered with linoleum remnants, had slivers. The two girls both found it intolerable. Beatrice went to see westerns at the Rex or Lux Theaters just outside Chinatown. Hing, thinking that an unwise use of her time, made the Municipal Library her second home. If she had no homework to do, she looked up books on self-improvement. She did what they said to do and practiced her smile in front of the mirror in the washroom. For the scars on her legs, she tried out the "miracle spot remover" that she had sent for from a mail-order advertisement in one of Beatrice's magazines about Hollywood and its movie stars. Only at closing time did Hing head back to the Los'.

Hing could see herself that Beatrice's mother was too busy lacquering her nails, doing her hair and juggling boyfriends to worry about the teenaged girls in her care. On Saturday nights, when her husband came back to town, Mrs. Lo showed more decorum. Then she retired alone, and it was he who would come in late, dragging several friends behind him, all smelling of whiskey. "Beatrice!" he'd holler, waking up the entire household. "Get up! Make me a pot of coffee!" Mr. Lo was not even Beatrice's real father; hers had run out on them when she was two weeks old.

A feeling that she was tainted by Mrs. Lo's loose reputation came one night when Hing happened to overhear her guardian talking at the Pender Café. That night she and Beatrice had decided to have dinner there instead of cooking for themselves at home. Beatrice had already gone, but Hing had not yet left for the library.

"Hing, the poor girl, it's her I need the money for." Mrs. Lo's voice was coming from the adjacent booth; she was probably taking a coffee with a customer.

"Her *Mama* is not here, and I have the feeling she isn't even concerned about her," she continued. "The girl doesn't even have a winter coat. Forty dollars would buy one."

"Is forty enough?" said a man's voice.

"That's enough," said Mrs. Lo. "Her *Mama* will never be able to pay you back though."

"Oh, that's okay, that's okay," the man's voice said. "You take the money and don't worry about it."

Hing's cheeks flushed. She felt like she had been used to get money from a man, and the images flashed before her mind of her mother currying favors with men in Nanaimo. She'd been just a child then, and didn't know what that was all about, but she thought she knew now. Mrs. Lo's concern turned out to be legitimate; a new green wool coat did show up. However, Hing could never wear it without feeling tarnished.

The excuse Hing needed to find her way out of Mrs. Lo's came on her fifteenth birthday. It was Mrs. Lo who encouraged her to invite a few girlfriends over for a party. Hing had a brown paper bag for each girl as they left. Mrs. Lo emptied one, saw the individually wrapped cake and the colored feather fan and bawled out Hing: "I don't have the money to spend like that! Why do you waste my money like that?" One of Hing's few measures of self-respect—being good, obedient and doing no wrong—had been publicly violated. Humiliated and overcome for the first time ever with missing her mother, she later hurriedly scribbled her a letter: "I'd like to see you, *Mama*. Could I come to visit? She doesn't treat me right." She knew that her mother would see that it was out of the ordinary.

A few days later, a long-distance telephone call came from Calgary: "*Ah* Hing, I got your letter. What's the matter?" For once, Hing did not hold back her tears. She cried into the receiver and repeated how much she would like to see her. A train ticket arrived in the mail.

On the way to the station, Hing stopped at the Notte Bon Ton Pastry and Tea Shop on Granville Street. It was a favorite bakery of the Chinese; they used their butter and sugar ration coupons to pay for the shop's trademark "Religious cake," a sponge cake layered with pastry and topped with butter icing. Hing, who'd never tasted the cake herself, bought one to take to her mother.

May-ying accompanied Hing on the train back to Vancouver when her two-week visit was over. Only when a crushed Mrs. Lo showed May-ying a letter Hing had written to Beatrice did she know that her daughter did not want to stay there. "When I come back to Vancouver, I don't want to come back to 124 Market Alley. It stinks and it's filthy..." it said. A mortified Hing waited for a reprimand. None came. May-ying showed a tenderness Hing had not seen before: "But where will you stay, *Ah* Hing, if you don't stay with Mrs. Lo?" Fortunately, a forgiving Mrs. Lo wanted to forget it, and besides, nobody was debating the truth of Hing's words.

Hing felt hopelessly trapped at Mrs. Lo's when, a few weeks later, her mother and her brother showed up there. The spare room wasn't being used, so May-ying moved in with Hing and Gok-leng. The arrangement between the two women to share the electricity and food bills turned into a routine of gambling, smoking and drinking together. Hing surprised herself with how she dared speak up: "Not so much, *Mama,* you've had enough," she'd say when Mrs. Lo refilled her mother's glass. It fell to Hing to see to it that Gok-leng was clean and dressed for school; it was she who usually cooked dinner for them both.

May-ying turned out to be biding her time until Chow Guen's return to Vancouver. Were it not for him, her slide back into her old habits may have gone unchecked. When he came back to Vancouver a few weeks later, they took two rooms at Vancouver Rooms, which occupied two floors above a shoemaker and a vacant storefront. May-ying, Hing and Gok-leng shared a room on the third floor, Guen's was on the second floor. He opened his own gambling club around the corner on Pender, in a sub-basement room behind a steel door that opened onto the street. He hosted the traditional gambling games of dominoes, *fan tan* and dice, and on the side were two tables for mah-jongg, which remained May-ying's game. She went to work there.

Hing now saw a side of her mother that she had never seen before. In contrast to the deliberate spareness of how she and Chan Sam had once lived their lives, May-ying set about making some home improvements. She hired a carpenter to build a partition. On one side were two beds—the three-quarter bed that Hing and Gok-leng shared and the single bed that was May-ying's. On the other side were the sink and a four-burner gas stove. May-ying added four chairs and a table, which she bought at Woodward's on a monthly installment plan. When that was paid off, she bought a cupboard. She also bought some fabric remnants, hung one over the window and another over their clothes hanging on hooks on the wall. Inspired by her mother's attempts at homemaking, Hing asked for an easy chair. May-ying found a clan association with one they were prepared to give away. Hing would sit in the easy chair listening to the radio, which she borrowed for the weekend from the shoemaker downstairs when he closed up on Saturday night. Forgetting the slivers in the floorboards, the cockroaches around the sink and the bedbugs that came with every rooming house, she would say to her brother, "This is like a dream come true."

When Hing and Gok-leng returned from school, they would open the door to the sight of Guen trimming greens and meat or fish. Soup and rice already on the gas burner steamed up the windows and warmed the room. The table was already set for four, awaiting May-ying's return for dinner. Hing saw that he wanted her to like him. He rewashed her bobby sox, which had been hanging on the laundry line above the gas burners. "*Ah* Hing, see? I can get them whiter," he said. She saw that he could be generous if there was a purpose. When her mother said she could use a sewing machine to finish the edges of the makeshift curtains, he bought her one.

Another sign that life in Chinatown was settling into a pattern of mutual acceptance was that Chan Sam rather casually appeared in the presence of both May-ying and Guen, with nobody showing any hint of animosity. When he came into Chinatown from whatever job he had, he put his face to the cubbyhole in the steel door in Guen's gambling club, and the bolt was always drawn to admit him. He came to pass the time, chat, watch the gamblers, but never to gamble himself. Less often, he stopped by Vancouver Rooms, where an extra pair of chopsticks would be set for him at the evening meal. Chan Sam, Hing and Gok-leng ate happily as Guen and May-ying's chatter dominated the conversation. In the same unobtrusive manner, he fell into step with Hing's life. Twice he surprised her with his generosity and consideration: noticing that she had to wait until the table was cleared of supper dishes before starting her homework, he had a used desk delivered; another time, seeing how she had to borrow the shoemaker's radio, he showed up with a brand new Viking radio in a gleaming walnut cabinet. Eaton's department store had a special shipment in, and Chan Sam, knowing there would be a line-up as radios were scarce during the war, had come especially early into town to buy it. Chan Sam also made an effort to befriend Gok-leng. Once he took him on the streetcar out to New Westminster and back; another time he brought him a jacket with a Nationalist flag sewn on the back. Gok-leng did not address either Guen or Chan Sam as *Baba*; he never saw either as a father.

Though pleased that living with their mother had settled into some routine of a home life, Hing was still not satisfied. What more she wanted her mother could not deliver. May-ying still had the same frailties; there were still the same aches and pains. She used the same pickle jars to store her medicinal potions. Though she had curbed her drinking upon Guen's arrival back in Vancouver, she continued to gamble. If anything, she gambled more; she saw it now as her profession rather than a pastime. One evening, when Hing and her classmates had just left Chinese school, they came across a police raid in progress. Three paddy wagons were being loaded with gamblers. "Isn't that Hing's mother?" asked one of the boys. "That's not her," Hing said, her cheeks flushing at the sight of her mother, the only woman among the men. What Hing did not know was that the police were alternately zealous and lax about enforcing anti-gambling laws. Club owners usually had enough warning of a raid to clear out all but a few patrons, leaving them with enough money to pay the requisite fine. That hadn't happened this time. Though the owner made good on their fines, it was Guen, not May-ying, who was chagrined by what had happened. "Your mother goes all over Chinatown to gamble," he said to Hing the next day, as he recounted what she already knew.

For the first time since Guen came into her mother's life, Hing started to resent him less. There was no denying his steadying influence. Still, she could hear the echo of her godmother's words when her mother had first chased after him: "Why are you so foolish to follow that man... He won't provide for you. He won't give you the comfort of a house..." Six years later, her mother was still living in a rooming house, still making trips to the pawnbrokers. This was the man she cared for enough to leave Hing behind. Yet she was still reduced to creeping back from his room in the middle of the night. What honor was there in that? Hing wondered. She wasn't sure what annoyed her most about it—having to pretend she was asleep, or worrying about whether her younger brother was asleep, or thinking that her mother was pursuing the wrong man. As she lay there in the dark, Hing said the same prayer night after night to herself: "Dear God, I hope my life will be better. I hope some day I will have a good life, a good family of my own, and someone who will care for me."

In the midst of it all there were moments to be grateful for, when the shame of their lives was forgotten in shared laughter. Some of the best of times were when Hing was listening to the *Hit Parade* on the radio. There was one tune in particular that her mother liked. When it came on, she always asked Hing to turn up the volume, and she swayed and tilted her head to the music.

Hing bought the songsheet, and May-ying herself translated the opening lyrics of "Doing What Comes Naturally" as "*Mo yin mut jo li,*" so that she could sing along.

As Chan Sam approached sixty years of age, the letters that he wrote home to China became steeped in worry as to what would happen to his family there when he became too old to work, or to find work. From afar, he willed a sense of purpose to his son's life, which had started out so badly. "Study hard," was the advice he pressed on Yuen, "doing well in school is your only hope." It did not need to be said that, with crippled feet, Yuen would never be able to work his father's land.

After Nan's death, which took away a helping hand in the family, Chan Sam urged Yuen to find a way to walk so that he did not have to rely upon someone to carry him about. The timid Yuen had hidden behind the protectiveness of Ping's strong personality, and behind her back, as if the sling was his cocoon. But steeled by his father's words of encouragement, the boy, at seven years old, finally dared to try to walk. He tried the soft grass and mud of the canal bank, bending his knee and pulling his ankle behind. When he could fashion a limping forward motion, painful though it was, he persevered on the pebbled village paths until the tops of his feet and toes had callused. His proud father then encouraged him to try riding a bicycle. Ping approached a neighbor's son, the only villager who had one, and persuaded him to let her brother try it. Yuen, finding riding easier than walking, was emboldened to ask his father for his own bicycle. A bicycle would be best bought in Hong Kong where they were cheapest, his father wrote. But, he said, it was impossible at this time to find one single person from overseas going into China to bring one.

The loss of her sister drew Ping closer to her family at a time when most girls her age were preparing themselves to "go out the door." Ping was seventeen, at an age when she ought be married. Despite the protracted war with Japan, Huangbo had rebuffed every matchmaker with the excuse that her daughters were going to return to Canada. Ping herself lost faith when Nan was buried.

She did not see how she, or her mother or brother, could endure having to part ways when the day came for her to live as a daughter-in-law in another woman's household in another village. Huangbo obviously felt the same. Her eyes watery, she was already grieving for the loss of another daughter when she said to Ping: "You are the only daughter I have left. My heart will be heavy when you go from the house."

It was Ping who picked out a boy from Chang Gar Bin who would do as a husband. To marry someone within the same village was considered incestuous, like brother marrying sister, but wartime provided a convenient excuse. Ping chose the boy who owned the bicycle. He was tall and strapping, a few years older than her, and the bicycle meant he could sometimes find work delivering messages between the nearby villages and Shekki. His was a peasant family without land. But at least the family home was one made of brick, not adobe, and as the only son, he would inherit it.

Huangbo wrote Chan Sam asking his permission for Ping to be married. She said she had found a family in the village whose son was a suitable husband. In all their years of separation, Chan Sam had not so much as hinted at any displeasure with Huangbo, until now. "Why are you marrying Ping off so young?" he wrote back. "Seventeen years old is too young to be married." Yet his next instruction acknowledged what the family was feeling, that they didn't want to see Huangbo lose the company of another daughter: "If Ping wants to marry this boy from the village, then she can get married."

Huangbo gave Ping a chance to change her mind. "*Mama,* at least you'll have one less mouth to feed," Ping replied. "Don't worry about me, I won't die of starvation nor will I die of overeating."

Chan Sam arranged the transfer of four of his twenty-eight *mau tin* to Ping's husband-to-be as her dowry. Had her family been the poorer of the two, it would have been Huangbo instead of the new mother-in-law who would have been on the receiving end. Instead of a dowry, there would have been a bride-price paid.

But as it was, no one in Chang Gar Bin would have believed that the family living in the chalk-blue two-story house wasn't better off than any other family in the village.

The day came for Ping to leave her mother's house. It was to be without ceremony—there would be no raiding party of flag-bearing village boys and musicians to take the bride away, no enclosed sedan chair for her, no pretense of loud weeping on her part. Ping simply waited inside the house. She had risen early, and her mother had helped dress her in a new blue cotton tunic top and a red silk skirt, red being the color of happiness traditionally worn by brides. Huangbo could only afford enough silk for the skirt, but she improved the cotton of the tunic by having it lacquered so that it afforded coolness in the sun.

At midday, a boy's voice called out: "*Ah* Ping; are you ready?" He didn't get an answer. He hesitated. "Take your time," he said. The boy had come on his bicycle to double-ride his bride to his mother's house. Three people came out of the chalk-blue house into the courtyard: Huangbo, Yuen and Ping. Huangbo was holding the bundle of Ping's belongings. It contained two tunics and two pairs of pants (one each to wear when the other was being washed), the down comforter that had crossed the ocean with her from Canada, the Big Ben alarm clock from her father and a single photograph: one of the foreign mother and Ping, taken on her Full Month. Any photographs of herself and her father had been among those destroyed by the Japanese soldiers that had occupied their house at the start of the war.

The boy tied the bundle onto the back of his bicycle. He motioned for Ping to hop on. Yuen, his face tear-stained, clung to his sister's skirt. "Don't take my Ping, don't take my Ping," he pleaded. Huangbo, also crying, had to pull him back.

At the boy's house, there was no celebration, only a waiting mother-in-law. But three days later at Huangbo's house, when by custom the bride returns to pay last respects to her former house, there was a proper wedding banquet. Though it wasn't customary for the in-laws to be included, they were among the guests. No villager there had seen the likes of such a feast since before the war. It was Chan Sam's doing; he had arranged from afar for one whole roasted pig.

⊷⊷⊷⊷

In 1945, in the second year of Ping's marriage, atomic bombs fell on Japan, bringing its surrender and ending the Second World War. In China, the tail end of the war had already dragged its course through the country. After 1943, when the Allies assumed the offensive against Japan in the Pacific and brought the Japanese advances in China to a halt, Chiang Kai-shek's Kuomintang and Mao Zedong's Communists brought their differences out into the open and began to skirmish for the spoils of China. The prolonged war with Japan, fought separately by these two rivals, had had opposite effects. It had severely weakened the corrupt and badly led Kuomintang, but had strengthened the Communists. Communist forces grew from a guerrilla force of a few tens of thousands when the conflict with Japan first began to a million strong. By war's end, they were firmly in control of northern China. Mao ignored Chiang's demand to disband his army. The equally egotistical Chiang, faced with a choice of ceding the north to an enemy he hated more than the Japanese or trying to crush him militarily, chose the latter. By the summer of 1946, the country was plunged back into open civil war.

On V-J Day, Hing and her friend Doreen went to join the thousands congregating on Granville Street to celebrate the victory over Japan. The crowds spilled over the sidewalks, car horns blared, and people sang and laughed into the night. In Chinatown, there was no such revelry for the older generation, who were too preoccupied by fears of the next conflict that was sure to come in China. But for young people like Hing, a generation of Canadian-born children, the images of war were gone as abruptly as were the newsreels that came on before the feature films at the movie theaters. Their fear of war was replaced by youthful hopes and dreams of a future full of possibilities, one that ignored the reality of lingering discrimination.

Hing became obsessed with school. She didn't just throw herself into her studies; school became the *only* thing that mattered.

She was on the student council, worked on various committees, helped edit the school year book, all of which required her to stay late after school. She told herself that even though "smart" girls were not among the most popular, high marks were her only chance in the lottery of life, her one ticket to changing her life for the better. Hing reapplied the severity of the discipline her mother had meted out when she was young to her own academic performance: she was disappointed with any score short of 100 percent. On nights that she had to study for tests in both Chinese and English, she tied one end of a string to her hair and the other end to the light bulb fixture overhead. It was a scene borrowed from a Chinese classic; if she happened to nod off, the tug on her hair would wake her. She was studying Latin at school and in her spare time, for she had indeed set her sights on becoming a doctor. She did not know then that the University of British Columbia in Vancouver, then among the top schools in the country, had yet to admit a Chinese student, male or female, into its faculty of medicine.

So proud was Hing about graduating from Strathcona Junior High School that she asked her mother if she could have her portrait taken. She went to Wand Studio on Hastings and posed in the graduation dress that she and her mother had gone shopping for, a powder-blue crepe with tiny squares of mirrors sewn in the gathers around the neckline. For their senior secondary schooling, students had to decide whether to attend a technical, commercial or academic high school, depending on whether they were looking only to complete high school graduation or to go on to university. Hing and Doreen, who had become best friends, chose the latter. They made a pact to stay together at Britannia High School until graduation, to give each other the encouragement and support to study hard, and to do well enough on the day they would write the university entrance examinations to win the scholarships that would help pay their way. If they succeeded, they would be among the earliest generation of Chinese youth in Canada going on to higher education.

That generation's optimism in looking beyond the confines of

Chinatown was not misplaced. During the Second World War, Canadian public opinion had swung because of the patriotism shown by Chinese men who volunteered for active wartime service (Chinese were initially excluded from the draft; politicians on the west coast convinced the federal government that the risk of allowing the Chinese to go to war for the country was that they might then demand the right to vote). Both the Canadian Parliament and the U.S. Congress wrestled with their past "mistakes" against the Chinese. Congress had already taken the step of repealing its Exclusion Act in 1943, when China became a wartime ally, and after Madame Chiang Kai-shek made a celebrated tour of America, where she was the toast of the salons and of Washington. The United States put an annual quota system in place for Chinese immigration (the initial level was set at the level deemed acceptable in 1924—105 Chinese, which for some years the immigration service declared could not be achieved because there were so few qualified applicants), but eventually, wives and children were permitted to enter without restriction.

In 1947, Canada finally ended almost twenty-five years of exclusion, during which time only twelve Chinese, ten of whom belonged to the exempted class of merchants or scholars, had entered as immigrants. Canada lifted the barrier more tentatively than did the United States regarding wives and children: only family of those Chinese holding Canadian citizenship were to be allowed in (in contrast, whites wanting to sponsor family only had to be residents of Canada). When Chan Sam learned of the change in the law, he got himself before a judge known to be sympathetic to the Chinese, to apply for his naturalization papers. He had not given up hope that he might return to China, but he feared that if he didn't become naturalized, it might be held against him. However, he was pleased enough with the official photograph taken for his application that he ordered an eight-by-ten enlargement. It came in a cardboard frame and he kept it among his valuables.

# CHAPTER NINE

WHILE HING WAS determined to stay focused on school, other girls her age were thinking more about boys, and about having fun. May-ying, despite her own past behavior, had strong views on the conduct expected of a virtuous daughter. "Having fun" was acceptable. Choosing boys, however, was May-ying's responsibility—she still planned to act as matchmaker. "I don't want you to mix with boys," she instructed Hing. She found more comfort in this blanket ban than in the thought that her daughter might be keeping company with boys of whom she had not approved beforehand.

In May-ying's eyes, Hing showed disrespect and rebellion simply by asking to go to any organized teen social events in Chinatown or at school. When she dared ask, May-ying implied her motives were suspect: "Why do you want to go?!" If Hing sulked, her mother simply put it another way: "What's the point of going?" Hing, already cowed by the spankings and lectures of her childhood, retreated further behind the walls of obedience. On the day she graduated from Strathcona school, which she then considered the most exciting day of her life, she did not even ask if she could attend any of the parties that followed the ceremony.

However, May-ying did not object to Hing keeping company with her girlfriends in Chinatown, provided that she lived up to an elder sister's responsibility and took Gok-leng wherever she went. Hing was one of about eight girls from Chinatown who were classmates at both Chinese and English school. Among them, Doreen Jang and Amy Gee were the magnets around whom the others gathered. Both girls' homes were like social clubs for Chinatown's youth. Doreen's mother—who lived with a man in the business of trucking live chickens—was happy to see that her boisterous, fun-loving daughter was so popular. Friends of Doreen's older brother came and went too. Amy Gee's father, twice widowed, in China and in Canada, lived with his six children in the flat above Kuo Kong silk store. He liked to see his children make friends, never complaining about the crowd dancing around the hi-fi or about the extra places set at supper. When Amy's older siblings started dating, he told them: "As long as you don't marry a Japanese or a gambler, I don't care who you marry—Chinese, black or white." It was an attitude that set him apart as much more liberal than many of his or even of his children's generation; certainly any Chinese boy who dated a white girl avoided Chinatown, knowing that the talk would be that he'd been seen with a prostitute.

On weeknights, Hing studied. On weekends, she told her mother over supper she was meeting her girlfriends later either at Doreen's or Amy's. May-ying approved of both homes: Doreen's mother had been a waitress, and Amy's father ran Chinatown's daily pigeon lottery. Hing felt she was violating one of her mother's rules by not telling her that older boys were often present. But it didn't matter much; what her girlfriends did was innocent enough.

From Doreen's or Amy's, the group went on their own outings outside Chinatown. Sometimes they went to the municipal swimming pool. Although the rules at Crystal Pool had recently been changed to allow Chinese into the pool, they went only to watch the other swimmers. Most often the girls walked to a cinema on Granville to take in the latest Ingrid Bergman film and afterwards stopped in at one of the fashionable cafés—the Pa Ma, Scott's or Purdy's. They ignored the looks of disdain from the waiters and waitresses, and they understood the message at the bottom of a menu: "White Help Only." The main reason they went was to ask the resident fortune-teller to read their tea leaves, hoping she'd see in them the initials of future boyfriends.

❦

The teapot that was Chinatown continued to empty, rather than to fill. As soon as the Second World War ended, a few elderly *Bak*s bought one-way passages to China. They took no heed of the renewed and bitter civil war, the fight to the finish between the Kuomintang and the Communists; they wanted only to see the homeland a last time. The Canadian government's repeal of the exclusion law in 1947 did nothing at first to reverse the decline in the population of Chinatown. In the first year after its repeal, only twenty-one Chinese immigrants would be admitted to Canada, in the second year, thirty-three. The birth rate remained low, as in later years sponsoring fathers preferred to bring their sons rather than their daughters.

The postwar trend in Chinatown was for anyone who could afford better accommodation to move out. Like other Canadian families, Chinese families had aspirations to own their own homes. However, they did not necessarily have their choice of neighborhood. Mr. Gee had put down a deposit on a house in Kitsilano, a crowded middle-class neighborhood that rose up the slope from English Bay. When white neighbors got wind that a Chinese family wanted to move in, they amassed a petition against him. He walked away, losing his deposit. Some years later when he did succeed in moving his family out of Chinatown, he got his own back by quietly moving into the former home of the Japanese consul, then going cheap, in the upper-crust white neighborhood of Shaughnessy. By then, the number of families left in Chinatown could be counted on the fingers of two hands.

"Why don't you buy a house on Keefer?" May-ying's friends suggested when she suddenly had a cash windfall. Grandfather Eng at Sing Kee Confectionery had sponsored a weekend-long mah-jongg tournament. Play continued day and night; cups of tea and bowls of rice topped with stir-fried greens were brought along with chopsticks to the tables. On Sunday night, May-ying emerged the overall winner, taking home almost two thousand dollars.

Keefer was one of the first streets outside Chinatown where the Chinese bought houses. Some had been bought by clan or locality associations and rented out to bachelor men, some by Chinatown's early merchants, like Granny Yip and her husband, upon retirement. The houses were small A-frames, without basements or driveways, and with a patch of grass out front. What May-ying won would have gone a long way towards buying one.

She had her own ideas, however, on how to indulge herself. A friend had talked of going with her daughter, Margaret, to San Francisco to visit her future in-laws. Margaret and Raymond, who was currently serving overseas in the U.S. Army, had met in Vancouver and become engaged. May-ying decided to use some of her winnings to take Hing and Gok-leng with her to see the sights of North America's largest Chinatown and to drive across the Golden Gate Bridge. She suggested that the two sets of mother-and-daughter take the trip together, each paying their own way. The other woman had a friend willing to drive them in his car if they paid his expenses. Including the driver, Gok-leng and a girlfriend of the other daughter, they were seven. They planned a trip of three weeks. The driving was slow; though the summer days were long and the nights short, night was the only time the driver felt safe on the road.

Margaret, the other daughter, announced with some trepidation, just before they were to call on Raymond's parents, that the two of them had already married just before he was sent overseas. It came as a bit of a shock, but for Margaret's mother, a pleasant one. She quickly forgave her daughter's transgression. It served as a lesson to Hing of the difference between a liberal-minded mother and her own, who seemed anything but. Hing's own wrongdoing during the trip, judging by May-ying's reaction, was far worse.

The three girls, chaperoned by Margaret, twenty-one and

"married," went out on their own to meet some of her friends at a nightclub. The friends turned out to include boys. Hing, who remained painfully shy around boys, exchanged barely a few words with them. As the evening wore past eleven, her curfew at home, Hing grew nervous about what her mother would think. It was two before the club closed, and later before the girls were back at the hotel. Hing went to bed knowing that May-ying would conclude that her lateness could only be explained by the presence of boys. To compound Hing's guilt, they were boys her mother didn't know.

The next morning, Margaret's mother was unperturbed. Not May-ying. In front of everybody, she asked Hing accusingly: "Where were you last night?!" She answered for her: "Why bother to come back?! Why don't you just go and die right now?! Go and die!" That evening, when the others went out to a Chinese film, Hing stayed behind and tearfully penned a letter to her girlfriend, Elsie. She said she was having a terrible time, that she didn't want to go on with the trip. She felt like doing as her mother said. "What is there to live for?" Hing thought to herself.

The answer, as always, was school. In English school, all the Chinese students used their English names. Hing used "Winnie," the name she'd chosen for herself in kindergarten. That autumn, Hing and Doreen entered the ninth grade at their new school, Britannia High. The two weren't in the same division because of the difference in their grades, but they remained best friends, Doreen's infectious laughter providing a foil for Hing's weighty seriousness. The two were locker partners and met for lunch. Sometimes they treated themselves to a half-cantaloupe filled with ice cream at a coffee shop down the street, across from the Grandview Commercial High School for Girls.

It was at the coffee shop one day in the closing months of the ninth grade that Doreen dropped what to Hing was a bombshell. She said that next year she was dropping out of the academic stream and instead going to finish her high school education at a technical school, at Grandview High. "Science, geometry, algebra—they're tough, I'm not cut out for it," Doreen said.

The real reason came out soon enough. "How can I even think of going to university, Winnie? Where am I going to get the money?" Doreen gave voice to Hing's own sad truth. The girls' decision to pursue the dream of university had been their own; nobody was pushing them. Hing knew personally of no university graduates in Chinatown to look to as role models, other than an aunt of a classmate, who had reportedly become a dietitian. The few who went to university came mostly from middle-class families living *outside* Chinatown, families that had taken one step up the social ladder. Living among white neighbours, some of whom were professionals, encouraged their own children's ambitions. There were virtually no professionals among the generation of Hing's immigrant parents, most of whom were rural-born and poorly educated. Enfranchisement—a requirement for practicing a profession—would come only after exclusion was lifted. However, the reality was that other barriers would have to fall before there were more Chinese engineers, lawyers, accountants, pharmacists, doctors or dentists. Most parents in Chinatown, even if they could afford it, saw little practicality in paying for a university degree only to have their children end up no further ahead than they were—waiting tables, driving taxis, working in laundries, mills or wholesale houses—in other words, either working in Chinatown or where whites allowed Chinese to work.

Hing, along with Doreen, was forced to acknowledge this harsh reality; she decided to make the transfer to Grandview with her friend. Knowing her disappointment, Doreen tried to console her: "Of all of us, you were the one to go on to university, Winnie; you had the marks." But Hing was already putting any regrets behind her. She recalled the success story of Jessie Chang from Nanaimo, from the family who owned the store and the pig farm. Jessie could reportedly type seventy-five words a minute and worked in Ottawa for the federal government, an employer that offered the job security few Chinese had. "We'll be very, very good at commerce, Doreen," Hing told her girlfriend. "We'll graduate at the top of the class."

The two girls were locker partners again at Grandview. Hing got top marks in her commercial courses—business English and spelling, shorthand and typing—and even in one of her electives; in home economics her dress was judged the best sewn. When Chan Sam happened by Vancouver Rooms on one of his infrequent visits, she told him of her new ambitions, and he promptly bought her a used typewriter. Every evening before supper, as Hing pounded away on the keys trying to get her speed up and the number of mistakes down, she told herself she loved school more than ever, that she couldn't remember loving anything, or anybody, as much as school.

One year after that conversation in the coffee shop, Hing arrived at their locker one morning to find a note taped inside. It was from Doreen. "Winnie, I've quit school," it said. "I can't tell you why. Your hair would curl if I did. Some day you'll understand. I shall miss all our laughs, I shall miss having you as a locker partner and friend. Goodbye, Doreen."

Hing was stunned. She found Doreen in tears at home. Were it not for Doreen's mother noticing her daughter's uneaten lunches, Doreen herself would have seen no reason to quit. Her mother asked if she'd been feeling sick to her stomach. When Doreen said yes, her mother demanded to know when she'd had her last period. When she couldn't remember, Doreen was marched to the doctor, who confirmed her mother's suspicions that she was pregnant. "I'm going to give you the spanking of your life," her mother said. A few weeks later, dressed in pink and clutching a matching handbag in front of her belly, Doreen would walk down the aisle of a United Church near Chinatown to marry the boy who got her "into trouble." They were both sixteen.

In the days following her girlfriend's sudden departure from school, Hing was mired in depression. Her mind whirled in confusion. Two more years of school stretched ahead to graduation, without her best friend for company and encouragement. Until now, she had thought, naively, that nothing could be more important than school, that nothing could get in the way of finishing her education. She saw now that life could throw up one hurdle after another. For the first time, Hing questioned her devotion to getting the highest grades, to getting to the top of the class. What Amy had once said came to mind, when she'd silenced her talk of how she'd done in a school examination compared to her rival, Norman Wong: "Oh come on, Winnie. Marks aren't everything! It's how you do in the work world that matters." Hurt by Amy's words at the time, Hing now wondered about their truth.

Unable to sleep one night, Hing heard the telltale click of the door opening to admit her mother. This was nothing new; May-ying often came back from Guen's room in the middle of the night. But this time her mother had company. It was a man.

"I wouldn't have any tonic like that—I wouldn't know what to buy," he said. Hing did not recognize his voice.

"Sit yourself down, sit down," May-ying said. "I'll let you taste some and I'll give you some to take home." Neither was making any effort to keep their voice down.

Hing checked the time; it was three o'clock in the morning. She lay there seething. She did not like the idea of her mother bringing a strange man home in the middle of the night. They must have been among the last people chased from the gambling clubs at closing. She looked over at her brother; at least he had not woken. Still, the sound of the scraping of chairs on the wood floor, the banging of the cupboard doors, of the lid being unscrewed, and the splash of gin being poured from one of the pickle jars rattled inside Hing's head.

"Taste this," May-ying said. "I use it for my general health, and whenever I have insomnia. It will be good for your circulation…"

Hing was digusted. The tonic was far more potent than ordinary gin, because the herbs had been left to ferment for three or four months. This business of her mother's showing off her herbal concoctions was just another of her excuses to drink alcohol.

After the man left and May-ying passed out asleep, Hing was wider awake than ever. The things she hated most about her mother's life—the gambling, the men, the drinking, her frail health—had that evening come rolled into one. Before she knew it, she was out of bed and around the partition, and she had both hands on the heavy pickle jar.

She was mad enough to smash it, but her rebellion against her mother sputtered. She managed to check herself and catch the heavy jar to set it back upright. But the lid slipped off. She rescued it as it rolled across the floor. Still, some of the tonic had spilled. Hing, shaking with fright at what she'd done, screwed the lid back on securely and wiped up the spill. She crawled back into bed, thinking, "She would have killed me if the jar had broken."

When her shaking subsided, the confusion that had preyed on Hing's mind cleared. She told herself calmly, "This can't go on with *Mama* like this. She's gambling; she's sick half the time; she drinks. If this keeps up, we won't even have food on the table." She thought of worse misfortunes: she could get seriously sick; what if she should die? What would happen to Gok-leng? Hing suddenly saw that she had to sacrifice her love of school for the good of the family, that it was important that she be in a position to support her mother and brother if necessary. She knew what she had to do.

In the morning, she went to see the principal for the second time in a week. The first time, she had gone on Doreen's behalf, and she had been impressed with Mr. Webster's sympathy. Hing confided in him her worries about the insecurity at home. She told him that her feeling was that time was running out; she could not see how her mother could manage to support her brother and her for another two years until her graduation. She told him her decision: she was quitting school. She would try to find the money to go to a private secretarial school, where she could earn a business diploma in six months' time and then try to find a job.

To her surprise, Mr. Webster was suppportive. "I hate to lose one of Grandview's best students, but what you are doing is a good thing." He brought up the word "prejudice." He said that high school standing wouldn't necessarily improve her chances at getting a job. He confessed that he had failed to place his top Chinese graduates, that every one he'd sent to a job interview had been been turned away with "The job is taken" or "We don't hire

Chinese." When she left Mr. Webster's office, Hing took with her a certificate granting her standing in the tenth grade, even though she was two months short of finishing.

That evening, Guen came to their room with groceries in hand to prepare supper. He found Hing sitting in silence. "Why aren't you practicing your typing?" he asked. Hing told him that she had quit school. She wanted to go take a private secretarial course, she said, but didn't have the money for the monthly tuition or for the bus fare to get there and back on the city bus each day. As she had hoped, Guen came through. He said he'd pay her way. He also agreed to keep from her mother what she'd done; the hours that she left and returned home would be the same as before. She didn't want to have to explain her decision.

Within two months at Pitman Business College, Hing's typing surpassed seventy-five words a minute. In another four months, she could begin to look for a job.

All the time Hing was keeping her career plans from her mother, May-ying continued to steer her in a different direction. Once her daughter turned seventeen, May-ying took it upon herself to get her "used to the idea of boys." Having few connections with other families, and presuming that those in Chinatown would think her daughter beneath them, May-ying looked to introduce Hing to some of the boys that came up from San Francisco to Vancouver on whirlwind "wife-hunting" trips.

With the shortage of girls of marriageable age on both sides of the border, there was a lot of bachelor traffic from San Francisco. It was said that Canadian girls were prettier, but American boys had their own attraction. Though many worked in San Francisco's Chinatown, some held university degrees and were assumed to have money. To May-ying, money was the most important attribute in a prospective son-in-law. Marrying her daughter into it would also take care of her son: "After you marry, *Ah* Hing, you take Gok-leng with you and give him a proper home. That would make me happy," May-ying often said. "Promise me you will."

When friends passed along word of boys up from San

Francisco, May-ying would arrange for one to meet her daughter. She came along as chaperone, of course. Hing protested her mother's attempts to choose for her with a Chinese expression: "What if he likes salty food and I like sweet?" Such complaints were ignored. The outings, paid for by the boy, were pleasant enough—typically, a day's boating on Horseshoe Bay. Guen and Leonard would also come along.

One boy was interested enough to ask Hing if he could see her again the following day. A group from Chinatown was going on a day trip to Harrison Hot Springs, they were leaving at six the next morning, could he come by to pick her up? "Don't come—I can't go," said Hing, in a hushed and hurried tone, anticipating what her mother, within earshot, would say. One outing was enough time spent with any one boy, in May-ying's view. A second was necessary only when choosing one who would make a suitable husband. Until such time, she had no intention of allowing Hing to go out alone with one.

It didn't matter that other parents were more lenient, more trusting or more relaxed about what their sons and daughters did. The obedience that May-ying had instilled led Hing to police herself almost as tightly as her mother did. One girlfriend was so peeved at Hing's refusal to go out on a double date that she sent her a note: "Winnie, get off your high horse. Why try to live up to your mother's expectations? If you go out with a boy, do you think you're going to come home with a baby?" It resonated, but not enough for Hing to challenge her mother's authority.

It was not just her mother but the whole Chinese hierarchy of kinship that came bearing down on Hing when she was three months into her course at Pitman. Yoong Fong wrote from Calgary to summon Hing to her side. She mistakenly thought her goddaughter was out of school for the summer—it was July—and she wanted her to come work for her. She said staff at her Sunny Side Café had quit because of troubles with her boyfriend. Hing was too afraid to own up that she had quit school and was enrolled at Pitman. Besides, May-ying made it clear—a godmother's call had to be heeded as if it came from one's own mother.

Hing arrived in Calgary to find Fong and her boyfriend wielding cleavers at each other. A month later, taking Hing with her, Fong left for Edmonton to join her newest boyfriend, the owner of the New Way Café. She tried to interest Hing in the cook there, a man from China who was twice Hing's age: "He's a good person. Wouldn't it be nice for both of you to work here? He could be the cook and you could look after the till." Hing had enough of her godmother's meddling ways when she accused her of "looking" for boys just because a local boy telephoned for her. She wrote May-ying, who gave her permission to come home early.

Hing would have resumed her course at Pitman but for Amy. She had heard from her white girlfriends that the provincial government was advertising a three-year program for resident student psychiatric nurses at Essondale Mental Hospital. A minimum grade ten standing was required. "Trust Amy to have such contacts," Hing said to herself, recalling how her girlfriend had been the adventuresome one of their group, the one pushing them to go places they hadn't been, do things they'd never done before. Following Amy's lead, Hing and two others from Chinatown submitted applications. Fourteen whites and Hing passed the interview. The other successful applicants were told when to report for the first day of classes; Hing was told that her enrollment had to be approved by the hospital's board of directors.

That autumn, clutching one small white suitcase containing all her personal belongings—including a Chinese classic called *Moment in Peking* by the popular philosopher Lin Yu-Tang, won for an academic first in English school, and a jar of Noxema skin cream that she was never without—eighteen-year-old Hing moved out of Vancouver Rooms. After promising May-ying and Gok-leng that she'd be back to see them on her first day off, she walked to the downtown bus depot and got on a bus for the forty-five-minute ride to Essondale, a stop just beyond Port Coquitlam.

A nervous Hing walked across the extensive manicured grounds to the hospital's Main Building, and presented herself as Miss Winnie Chin. She was shown to the third floor where first-year students would live during their orientation, down the corridor from the patients. One week later, Winnie was assigned a roommate in the residence for student nurses. On a ridge above that building sat six well-kept houses for the graduate nurses, and on the next ridge, several larger ones for the doctors. Never was Winnie so proud as when she walked through the grounds in her uniform and cap and was addressed by the doctors as "Miss Chin."

The director of nursing, a muscular, gray-haired woman, summoned Winnie to her office after she handed in her psychological questionnaire in the opening-week examinations. Miss Pearson fixed a look on her and suggested that she was a mixed-up, disturbed person. Winnie saw, too late, that her ink had flowed too honestly on the questionnaire. To questions about her home life and whether her parents were happily married, she had spilled the truth. To a question about whether she was happy being a girl, she answered according to how she thought her mother felt, that she would have made everybody happier had she been born a boy. "Did you do well in high school?" Miss Pearson asked with a doubting tone. "I did all right," Winnie said, with characteristic Chinese modesty.

After that encounter, despite her consistently high scores in class and on the wards, she was the first suspect if anything questionable happened. She was accused of sleeping on midnight shift if the telephone wasn't answered quickly. She was told some senior nurses refused to be paired with her. She was called in when her weight dropped to ninety-nine pounds and asked what in her personal life would explain it. Everyone else passed their three month probation; Winnie's was extended by three months. Believing the aim of such harrassment was to make her quit, Winnie only strengthened her resolve to stay the course.

The year 1948 was a good time to be away from Chinatown. The mood had gone from anxious to grim. Aging sojourners like Chan Sam, then sixty-one years old, could talk of little else but the rapid Communist advance in China. Like other overseas Chinese, he had revealed his allegiance by buying bonds to help Chiang Kai-shek and by donating money to help outfit his Kuomintang troops and stock their arsenal. Men like Chan Sam who had raised a roof and bought a few *mau tin*, who had realized what their ancestors for generations aspired to, now lived in fear of a Communist victory over all of China. Communists were infiltrating the south. Talk among Chan Sam's compatriots was that they were already blacklisted, that their families would surely suffer reprisals, that they would lose what they had sacrificed all their lives for.

With the renewal of civil war, China began a twentieth year of war and conflict. Most Chinese, worn out by the strife and hardship, wanted only peace and stability. The coming end was predictable. The inept Nationalist government had inflicted economic damage. Corruption reigned; aid from America had gone straight into personal coffers. Uncontrolled inflation became uncontrolled panic. From mid-September to October in 1948, prices in Peking multiplied five times; on one day alone in November the price of rice at nightfall in Shanghai was six times what it had been in the morning. People were starving. In the cities, hundreds of bodies were thrown out into streets daily to be collected by trucks.

Whereas the disciplined Communist troops were self-sufficient in food, the Kuomintang—troops, officers and generals alike— scrounged and pillaged for enough to eat. The government paid its troops only irregularly. When they were remunerated, they were paid in paper currency so eroded by inflation as to be worthless. To buy food, some sold their weapons and army equipment, much of which was military hardware left over from the Second World War and supplied by the Americans in their continuing generosity to Chiang's regime. Ironically, much of it ended up in the Communists' hands.

In the winter of 1948, foreign journalists reported the Communists' claim that they had "obliterated" several Nationalist army divisions. Madame Chiang was back in Washington—this time, in contrast to her celebrated tour in 1943, she could not even get a meeting with American officials. Washington, acknowledging Nationalist corruption, subsequently barred any more American aid, deciding it would be futile.

Before that winter's end, Chiang's depleted troops would suffer a series of decisive and crushing defeats in the north, which would open the way in the spring for the Communists to cross south of the Yangtse River to take the city of Nanking, the Nationalist capital, and press on, in Mao's crusading words, to "liberate" the south and west.

In the village of Chang Gar Bin, Ping carried out duties expected of a wife. She rose each morning to place before her husband a basin of water. She cooked for him and washed his clothes, and at night she put before him another basin of water before retiring herself. Though husband and wife, their faces were like two lumps of clay to each other. Their eyes avoided contact, their tongues stayed silent.

Ping had maintained this demeanor for almost five years. This, and her refusal to allow him to share her bed, was her way of punishing him. Not three months after she'd left her mother's house for his mother's, Ping became pregnant. From that day, her husband would leave the house at nightfall and sneak back before dawn. Ping found out what other villagers already knew—that he was having an affair with an older woman whose husband, like Chan Sam, was "gone outside." At first, Ping voiced her protest by letting her husband's dirty laundry accumulate. But she had to back down when she was taken to task by her mother-in-law: "He's still your husband—go and wash his clothes!"

Even after their son was born, her husband did not change his ways. Unable to stand being the butt of the village gossip any longer, Ping decided to face down her husband's mistress. Villagers followed her angry footsteps to the mistress's house, and a crowd swelled for the meeting of the two women.

Ping ordered the startled woman outside and unleashed a torrent of indignation: "Why are you taking away my husband? I am the one who is the real wife. I am the one who cooks his rice and washes his clothes. In what way have I failed him?"

The woman spoke of love: "If a day passes that I don't see him,

I want to die!"

"If you die, I will be happy!"

The mistress tried to slap Ping first. The wiry and strong Ping emerged the victor, ripping her rival's dress, leaving her in tears and with a couple of smart bruises. "I'll strike you to the death before you can kill me," she said, before she marched back to her own home.

The confrontation did nothing to end the affair, but Ping had the satisfaction of swinging the villagers to her side. Regretting her choice of husband, she had someone write a letter on her behalf to Chan Sam. She confided that she had married a man "not of good character." She knew her father would see that the letter was out of the ordinary. A wife who involved her birth family in a marital spat was considered disloyal to her husband's family. Bringing upon them such shame was acceptable only if it prevented the worst—divorce. Chan Sam wrote back in a cajoling tone to Ping's husband: "My daughter is young. You could teach her a few things." When nothing changed, he tried a sterner tack: "I know where this woman's husband is in Canada. When he learns of your affair, he might find someone to get even with you."

The woman's husband owned a market garden farm in the Fraser Valley outside Vancouver and employed dozens of Chinese laborers. His surname was Wong. But Chan Sam's threat was a bluff. In Chang Gar Bin, he was a prominent figure; abroad, he was nobody. How could a laborer go up against a man of money, one connected to a clan more powerful than his own?

Feeling powerless to help his daughter, Chan Sam had a pang of conscience about having taken his two daughters from Canada to China and never returning for them. It was too late for Nan, but not for Ping. Late in 1948, just as the Communists were sensing victory in China, he wrote his eldest daughter: "You can start over in Canada. You can remarry here. Do you want to come?"

His understanding from a middleman in Chinatown was that Ping could enter Canada on her Canadian birth certificate provided she came alone. According to the British citizenship law governing countries in the Commonwealth, Ping was deemed upon marriage to have forfeited her Canadian citizenship and to have taken on her husband's Chinese citizenship. If she came to Canada, she would have to say she was unmarried. That posed little problem; it would have been her word against that of her husband's family. In China, no level of government kept vital statistics; only families kept record of the three "greats" of a person's life—birth, death and marriage.

"I'm coming," was Ping's eager reply. As her father instructed, she had photographs taken for the papers of passage. Her next letter, however, was unexpected. "I can not come," she wrote. "There is nobody here to raise my son." In the end, she could not bear to leave behind her boy, then aged two. She could not live with herself as a mother in Canada, knowing he was being raised in China by the indifferent mother-in-law, or worse, the cowardly mistress. She would not do to her child what May-ying had done to her and her sister—turn her back on him and leave him in China to go to Canada.

And so Ping, having made her choice not to start her life anew in Canada, the country of her birth, stayed in her adopted country. On October 1, 1949, in the sixth year of her marriage, before a cheering throng of tens of thousands in Tiananmen Square in Peking, Mao named himself Chairman of the new People's Republic of China. Chiang had already fled to Taipei, on the island of Formosa, with his Nationalist cronies and the loot he'd plundered from China's ancient treasures, including much of the collection of the Palace Museum inside the Forbidden City. Within weeks, Canton, the Nationalists' last southern stronghold, fell.

Once Winnie left for Essondale, a sense of home life for those left behind also began to fall away. With the number of places around the supper table dropping from four to three, Guen and May-ying rarely bothered to come back to Vancouver Rooms to have supper. With Winnie gone, there was also nobody to keep any eye on her brother Gok-leng—now known to his friends as Leonard—or to take him places. So he, like Guen and May-ying, also spent his free time at the gambling club.

As usual, Winnie came in from Essondale to spend her two days off with her mother and brother, and to stay the night with them. One afternoon after her shift ended, she found them at the gambling club. Leonard had a bowl of rice and chopsticks in his hand, eating the supper Guen or May-ying had cooked on the hot-plate there, while the gamblers continued play around them. Winnie felt embarrassed to join him in a bowl of rice. She thought to herself that it was acceptable for a nine-year-old boy to be hanging by his mother's side, but she, a grown girl, ought to have better things to do.

Later that evening, Chan Sam happened by the club. It was Thursday, his usual day to come into town. He sat, sipping tea, passing the time as he had on evenings before. Guen was minding his own business; May-ying was hosting one of the two mah-jongg tables.

May-ying went to start a new round. The players, discussing how much to play for, had virtually settled on a maximum win of ten dollars. May-ying proposed that it be raised to twenty-five; whenever her gambling instincts were to go for broke, she raised the stakes dramatically. Chan Sam, instead of keeping quiet as he knew he should if he was not to wear out his welcome with other club members, spoke out.

"*Ah* May-ying, don't play so big," he said. "When you don't have the money, all the more reason not to gamble so much."

If to him it was a statement of fact, to May-ying it was the spark that lit her temper. She did not like criticism, least of all from him. "What I do is none of your business. I don't ask you for money to pay my debts," she said.

He took her reply as an insult and the argument was well on its way.

"The way you carry on, you're not going to have rice to eat. You're going to starve to death."

"So what if I die? What is there to live for? Anyone who put up with you would have coughed up blood!"

Winnie, like Guen and Leonard, shrank into the shadows.

Some gamblers, in embarrassment, spoke up: "Don't be so hard on each other." Nothing could perfume the poisoned air.

"Look at you. You are so much like a man. A woman does not behave like this."

"If you're so ashamed," May-ying yelled at Chan Sam, "why don't you get a cleaver and kill me?!"

"I'm afraid with your drinking and your temper, you will kill me first."

"So we will both die!"

Chan Sam put on his fedora. May-ying stood up, pointing her finger at him in the way he used to point at her: "Next Thursday evening, after supper, you meet me at Vancouver Rooms. We'll have it out for once and for all. Let's see just who's going to kill who first!"

On the designated day of bloodletting, Winnie had arranged an early shift. She took the bus straightaway into town and hurried to Vancouver Rooms. As she came down the hall, her heart pounding, she listened for angry voices from the direction of her mother's room. There were none. She knocked. "*Mama?* Open the door! *Baba?*" She felt sick. All she could hear through the open frosted window above the door was the ticking of the clock inside. She summoned the courage to take her key from her purse to unlock the door, fully expecting to step into a room spattered in blood with two dead bodies. There was nobody inside.

Winnie went over to the gambling club. Her mother and Guen were there. Her father was not. Nothing seemed amiss, except for her own hurried steps. Her mother glanced up: "Oh *Ah Hing.* Did you just come in? Have you had rice yet?"

"Did I imagine this? Is something wrong with me?" Winnie wondered to herself.

⊰⊱

Winnie began, tentatively, to live her own life. She took advantage of her mother's ignorance about what shifts she was on to come unannounced into Vancouver and to go on outings with girl-friends. Her one nagging worry about her family remained Leonard. Amy had told her that he was spending every minute he could at their family home. At midnight, they practically had to kick him out. "I don't think he has much to go home to, Winnie," Amy said.

The truth was that May-ying, more lenient with her son than she'd been with her daughter, was finding it hard to keep Leonard in line. He would take money she'd given him for a haircut, cut his hair himself and buy comics instead. Bored with hanging around the gambling club, he would run off. He and some older boys he'd fallen in with would wander off into the tunnels under Pender, now used only by gamblers escaping a police raid. Or else they'd climb the fire escapes to the rooftops along Pender and sit up there letting off firecrackers or smoking cigarettes; Leonard stole his from his mother.

Life was starting to unravel again for May-ying. Winnie guessed the end was coming between her mother and Guen when, frustrated and weary, he confided: "*Ah* Hing, the trouble with your mother is that she'll gamble even on credit." As was his way, he abruptly closed down his gambling club. He headed east, ostensibly to size up business opportunities elsewhere in Canada, but also, Winnie suspected, to leave her mother to her own debts.

Feeling at loose ends, and looking more thin and frail than at any time before, May-ying left for Nanaimo, taking Leonard with her. She said she wanted to restore her ailing health. Winnie worried enough about her there to bring an electric blanket to her and, on Mother's Day, a cashmere sweater. That winter and spring, the misfortune Winnie had predicted came true. Her mother, without work and in ill health, depended on her for support. Each month, she sent May-ying her entire $105 paycheck. May-ying would cash it and send back $5 for spending money. Cashing the check at Tong Yick store allowed her to boast about what a good daughter she had raised.

When May-ying returned to Vancouver the following summer, Winnie took the first chance she had to bring a boy whom she'd been dating up to her mother's rooming house. Winnie had first met John Chong on Thanksgiving weekend on a crowded ferry from Vancouver to Nanaimo. Winnie, Doreen and Elsie had been going to a reunion there; John and two of his brothers had been on a weekend outing. Winnie, who had so absorbed her mother's strictness about boys, at first thought John rather forward. He suggested that the three girls take shelter in their car instead of standing out on the deck in the rain. "This is unheard of, sitting with strange boys in a car," she thought. He caught sight of her next in Chinatown. He was making pickups and deliveries for Keefer Laundry, and he leaned out the window of his truck and yelled, "Hi Winnie!" She pretended not to notice.

That Christmas, there was a Chinese roller skating party at The Barn outside Stanley Park. At Elsie's insistence, Winnie went. A slight but gracefully athletic skater in a black-and-white checkered shirt caught her eye. It turned out to be John. The girls on the bench talked admiringly of him as "the perfect gentleman." He was with an older, sporting crowd who, like him, lived outside Chinatown and roller skated, swam in English Bay and played tennis at Stanley Park. John surprised Winnie by asking for a skate. Misled by her white skates into thinking she was an experienced skater—she should have rented the black skates of a beginner—he found himself practically holding her up.

"You'll never get a date with that girl, her mother is too strict," one of his chums told him afterwards. It seemed so.

"Why don't you two come back for some chow at my mom's place," he said to Winnie and Elsie. Winnie declined. He took out his cigarette package to write down her telephone number. Winnie would say only that she worked at Essondale Hospital.

The day after the party, John borrowed a car to drive there to look her up. Beneath a window of the main building, the car stalled, and a patient looking on sang "Slow Boat to China." "Hey Win, they're not so crazy after all," John said. His sense of humor won her over; the two began going steady. John bought a car so they didn't have to rely on the last bus from Vancouver. If the hour was past curfew, he hoisted her through a window. He wrote her letters every other day. What most impressed Winnie was how he included her in his mother's Sunday afternoon gatherings at the family home, when the married children came home.

At their first meeting, John and May-ying didn't have much of a conversation, partly because his Chinese was limited, and partly because she put him off by glaring at him. She derided him afterwards as a *fa-la doi*, in other words a "fella," and a nobody. As if Winnie wasn't upset enough that her mother and John had obviously not hit it off, her mother added, "You can tell by his physique and his ears that he won't have a long life." There was more. Her mother complained that his family was not well off. It was true—John had been eight when his father died, twenty years ago, leaving his mother with ten children, the youngest a baby, to raise on her own. The older ones were put to work in whatever corner grocery store she bought, most recently one in the white neighborhood of Kerrisdale that was sold by the government when it was disposing of assets confiscated from Japanese interned during the Second World War. But though the family had little money to spare, there was a legacy to the Chong name. Many old-timers owed their start to John's father. During the time of the head tax imposed on Chinese immigrants, his house and grocery store in Victoria was a depot for new arrivals: he was banker, postman, hotelier and friend. When he died, prematurely, a horse-drawn carriage carrying his coffin, draped with the Nationalist flag and surrounded by an honor guard of Chinese Benevolent Association officials from across Canada, wound its way through Victoria's Chinatown to the cemetery, on the westernmost point of land in Victoria that looked towards China.

May-ying would not be in Vancouver much longer to take a hand at matchmaking. She decided to give chase to Guen. Until she knew for sure if the on-again, off-again relationship was back on, she took Leonard to Nanaimo to be boarded out. Winnie, living up to what she believed was her responsibility, brought him back to Vancouver to be nearer her. She left him with the old lady Lee Yen. Granny Yip wasn't available; Winnie had come across her in the infirmary at Essondale, too ill to recognize anybody.

May-ying eventually sent for Leonard to join her and Guen in Winnipeg. When Guen sent Winnie a plane fare to spend her two-week annual holiday with them, she assumed all was well. It was with sorrow that she heard him complain to her one night, "*Ah* Hing, your mother hasn't changed one bit." That night, her mother returned at five o'clock in the morning.

Winnie returned to a life consumed with nursing and with John. As far as she was concerned, she had the stability she'd never dared dream of—a job, a future career and a boyfriend. Then she herself tipped the balance. On Chinese New Year's, knowing there was a party at The Barn and that John wouldn't miss it, Winnie came in specially after work to surprise him by showing up. It backfired. He arrived to see her skating on the arm of another boy, and he left without a word.

On her next day off Winnie tried to keep her mind off her heartbreak over his continuing silence by coming into Chinatown to stay with a girlfriend. In the night, she woke in severe pain. It was diagnosed as an appendicitis attack, but because Winnie, at nineteen, was underage, the surgeon needed the signature of a parent before he could operate. With her mother in Winnipeg, there was only her father. The hospital's calls to sawmills in and around New Westminster finally turned up Chan Sam and in the recovery room, Winnie awoke to the sight of him standing over her, but she had only one reaction—disappointment that it wasn't John.

It was Elsie's doing that John did show, on the day Winnie was to be discharged. He came to the point: his mother was getting old, and it would please her to see her boys married. John voiced doubts that Winnie would ever marry. "You are always telling me you believe in a career before marriage. Next year, you'll graduate from Essondale. I'm wondering when, if ever, you'll want to get married." He proposed: "I want to marry you, Winnie."

"I have to think," Winnie replied.

"I'll give you two weeks to think about it, to tell me yes or no," John said. "This is an ultimatum."

When Winnie returned to work, she was assigned to "J" ward, which housed the most violent patients, who often kicked or attacked the nurses. She protested that such work was unsuitable for someone recovering from an operation; her stitches had not yet been removed. Miss Pearson, accusing Winnie of trying to capitalize on her condition, refused to transfer her. In the two weeks John had given her, Winnie was torn between nursing and marriage, between finishing what she had started and putting her trust in family life, which had failed her so far. She finally put her faith in John and in her future mother-in-law, who Winnie liked and thought would appreciate the sacrifices of a good daughter-in-law.

Winnie told John yes, then carefully phrased a letter to May-ying. She expressed her desire to become engaged in March, on her twentieth birthday, and to marry the following September. She wanted to marry on the ninth day of the ninth month—the two Chinese characters together symbolized "forever." Winnie was nervous about how May-ying would react. She recalled how, during her visit to Winnipeg, her mother had still been trying to find her a boy. May-ying had arranged a day's outing for herself, Leonard and Winnie with a man who was a cook. After boating on Lake of the Woods and an elaborate dinner afterwards at a restaurant, she asked her daughter what she thought.

"What do I think?!" Winnie had exclaimed, her mother's intentions only then dawning on her.

"So you still like that *fa-la doi* then?" her mother had said in disgust, referring to John. "I don't care about you then. It's your life. If you want to be in the dirt and the gutter, go ahead."

Upon getting Winnie's letter, May-ying sent a letter back saying she would be taking the train out to Vancouver, with Leonard, to help with the wedding plans. Winnie assumed that she had her mother's blessing to marry John. Yet when she explained to her mother that she would need her to accompany her to the marriage bureau to give the parental approval necessary for the licence, May-ying chose to be difficult. "I don't have the money to put on a proper wedding banquet," she said. Winnie had no choice but to go in search of her father. She asked at a mah-jongg club where people of his county gathered if anybody knew when he was next coming into Chinatown and where he stayed. On that day, she went to the Sun Ah Hotel above the Ho Ho

Restaurant. "*Ah* Hing, it's fine; I trust your judgment," Chan Sam said when he learned of her plans. When Winnie saw "Father" beside his signature on her marriage licence, she finally felt she had a father that no one could deny her.

There was one obligation to her mother that Winnie had promised to fulfil upon marriage: taking Leonard with her. May-ying had brought it up again when Winnie entered nursing, and again when she toured the hospital and the nurses' residence. Winnie had not said a word about it to John. But when she had to tell her mother she was going ahead with her marriage plans, she felt she had to soften the blow.

"Of course, I'll take Gok-leng with me," she said in the same breath.

"Can your *fa-la doi* give me a good bride-price?" May-ying replied.

When Winnie broke the news to John of the $500 bride-price and the issue of Leonard, it was the latter that he was quietly, resolutely against. Winnie tried in vain to get Amy's support. She took John's side: "It's your new life, Winnie. You shouldn't have to do that." For the first time in her life, Winnie felt she was letting her mother down, that up until now she had been the good daughter her mother raised her to be. John provided her with the excuse to give May-ying: that his mother and brothers and sisters, with whom they would live after getting married, would not like Leonard moving in as well.

May-ying, with no choice, was disappointed. "*Ah* Hing, here I thought my worries were over—you were going to have a home of your own and take care of Gok-leng for me. But I guess that's asking too much." She was proud, without being acrimonious. "Don't worry about us. We'll look after ourselves. I don't have to depend on you."

The red envelope of the bride-price money that John gave May-ying was more than enough to cover her plans to celebrate her daughter's betrothal: a ten-table banquet at one of Chinatown's fancier restaurants (which, by tradition, the bride, having left home, did not attend) and the distribution of sweet

lotus-seed cakes to her friends. Winnie's godmother delivered a
metal trunk filled to the brim with everything from a nightie to a
tea towel. May-ying gave Winnie what by tradition a girl left her
mother's home with, a down comforter and two down pillows,
which she had made by a man in Chinatown. She put them inside
a cedar chest bought from Woodward's on a monthly instalment
plan. The chest, with a swirling walnut grain and a bottom drawer, was an item of furniture more beautiful than either May-ying
or her daughter had ever lived with.

In early September of 1950, Winnie quit nursing short of
graduation. As she left the grounds of Essondale, she stopped by a
garbage can, opened her white suitcase and threw away her nursing shoes. One week later, May-ying watched her twenty-year-old
daughter walk down the aisle of an Anglican church, on the arm
of Chan Sam, to marry thirty-one-year-old John Chong. The
bride was wearing her mother's jade pendant around her neck.
"You should wear this with your wedding dress," May-ying had
said when she and her daughter were dressing in a room at the
Sun Rise Hotel. "It will bring you good fortune, and it will match
the green and yellow flowers on the bottom of your dress." After
the ceremony, the wedding guests gathered at Mrs. Chong's
house. The tea and white-bread sandwiches surprised May-ying,
who'd been expecting Chinese barbecued duck at the very least.

The newest daughter-in-law and newly married son were assigned
the third-floor attic in the Chong house, bringing to seven the
number of adults living there. With its veranda and patch of
lawn, the house was neat and well-kept, much like other houses
on the block. In another lived Mrs. Chong's eldest daughter and
her husband. In yet another, some of his relatives. The neighborhood was part residential, part industrial. One block over were
Acme General Woodworks and Davis Junk Company.

Winnie busied herself setting up house. John used the savings
that he had set aside to get married and set himself up in business
by buying a dry cleaning operation from one of his sisters. He
renamed it Felix Dry Cleaners, after the cartoon cat. Winnie

helped out there and took home his customers' alterations and mending. Within a few months, she was pregnant and getting ready for a new baby.

# CHAPTER TEN

I N THE SPRING of 1950, Chiang Kai-shek sent planes from Taiwan (formerly Formosa) to carry out harassing attacks on the port of Canton and other southern coastal targets. By summer, Chiang had ordered the planes grounded, finally abandoning the Chinese mainland to Mao Zedong and the Communists. While Chiang and his discredited Nationalists declared they would defend China from socialism, the youth of China were clamouring to help rebuild their war-torn country. To them, the Communist People's Liberation Army became a symbol of hope.

The first sign of the new order in the village of Chang Gar Bin was the arrival of a regiment in khaki uniforms and caps with the soon to be familiar red star. The new recruits were traveling throughout the county to repair bridges, roads and public buildings, and to plant rubber trees to create future jobs. There was no military academy, despite what they had been led to believe before they joined; their training would be undertaken in the countryside itself.

Before the regiment's arrival, Huangbo had been visited by the local Communist cadre. She was told that she would be "inviting" three officers to stay at her house. This was the army's practice in housing their troops: in the villages they stayed in, the best house, typically that of a landlord or a better-off peasant, was assigned to the commanding officers. Often there was no need to call on the owners, as the largest houses were generally owned by Nationalist officers or sympathizers who had fled the country. The rank and file soldiers were usually housed in a temple or a school, whichever was the largest public building.

Huangbo, like other villagers of Chang Gar Bin, was won over by the discipline and uprightness of the officers and soldiers alike —a welcome contrast to the tax-collecting, thieving troops of past regimes. She was impressed by what she assumed to be Communist ways. Except for drawing water from the well in her courtyard—which the guards tested frequently to make sure it wasn't poisoned by Kuomintang infiltrators—her three guests did not take or disturb anything that did not belong to them. They did not eat with her; they ate with the rest of the regiment. Their cooks paid politely for fish and vegetables they bought at the local market. The entire regiment rose before dawn for thirty minutes of exercise, followed by a two-hour lesson from the political officer in basic literacy and Communist thought according to Mao. The rest of their waking day was devoted to cleaning up the debris of wartime and rebuilding for the future. Occasionally, the regiment practiced limited military maneuvers, but there was no actual shooting because bullets were too expensive.

A sense of calm and order prevailed. The villagers of Chang Gar Bin, who had lived in the frontlines of war for most of the last decade, finally believed that the fighting was truly over. They told each other that an era of peace and stability had begun. Village girls, like girls everywhere, fell in love with the soldiers in the caps with the red star and dreamed of marrying an army man. And so it was with great disappointment that the village awoke one morning to find the entire regiment had moved on in the middle of the night. Nobody but the commanding officers had known the departure date, for it was part of a soldier's training to move quickly, in silence and in darkness, not even using torches to light the way, so as to keep their wits sharp against the enemy Kuomintang, should they rise again.

Hardly had the army left when the villagers heard rumors that Mao's radical "land reform" was coming to the south. The program to confiscate land held by landlords to give to landless peasants had wooed poorer peasants of the north to the side of Communism during the civil war. The program had none of the same appeal in the south, where there was a long tradition of land-ownership among even the very poor peasants. In the south, some of the largest tracts were owned by wealthier clans, which often dominated whole villages. Such landowners were like public benefactors, paying for schools, temples, roads and bridges that served their village. The tyrannical absentee landlord who owned massive tracts was becoming the exception; in the last couple of decades, the lure of investing in land had diminished, because of low returns on investment and because of recalcitrant tenants who had made rents difficult to collect. But now that the war was won, a confident Mao pushed ahead with the land reform, using it as a blunt instrument of oppression to remove those that stood in his way, thereby extending his reach down to the local Communist cadre.

The rumors of land reform were confirmed when a contingent clad in uniforms of blue cotton came to Chang Gar Bin. The Work Team was met by the local cadre. Nobody in Chang Gar Bin knew their faces or where they came from. This was deliberate, so that acquaintance, relation or personal sympathy would not compromise their work. The voice that boomed over a loudspeaker was also anonymous. Quoting from Mao, it condemned the enemies of the poor—the usual local bullies, thieves and speculators—but then classified other "uniformly counterrevolutionary" elements in the village: "All Right-Peasants, Small, Middle and Big Landlords." The Work Team was there to root them out. The broadcast ended with "Long Live Chairman Mao." Every day the broadcast was the same and called upon the peasants to fight the enemy, who was anyone who opposed the land reform.

Each day, the Work Team rounded up bewildered wrongdoers from the village and the surrounding countryside. The so-called "Big Landlords," the ones who owned hundreds or thousands of *mau tin,* were not among them. They either lived in the cities or had already fled. Instead, the Work Team, like others throughout China, found only the "Small" and "Middle" landlords, who owned generally more than thirty but no more than two hundred *mau tin.* They were condemned as guilty and held in detention until it was their turn to appear at a "struggle session." Their peasant-tenants were assembled, along with other villagers of Chang Gar Bin—who dared not be conspicuous by their absence—to "speak bitterness" against them. Once publicly denounced and humiliated, sentence was passed: their *mau tin* was confiscated; and for some fifteen landlords, the sentence was death. "Kill not one or two, but a goodly number," were Mao's instructions to the Work Teams. The condemned were prodded and pushed at the end of a bayonet to the field by the school, where they knelt, hands tied behind their backs, to receive a bullet to the back of the head. By the time Mao's land reform was completed in 1953, some five million would be tried in all of China. According to Chinese figures, two million were executed. Foreign observers would put the number as high as fifteen million, but it was later thought that a more accurate figure was three to four million.

As the public trials continued, Huangbo saw the net cast ever wider. Her husband's land holding of twenty-four *mau tin,* excluding the four he had given Ping as a dowry, was not what she feared most. Rather it was the showiness of the house that would label Chan Sam, and therefore his family as "Right Peasants"—in other words, with leanings away from socialism. When Huangbo saw the authorities come to the door of the grain dealer's house, she feared hers was the next place they'd come calling. The grain dealer's wife, who had not fled with her husband, protested her arrest, but the more she resisted the more severely she was beaten. When the Work Team came for Huangbo, she offered no resistance, as Ping had counseled her. Though cuffed, shoved and pushed, she met neither heavy sticks nor brutal bayonets. In the market square, with her children watching, she was made to stand on one leg, with her head bowed in penance and her hands tied behind her back. For hours on end, the villagers railed against her and other victims there: "You are rich only because you have exploited the people!" "You are an enemy of the people!"

Chan Sam's *mau tin,* for which he had sacrificed years of his life overseas and which he had purchased to provide for the future security of his family, was confiscated. Huangbo was spared death, but there was more to come. The Work Team entered Chan Sam's house and removed all papers, letters and photographs that it could find. Included in what they took was correspondence from Chan Sam in Canada that spanned more than thirty years. What the authorities were looking for were the deeds to the *mau tin* he owned and "evidence" that his family was "counterrevolutionary." The house turned out to be evidence enough. It was condemned for its "unsightliness." The Work Team remedied its excesses: they smashed the glazed green tiles on the roof, removed the wrought-iron gate and grills over the windows and the glass itself and gouged out the carved panels in the wooden screens upstairs. They took away "extravagances": the overseas dressers and the large mirrors, several clocks, wool blankets from Canada. With the mindlessness of vandals, they destroyed the large painting of Chan Sam's parents and the smaller double portrait of him and Huangbo that watched over the main reception room. In a final condemnation of Chang Gar Bin's largest house, the Work Team declared that it was too big for one family, that there was room enough for three. Two new tenants—two brothers and their families—were moved in. A brick wall went up across the courtyard and connecting passageways were bricked in to divide the old tenants from the new, the village outcasts from the new ascendency.

When their work was done and the Work Team left Chang Gar Bin, Huangbo, Ping and Yuen were among the village's most vilified inhabitants. Others shunned them. No one talked to them unless it was in ridicule. During Ping's daily visit with her mother, the two spoke in hushed tones. They no longer dared wash rice in the courtyard, where it was easier to draw water from the well and to drain the pot, because they were unnerved by the prying eyes of the neighbor on the other side of the wall. A villager passing by overheard the telltale *chop-chop-chop-chop* of pork being minced. "The cadre might like to hear that you still have enough money to eat meat!" he had said accusingly. Thereafter, Huangbo took her chopping board underneath the stairwell at the back of the house, where the sound of the cleaver was more likely to be muffled.

Ping herself saw one small victory in the terror visited on the village. Her husband's mistress, fearing reprisal for her own absent husband's wealth, had fled Chang Gar Bin for Hong Kong. Ping let her husband back into her bed. She decided that if she was going to have any more children she ought to make sure they came one after the other, lest her husband think of following his mistress. In the next five years, she was to have three more children, a girl, then a boy, followed by another girl.

The Communists left thirteen-year-old Yuen with no heart for his own prospects. Most of his prospective inheritance, the *mau tin* and half the house, was gone. Following his father's advice that education was his only hope of overcoming the disadvantage of his feet, he had put everything into his studies. He had clung to the slim hope of going to university in the belief that his family might sacrifice for him. His father had told of a friend who sold his *mau tin* to send his son to Canton to study medicine. The son, in turn, had become successful enough to rescue his family from poverty. Yuen's hope of following that example was dissipated when he was visited by the local cadre and informed that he would have to leave school. Apparently directives had come down that landlords' children were to be entitled to no more than five years of public education.

After the land reform, Huangbo dared not ask anyone in the village to write letters on her behalf. Fortunately, Yuen had learned to read and write enough to take up the task of corresponding with his father. His father sent him the necessary writing supplies from Canada: some airmail paper and some ballpoint pens.

Yuen's first letters to his father reflected the family's despair at the turn of events: "*Baba, Mama* says it would not be possible for you to return home now. She could not stand for you to see this. You would be heartsick to see what has happened to what you worked so hard for with your sweat and with your ten fingers."

The reply was stoic: "You two better not cry over it. Times have changed and there's nothing that you can do about it. You have to look at it that way. From now on, don't even bring it up."

The Communists still allowed Chan Sam to continue sending money back, which only heightened other villagers' resentment. The fact was that the Chinese government had found its trade links severed with the non-Communist world, which refused to recognize the new government. Though it renounced much of its massive, foreign-held debt, the government was anxious to get its hands on foreign currency to meet its balance of foreign payments. The only restriction was that remittances had to be routed through the new government's Overseas Chinese Affairs Commission, which fixed a low rate of exchange into official Chinese *renminbi,* instead of through banking institutions in Hong Kong. Chan Sam had no choice but to put his trust in this new system.

As Yuen sat idle, he pondered the fate that awaited him when his only lifeline of support, his mother and his father, were gone. Even ignoring his feet, no one was going to give him, a landlord's son, work. Ever since the public trial, his mother, her back already stooped from hard work, tired easily. His father had voiced his son's worries: "What if something should happen to me? What if I should die? Who's going to be responsible for you? I think of that day and night." Yuen wanted to know more about his father's circumstances. Where did the money come from that he sent home? How was it that, if he had work only sporadically, he was able to send money home on a regular basis?

"This is how I do it," Chan Sam replied. "I have no work at the moment, so I can't earn any money. But I am always worried about the difficulties of your mother's and your life. You have no means of livelihood, so I can only borrow money from other people to send home. In some years the money I send you for living expenses isn't mine, but I treat it as such. Don't worry about me."

He bared the more cruel truth: "Regarding your feet, it's so inconvenient, everybody knows that. It's a pity, otherwise your mother and you could have joined me overseas. But if you were here, you would find it very difficult to get a job. If I sent for your mother alone and left you home by yourself, then I would worry..." In ever-deepening sorrow and self-pity, Yuen asked himself why it wasn't Nan who'd been born with crippled feet, so that in death, she could have taken the family's curse to the grave with her.

<hr>

Year in and year out, Chan Sam had awaited the "right time" to end his sojourning days and return to China. Most other sojourners did not hang on to the Gold Mountain dream as long and simply packed it in and went home. As the decades came and went, Chan Sam's hopes that the latest tumult in China would end, that things would stabilize again, had been raised and dashed many times over. When exclusion ended in 1947, other sojourners who still had any sentiment left for China or the families they'd left behind either went home or brought their families over. Chan Sam got his naturalization papers, so he could come and go as he pleased. But in China civil war was being waged to its bitter end. In 1949, when the Communists took over, he waited to see how other southerners like him would be received when they went home.

Chan Sam knew of the land reform visited on his family from what Yuen wrote. He thought seriously of going to persuade the strangers in his house to move out, and to see if the authorities might have overlooked some deeds to his *mau tin*. He dropped the idea when more stories came of arrests, beatings, torture and executions. Among the victims were compatriots who had only just gone home, who had spent their life's savings on a few *mau tin*. Chan Sam and his friends all said the same thing: "In earlier times, ninety-nine of one hundred overseas Chinese here wanted to go home. Now, because of all the fast changes in China, not one in ten thousand wants to go back."

So averse was Vancouver's Chinatown to dealings with the

Communists in China that its Canadian-Chinese organizations decided jointly that some 860 sets of bones awaiting shipment to China since 1939 would be buried in Canada instead. Men with families left behind and with the money to bring them out turned their backs on China and made Canada their new home. The horror of the land reform convinced many who were abroad to get their families out of China. Certainly, their governments were sympathetic. But Chan Sam never saw that as an option. In the end, it was the predicament of Yuen's feet that dispelled any wish he had of bringing Huangbo and Yuen to Canada. It was the same story spun from the time he first came: he had nowhere to install them in Canada, and the few dollars he earned abroad could be stretched many times further at home. He could not support them in Canada, but he could if they remained in China.

As frightening to Chan Sam as seeing the political situation at home turn against him was to see his working prospects in Canada decline. For almost forty years, he had relied on his contacts in the shingle mills. In the 1950s, unions started organizing Chinese laborers, beginning with the lumber and fish canning industries. The contract labor system, where a Chinese foreman could hire who he liked, disappeared. Chan Sam registered with an employment agency in Chinatown that placed workers with interested white employers for a cut of the wages. Now in his sixties, his graying hair turning white, his cheeks hollowed and his face lined with worry, he was not a prospective employer's ideal of a laborer. When he was hired to scrub the floors at a cement factory, wash dishes at a café or clean the hallways of a hotel, he lasted only until someone younger, usually white, came looking for a job or until he himself, exhausted and suffering from dizziness, had to give it up. The doctor he'd seen, when he twice hemorrhaged internally, had repeatedly warned him that, because of his bleeding ulcers, he should look for "light work" only.

Were it not for his own people, whom Chan Sam could depend on to lend him a few dollars to cover his own expenses and some extra to send home to China when he was out of work, he would have slipped into despair. Some more elderly sojourners left of his clan lived as if there was nothing for them to do but wait to die. His Association housed them in its cramped bachelor cubicles on one floor of the building. To Chan Sam, a dingy rooming house was one step removed, but preferable. It made it easier to believe one could live long enough to see things change for the better in China.

He tried briefly a shared arrangement. A three-story building on the edge of Chinatown had been newly renovated into two bedroom suites, offering the novel idea of apartment-living to the Chinese. Chow Guen moved back from Winnipeg to Vancouver, and when May-ying and Leonard followed, it was Chan Sam's idea that they rent one of the new suites. Chan Sam and Guen took one bedroom; May-ying and Leonard took the other. Chan Sam rather enjoyed the times when Winnie, newly married, on her way to or from her husband's cleaners, would come to share supper with them, or would stop by to pick up or drop off Leonard. But three months later, Guen left abruptly, this time for Toronto. Chan Sam and May-ying gave up the apartment. As usual, they went their separate ways.

The one bright spot on the horizon for Chan Sam was the prospect of collecting a monthly pension from the Canadian government upon turning sixty-five, a benefit once available only to whites. But it would do little more than meet his rent and his two meals a day. He held out hope that he would reach seventy, when the pension would increase by a few dollars. However, he could not deny that he was feeling the onset of old age—weakening eye sight, worsening circulation in his feet and legs.

Like a man contemplating his will, Chan Sam's mind turned to the last of the family's assets that he still held title to: the Canadian birth certificates of his daughters, Ping and Nan. They had once symbolized the only chance to unite the three daughters. Believing such sentimentality would be pointless after he was gone, Chan Sam decided it would be better to trade the certificates for money that he could send to China, to support his surviving family there.

He didn't have to look far to get the name of a middleman. A Mr. Lum confirmed that ever since the Communists took over

China, there had been a brisk trade between China, Hong Kong and North America in "buy paper" families. Although North American immigration laws had opened the door wider to the Chinese, few, other than wives and dependent children, were being allowed in. Families already in North America were just as worried about their non-admissible relations—grandparents, siblings, uncles, aunts and cousins. At the same time, there were people waiting in Hong Kong who had fled the Communist mainland and were eager to buy the papers that would get them into the United States or Canada.

Mr. Lum offered to find buyers for Chan Sam's birth certificates. He contacted his middlemen in Hong Kong, and two separate deals, each worth several hundred dollars, were made with women whose ages roughly matched Ping and Nan's papers. Mr. Lum asked Chan Sam for the essential details that immigration authorities in Vancouver and in Hong Kong would expect the real sisters to know: names and ages of himself and May-ying, when the sisters left Canada for China, what village they'd been raised in, who the other mother was. To support his application to bring his "daughters" to Canada, Chan Sam had to choose between involving their mother, May-ying, or their sister in Canada.

It was during the busy first year of her marriage that Winnie's father came to her with a request that she accompany him to the immigration authorities in Vancouver. On the way, they stopped to see Mr. Lum, who told Winnie she would be questioned about her sister, Ping. He advised her to say that she knew nothing other than that she had a sister by that name. In the end, the authorities asked only that she make a sworn declaration to that effect, which she did. Years would pass before Winnie would be reminded of what her father's business had been that day.

Some months after the deal was finalized, Chan Sam went to the train station in Vancouver to meet the first of his false daughters. The false Ping had sailed from Hong Kong to San Francisco and boarded a train for Vancouver. He took her to a nearby hotel where he handed her off to a man who, she learned, had paid for her as his bride. Some weeks later, Chan Sam, accompanied by

Mr. Lum, escorted this Ping to immigration authorities in Vancouver to be interviewed about her sister, Nan. The second false sister was waiting in Hong Kong, with her husband, to get into Canada. There was a rather tense moment when the official asked the false Ping why the two sisters spoke different dialects. She stumbled over what she'd been coached to say—that the sisters had been separated during the resistance against Japan, had been raised by their respective godmothers and had never returned to the village. Luckily, the officials wanted to hear most that she would put up her sister and brother-in-law, and that she could find them work, at the same sewing factory she worked at. That part, at least, was true.

At her mother-in-law's house, Winnie was causing problems for the other daughter-in-law living there. Thrifty enough to have had the house telephone removed to save money, she thought Winnie was driving up the gas and electricity bills. She was; Winnie thought nothing of leaving soup to simmer all day, or brewing the herbal teas to build strength before her confinement with her firstborn and to replenish the blood after the birth. Winnie knew relations were strained with the in-laws when someone below took to banging a broomstick on their ceiling—the floor of John and Winnie's quarters—whenever they heard the sewing machine whirring into the night. When not reversing cuffs and collars or draping trousers for John's customers, Winnie was sewing diapers. But Winnie herself was tiring of living in an attic; there was hardly enough water pressure to wash rice, never mind diapers. She convinced John that two and a half years living with the in-laws was enough. He agreed that they should find an apartment of their own.

Neither had the time to look for a place. Winnie was pregnant with her second child. After supper John always went back to the cleaner's to finish tagging the clothes for the next day's pick-ups and to hand-iron shirts and steam-press suits. Chan Sam told Winnie he was between jobs and offered to find them an apartment. He came up with the two upper floors of a house in a poorer, immigrant neighborhood east of Chinatown. Knowing the forty dollars a month rent was quite a jump from the fifteen Winnie and John paid the in-laws, he proposed, and they agreed, that he take the second bedroom and pay half the rent, which was half his monthly old age pension. Hardly had Winnie brought the new baby, another daughter, home from the hospital when they had the inconvenience of having to move again. The landlord living downstairs was annoyed when Winnie replaced the twenty-five-watt bulb in the hall with a sixty-watt without asking him first.

Chan Sam had his own ideas about what his daughter's next move should be. "Everybody is buying a house," he said. He persuaded them to look at what he'd found for sale, a modest two-bedroom house on Gladstone Street off the Kingsway, close to the Canada Dry Factory. Winnie and John liked the neighborhood. There was a United Church across the street and on one side was a gray stucco house with a white picket fence, and on the other, a purple stucco house. Both were immaculately kept. The house itself had an above-ground basement; the siding was of fashionable gray-green asphalt tiles; there was a gas fireplace in the living room, a sun porch, a well-tended lawn in the front and a garden in the back. It was being sold furnished. The asking price was $7,800. The problem was raising the $1,100 down payment. John's eldest sister was happy to lend him the money, and Chan Sam insisted he wanted to contribute. "Put a little more down," he said, "and then the monthly payment is just like paying rent." Winnie accepted his $900 graciously, knowing nothing would please her father more than to be able to boast in Chinatown: "I bought my daughter a house."

In return for his contribution, her father moved into the second bedroom. Winnie, John, their two-year-old and the baby, less than one year, shared the other bedroom. The closeness bothered no one. One of the jobs the employment agency in Chinatown found Chan Sam was cleaning a hotel three mornings a week. No matter how late she'd been up the night before, Winnie rose at four to cook him rice before he started work at five. Her father in turn sometimes babysat when she had to help at the cleaner's. He still spent most of his free time in Chinatown, taking the bus there, stopping in at his clan society to pick up his mail. He never came back empty-handed; he always brought back something for dinner—some greens, maybe a fresh rock cod. John was happy enough to propose a weekend trip together. Chan Sam had often said he'd always wanted to visit the United States. Except for being hassled on both sides of the border by officials suspicious that anyone Chinese might be a Communist and therefore have links to an enemy power, the trip to Seattle was pleasant enough, especially for Chan Sam, who was wide-eyed at the eight-lane freeways on the American side.

Winnie never insulted her father by asking, but it seemed to her that though he worked only periodically and drew a modest pension, he always had a few dollars to spare. There was the money he'd given them for the house, for example. She thought he must also be sending a few dollars here and there home to China, because he said to her: "*Ah* Hing, if things get better for you and I am gone from the world, all I ask is that you keep up sending money to China—twenty or so dollars every couple of months." Even though Winnie said she'd have to ask John, she knew she couldn't ask her husband to carry that obligation. He had been resolutely against taking in Leonard; how could he agree to support a family she herself had never met?

I was Winnie and John's second-born, and one of my earliest memories is of my grandfather, whom I knew as *Goong-goong* (the proper way to address a maternal grandfather), bringing me a red tricycle, the first present I remember receiving from anyone. I can also picture him coming through the back door of our Gladstone Street house, setting down a shopping bag of groceries and scooping me up. I remember too my sister and I sitting in pails of water in the backyard cooling off on warm summer days, reassured by his presence as he worked nearby in the garden.

It was on a day like that that he and my mother got into one of those silly disputes that blew up into something unintended.

Mother was down in the basement, standing at the wringer washer. She was diverting the hot soapy water from the wash cycle into pails, intending to reuse the water to wash the floors upstairs. My grandfather came down with the garden tools, put them in the sink and turned on the hot water to rinse them off.

"*Baba*, why don't you use the cold water to rinse off the garden tools?" she asked.

He was immediately offended. "I'm going to write to the family in China to tell them this is how you treat your own father!" he said. He went into a sulk, and Mother couldn't understand why.

Finally, he broke the silence. "If that's the way you're going to be, I don't think we can live under the same roof," he said.

Mother did not talk back, for only then did she realize how unhappy her father was living away from Chinatown. He'd been away three years. At the Gladstone Street house, only she spoke enough Chinese to converse with him. For company during the day, there were only the neighbors, old Mr. Penny, a night watchman, and his wife, tending their flowers behind their white picket fence, or else Mr. and Mrs. Stewart, a retired couple who rarely ventured out. Mother knew her father could hardly admit he no longer wanted to live in his daughter's house, not when it had been his idea to buy it. He moved back to Chinatown, to the Sun Ah Hotel where he'd lived before, and he rather enjoyed taking the bus when he came to visit us. I always went running to the door, my arms outstretched to meet his.

# CHAPTER ELEVEN

MAO ZEDONG'S LAND reform, even in the north of China, had proven to be a failure. In the less-crowded north, landless peasants were awarded three *mau tin;* in the south, such peasants were given only one *mau tin.* Such a tiny plot fell well short of the four or five that even the poorest land-owning peasant in the south achieved in his lifetime. It did almost nothing to alleviate the plight of the impoverished, for such plots were too small to be efficient. Even if their new owners had the money to cooperate with their neighbors and buy a water buffalo, such a draft animal wouldn't work for more than one master. As well, some of those awarded land couldn't work it themselves—like the infirm and the elderly—and couldn't afford to hire the labor to work it for them.

Instead of admitting the failure of his first grand plan, the impatient Mao declared 1955 to be the year China would forge further ahead with socialism. The answer to the problems of the land reform, he decided, lay in speeding up the program to turn farms into collectives. At the same time, he nationalized all commerce and industry still in private hands. Again, his overreaching ambitions would fail. Peasants who did not want to become tenants of the state would sabotage their equipment and land and destroy their pigs and chickens rather than surrender them to the collective. In regions where peasants fled to the cities, food production fell, hoarding became widespread, and famine hit.

Mao saw the Confucian family as a reactionary bulwark against Communism. He wanted the Chinese masses to see him as their substitute father-figure, so that he, rather than the family, became the central moral authority. He set up a nationwide movement to study "Mao Zedong's Thoughts." Those who rejected them were branded "Westerners" and were "reformed" in prison.

With such obstacles to truth and frankness, the communication between Chan Sam and Yuen became, in part, a charade to deceive the prying eyes of Communist authorities and villagers anxious to point the finger. As a consequence, Chan Sam honed his Communist rhetoric: "I hope things go well for China, that production will increase, that construction will increase, and people will live well." Such phrases became a standard part of every letter.

This made it difficult to find the true meaning between the lines. What was said in one letter would be contradicted by the next. Much of it was deliberate, so that the letters would not provide the "evidence" to victimize Chan Sam's family, an already easy target. Yet, since no one was traveling to China to hand-deliver a message for him, these letters were Chan Sam's only communication with his son and his wife. Chan Sam felt that Yuen, in his youth and in his enforced idleness, needed his fatherly guidance as never before. And as Chan Sam watched himself age, he became possessed with worry about Huangbo's health, about the day when she might need someone to care for her.

If only Yuen could find a way to earn a living, Chan Sam thought, he would have the solution to both his worries. In his letters, he tried to encourage his son to think that there were several possibilities open to him. He suggested Yuen find someone in the village to tutor him in tailoring or bookkeeping. Yuen dared not ask anyone; villagers still avoided him. In his replies, he suggested his father buy him a sewing machine so he could teach himself to sew. Or, implying he might escape the label of a "landlord's son" if he went where nobody knew him, he suggested he leave Chang Gar Bin for Shekki. He proposed going there to live and study, or perhaps to find "business partners," those who would ignore his label for the right price.

Discussion about what Yuen could do, seeing as the state had no interest in helping him, always came down to money. Chan Sam was compromised by the fear of the letters falling into the wrong hands. He wanted authorities to believe he had little to spare, yet he also wanted Yuen to believe that as his father, he would give him what he needed. So some letters would be a litany of personal financial woes—he was out of work; he couldn't find work; he could only hope to find work, but factories were closing down. He bemoaned unforeseen expenses; he had to undergo costly operations and take expensive western medicines. He often mentioned the burden of having to meet the living expenses of two families, one in China and one in Canada. In other letters, money would seem of no hindrance. Chan Sam offered to try to find someone in Hong Kong going to China to bring in a sewing machine for Yuen. He supported his son's plans to go to Shekki. He pledged to cover all the fees and expenses that went with study there. He bandied about sums of hundreds of dollars and more that Yuen might need to go into business, promising that "somehow or other" he could get the necessary money together. Then, inevitably, a letter would come setting aside everything that had been said before, blaming the lack of money as the insurmountable problem.

If it wasn't money, it was Huangbo whom Chan Sam worried about. He decided Yuen should not leave the village because of Huangbo: "If you go outside and leave your mother alone at home, what will happen if she gets ill? Who would help her? What will happen if she dies? Who would know?" He saw the answer to his worries in the daughter-in-law that Yuen would eventually bring into the house. Upon Yuen's reply that he did not want to marry, his father lectured him severely for having "unfilial" thoughts. "One generation should give way to another," Chan Sam wrote.

In reply to the charge of being "unfilial," the most grievous accusation a parent could make against a child, Yuen had to confess that he didn't think he could father children, because ever since he was young he'd had urinary problems. It provoked an angry reply: "Your mother should have taken you to the doctor long ago; why is it delayed until now? As soon as you get this letter, get going at once. Scour the place for a distinguished doctor of western medicine to go under the knife. Go to Canton." For this, money was of no concern. "Don't worry about the cost," Chan Sam wrote. "I will pay all your medical expenses."

On one of his visits to the Gladstone Street house, Chan Sam brought some letters from China to show Winnie. The first two were supposedly from Ping, who would have needed someone to write on her behalf. With her limited ability to read Chinese, all Winnie could make out was that her sister would "go crazy in the head" if her father did not send money—each letter asked for several hundred dollars. Chan Sam said the letters from Ping said she needed to go into hospital for treatment of some unspecified illness. He said it wasn't like his daughter not to come right out and say what her illness was, or to tell him what her real reason for needing the money was. The amounts she asked for weren't credible; it was enough, he said, to go into business. But what made him doubly suspicious was that although he recognized Ping's signature at the bottom of each letter, the two letters were unmistakably of a different hand. Neither was Yuen's, whom he expected Ping would ask for help in writing a letter.

He then showed Winnie letters from Yuen. He said Yuen had always written in ballpoint pen and on airmail paper, which Chan Sam himself had supplied from Liu Kiu Exports and Imports, a shop in Vancouver's Chinatown. But oddly, a recent letter from Yuen was written on rice paper and in Chinese brush. Winnie agreed; it was hard to know if the same person had written both. The difference between the two was like the difference between printing and writing.

Chan Sam told Winnie that it was not the first time he had received suspicious letters from China. Two people, claiming to be relatives, whose names Chan Sam had not recognized, had written asking for money, one to bury a deceased relative, the other for an undisclosed business. Chan Sam feared that he and the family in China were targets for extortion. People needed only an overseas address, he said. He said talk in Chinatown was that the Communists were intercepting remittances: "It's happening all the time. Everybody is scared to send money home," he said. "Those that do don't dare send much." Winnie was left with the impression that her father thought it best if he cut off contact for awhile, if he waited until the situation at home improved.

"Who are these people?" Chan Sam wrote to Yuen when the two unsolicited requests came from the supposed relatives. "I don't think they are related to us. Go tell them my father is getting on in his years and he cannot find work. He cannot give you money." Chan Sam also told Yuen that Ping had asked him for money for medical expenses. He told him to explain to Ping that "according to the father-child relationship, *Baba* should help you, but he doesn't have the money." He also instructed Yuen that, in future, he was to write only in ballpoint pen.

While Chan Sam believed imposters were behind the suspicious letters, he also worried that his children may have been trying to get more money from him. Such a thought annoyed him, but it also provoked his guilt because he couldn't provide it. The letter he wrote to Yuen was a sermon-like discourse:

...Some children of overseas fathers behave as if their fathers have found the golden mountain and planted a silver tree. Some of these playboys spend the money wildly, they take it easy in China and don't work. They just live on the money sent home. They don't realize the misery their fathers have been through, that the money comes from blood and sweat, that their fathers have to subject themselves to exploitation, that they have to take a lot that comes out of the white man's mouth.

Most of the overseas Chinese here have worked so hard for so long and have sent home so much money. Some have gone bankrupt, some have died prematurely. When things are good here, they are many times better than in China. But now when the economy turns down, when someone's fate is bad and he has no work, what can be done then?

Yuen, in his youthful insensitivity, saw only the need to protect his overseas connection. He asked about the Canadian side of the family, the third sister, Hing, her younger brother, Gok-leng, and the concubine. He wanted them to write to him. Chan Sam made excuses for Hing, said she ought to correspond with the family in China but that she had her hands full with two young daughters. He promised to ask her to add a few lines at the bottom of his next letter home. When that didn't happen, Chan Sam explained to Yuen that his sister couldn't very well write without sending money, which, he said, she and her husband could not afford to do. As for Gok-leng and the concubine, Chan Sam said that the boy and his mother had moved away several years ago to another city. "I have no concern for how their life is," he wrote.

It had been more than four years since Winnie had last seen her mother. Shortly after her daughter's wedding, May-ying had left Vancouver again in pursuit of Chow Guen. For a time, the relationship was off, and May-ying, with Leonard, made her own way waitressing in Toronto. But eventually, it was back on again. She joined up with Guen when he had an opportunity to take over a restaurant in London, Ontario. He was both manager and waiter at the Nanking Gardens; May-ying did the cooking, and Leonard helped out at the till. Business was slow during the week, but on Sundays, when *dim sum* was on offer, the place was filled.

Winnie kept up a regular correspondence with her mother. She even wrote when her waters broke signaling the inevitable onset of labor, thinking a daughter ought to share with her mother the important moment of going to the hospital to give birth for the first time. She always enclosed photographs with her letters, especially now that there were two granddaughters that her mother had not yet met. Since the letters back never said much, Winnie assumed that all was well, that they were making a go of everything.

Then one day came a letter from her mother that said Leonard had run away from home. Guen had added that he was in the care of the Ontario Children's Aid Society, in a detention home for teenaged boys. Winnie immediately contacted a social worker in London.

She reported that Leonard had been picked up by the police several miles from London in a resort town on the shores of Lake Huron. He'd been gone from home three days and nights. Out of money, he'd pilfered watches off towels on the beach, then turned them in to the police station in hopes of claiming a reward. The police were going to drive him home, but Leonard was adamant that he would not go. That was when a social worker was called in.

"Are you aware that your mother has a drinking problem?" the social worker asked. Sadness overwhelmed Winnie.

She convinced John that they should go back east to sort out her brother's living situation. They decided to travel by train and make a three-week holiday of it. Winnie bought her daughters, aged four and two, matching mustard-colored coats and hats trimmed in black velvet so they'd look nice when they met their grandmother for the first time. The family boarded the transcontinental train in Vancouver. During the stop in Winnipeg, they went to a nearby Chinese greasy spoon, where Winnie thought *Fee Bak,* the one who used to cook on the tugboats, might be working as a chef. Nobody knew of him, but the family stayed and ate a meal there anyway. By the time they disembarked two days later in London, the younger daughter was feverish and vomiting. May-ying put her granddaughter on a diet of rice meal liquid and turtle soup, her remedy for "flowing-stomach" disease. By early morning, a doctor had to be called, and the child was admitted to hospital with dysentery.

In between visits to the hospital, Winnie tried to deal with Leonard. She knew he was a discipline problem. When he was last living in Vancouver, he'd spent time with John at the cleaner's.

Once, John caught him stealing a wallet from a car, another time money from the cash drawer. Guen once added a comment to a letter that Leonard was not an obedient child. In London, Winnie saw plainly, however, that her brother was but one of many problems and disappointments in a household that was breaking apart.

Leonard felt he had no home life. He had been expected to help out after school at the restaurant seven days a week. He would run off, leaving the front counter and the cash unattended. He was in awe of how his white classmates lived—with two parents, a living room, a basketball hoop over the garage door—and was ashamed of how he lived with his mother, in a room above a second-floor restaurant. When boys at school didn't have much time for him, he got to thinking money could buy him friends. He rang in "No Sale" a few times, pocketed the customers' money and took to the streets.

The police brought him home a week later. He was turned in by the owner of the car he was found sleeping in. Guen said to May-ying, "He's your son; I take no responsibility." She punished him in her usual way, made him kneel on a broomstick in a corner and listen to her berate him, without allowing him to look around or get up until she said so. May-ying's drinking made a mockery of such punishments. She'd fall asleep, forgetting he was there. When she awoke to find he'd gone to bed, she'd wake him to start scolding him all over again. The more drunk she was, the more she brought up his past and long-forgotten misdeeds. Sometimes it was Guen who woke him, to tell him to get his mother upstairs to bed. Leonard practically had to carry her. Guen, even though he too had the smell of whiskey about him, could always manage to get back to his own room on his own two feet.

Even as Leonard was being brought home by the police the first time, he was making plans to run away again. This time he vowed to steal enough money to stay away. The problem he had to overcome was getting into Guen's locked room. He solved it by finding the way to unlock an unused back entrance. On the day he planned to leave, he went to the third floor of Fielding's Arcade next door, where the broken pinball machines were kept. He unlocked the dead bolts on the passageway between the buildings and on that back door to Guen's room. That night he came back the same way—the Arcade was open twenty-four hours a day. He took whatever money he could find in the pockets of Guen's trousers draped over the chair, and he bolted.

Winnie heard the story of Leonard's more serious theft from Guen. The several hundred dollars in Guen's pockets had been for the next month's supplies; business wasn't good enough to establish credit. That the business was suffering was apparent from the hollow dinginess of the place and the few white customers who straggled in. Guen was also looking for a sympathetic ear to listen to his complaints about May-ying. Obviously exasperated, he told Winnie that her mother was drinking too much. He said that the more she drank, the more MSG she put in her cooking.

The visit became intolerable. Winnie observed that it took less than a day and a half for the bottle of whiskey kept in the restaurant kitchen to disappear. Guen and her mother made no effort to have any regular meals. Nobody seemed to care about sleep. By the time the restaurant closed at midnight, May-ying, already drunk, wanted to talk. She would rehash the past, talk about the hardship she'd gone through to raise Winnie. She repeated, again and again, that she'd tried to raise her daughter to be a good girl. Winnie, wanting only to sleep, swallowed the familiar guilt. She answered as her mother bade her. Yes, she ought to be indebted to her; yes, her mother had sacrificed a lot for her sake. All the time she was thinking to herself, "I'm sick of listening to all this; I can't take it any more."

After their daughter was discharged from hospital, Winnie and John were only too anxious to cut short their trip. They settled the issue of Leonard with the Children's Aid: he was to be made a ward of the province and placed in a foster home in Ontario. The Society was to look into the jurisdictional issue between the provinces, and if it could be sorted out, Winnie and John could think about having him transferred to Vancouver. When that was done, the family was on the next flight home.

Several months later, Winnie got a telephone call from May-ying. She had seen her mother cry once before, upon Nan's death. Never had she heard her sob like this.

"*Ah* Hing, I'm all by myself. I'm alone in this world. I have no one else but you. What shall I do?" Guen had walked out on her and the business; she had no idea where he'd gone. She hadn't been able to meet the restaurant's debts and the bank had moved in and foreclosed on the place. Winnie felt sorry that her mother's seventeen-year relationship with Guen had ended on that note.

"You can move in with us, *Mama*," she said. Her mother was almost fifty years old; who, if not Winnie, would support her? They would be hard pressed, especially with another new baby in the house, John and Winnie's third child. However, John quite willingly sent May-ying the train fare and arranged for a railway escort. She moved into the bedroom that Chan Sam had vacated a year earlier.

<hr>

My grandmother, whom I called *Po-po* (the proper way to address a maternal grandmother), arrived after the birth of my younger brother. My sister and I called him "*Dai-dai*," not Greg, and he called us "*Jeh-jeh*," not Louise and Denise. Similarly, my sister and I used the appropriate Chinese titles of respect for each other of "Elder Sister" and "Younger Sister." We would address each other so only until we started school, when English overtook the use of Chinese at home.

I knew Louise, the firstborn, and Greg, the first grandson, were my grandmother's favorites. Both could light up her face, turn on her girlish laughter. Louise was gregarious and could speak Chinese well, and Greg was a happy child, with a smile and the chubbiness of a cherub. My grandmother had a down comforter made for Greg, by the same man in Chinatown who had made the comforter and two pillows that she'd put inside the cedar chest for my mother's wedding present. Greg was to carry around that burgundy satin comforter for years, until it was in tatters. I knew my grandmother had observed Louise's birth with a gift, an intricate bracelet linking hollow, lacey gold balls, filled with tinier gold balls that rattled together. I had nothing from my grandmother to mark my own birth, and I gave little in return. She intimidated me into a stony-faced silence. At two and a half, I held out my palm to her, burned on the side of the wood stove when I'd rounded a corner too quickly, and she applied a stinging salve of fermented oranges. I followed my sister in grooming sessions, tilted my head back for her to pluck my eyebrows, forward for her to plait my hair, always too tight. I knew that I mustn't flinch, that my grandmother didn't brook cowardice.

The rest of the household had different reactions to May-ying's arrival. My father, ever considerate, treated his mother-in-law well, and she found nothing to disapprove of in him. When he rolled his cigarettes, he would refill her MacDonald Export A tin, too. He happily gave May-ying a few dollars here and there. She needed some money to spend, for bus fare to Chinatown, for a round of mah-jongg, to buy the groceries she liked to bring home. Often she came back with a novelty toy for Greg.

Inevitably, there were whiskey and wine bottles concealed in her shopping bags. Winnie half expected it. She met disappointment soon after her mother's arrival; she went to store her suitcase under the bed and heard an unmistakable *clink* inside. Later she noticed that the garbage can under the back porch was full of empty gallon jugs that smelled of port wine.

Winnie, afraid of how much money would go to drink, kept May-ying in shorter and shorter supply. Within weeks tension pervaded the house. Winnie never knew if her mother was going to be pleasant or unreasonable, but she always expected the worst. If May-ying had been drinking, she would want to talk. Inevitably her monologue, interrupted only when she made Winnie answer, would degenerate into a harangue harping on past injustices— the same long-winded lectures she had subjected Winnie to during the visit to London. One night, she woke up the household muttering that there was no point in living, that she was going to go and die. She dressed to leave. Winnie, scared by her mother's talk of suicide, hid her shoes. At the same time, she couldn't help thinking how ludicrous the situation was.

In this unpredictable sea, Winnie was tossed between being a daughter and being a mother herself, of wanting to help May-ying but also needing to protect her family from the indignity of her drinking. When her mother, already terribly frail, suffered a rapid weight loss and had to be operated on for bleeding ulcers, Winnie took the opportunity to ask her doctor how to help her mother stop drinking for good.

"Alcoholics," he said—it was the first time Winnie had heard the word mentioned with respect to her mother—"don't actually stop drinking. They will drink behind your back. They will lie to you. Nobody can help your mother; she has to help herself first."

"I'm afraid I'm going to have a nervous breakdown," Winnie said.

"No you're not. An alcoholic's life is like a snake pit, but don't let your mother drag you down."

May-ying's enforced abstinence during the week she was hospitalized precipitated a destructive bout of drinking when she came home. She needled Winnie for money, ten dollars one day, ten dollars the next. It escalated into ridiculous amounts, a hundred dollars, two hundred. "I need the money to send to China," was a line she tried out.

"The doctor was right. It's no use then," Winnie thought.

She and John were in the living room one day when May-ying, her eyes glazed and her speech slurred, stumbled in from her bedroom demanding money. Never had she been so brazen as to behave so in front of John. She stabbed at her palm as if money were owed her. Hardly had she got her words out when Winnie cut her off: "I don't have the money for you, *Mama*." The denial touched off a maelstrom of desperate abuse.

"*Ah* Hing! Give it to me. You owe it to me; I raised you!"

As a stream of invective swirled by Winnie's head, something in her snapped. All the years of resentment and near-rebellion had come to the breaking point. She became her mother, wanting to hurl back worse than she got.

"You didn't raise me. I raised myself. You threw me out on the road, left me like a plant, without water or care."

Her mother always was a fighter. "Is this all the gratitude a mother gets? Is this all you learned from what I taught you?! Who needs a daughter like you? Go and die—the sooner the better!"

"If you don't want me as a daughter, if I can't please you, what else is there for me to do? You said you wanted to kick the life out of me when the labor pains were so bad. You should have killed me then. You almost spanked me to death; why didn't you just tie me to a telephone pole in the street, whip me until I died? Then I wouldn't have to live through such misery!"

John, whose limited Chinese had insulated him from his mother-in-law's past tirades against his wife, was not a person who liked confrontation. Never one to start an argument, he was the first to try to end one. He was particularly concerned about Winnie because she was pregnant with their fourth child.

His voice, in English, intercepted the insults mother and daughter were throwing at each other. "This has got to stop, Winnie. This has got to stop right now."

"John, you take her out of here then, take her out of here!" Winnie gestured towards the front door. She covered her face and broke down in tears.

John gave the order to her mother that she had to go. Spitting defiance, May-ying stormed into her bedroom and packed her suitcase. She got as far as the sun porch. "I refuse to leave," she said. She was such a featherweight that John practically carried her out. He put her into his car and deposited her and her suitcase at the door to Chan Sam's room in Chinatown.

When May-ying tried to get money out of Chan Sam, she somehow found out that he had sold the birth certificates of Ping and Nan. She demanded a share of the proceeds. He refused, reminding her that Chow Guen had never paid *him* for *her*. In a rare united act, Chan Sam wrote a letter, on his and May-ying's behalf, to their third daughter, saying that she owed her parents $1,500. The itemized account of what Chan Sam had spent included the $900 he'd given her towards the down payment for the house and the groceries he'd bought during the time he lived with her family. Winnie thought it petty that the list included even the red tricycle that he had given her youngest daughter.

Two days after the letter arrived, May-ying and Chan Sam showed up at the Gladstone Street house. A friend waited outside in a pick-up truck. May-ying marched in and said she wanted to take back what belonged to her. She went into the bedroom, threw the contents of a dresser onto the bed and had Chan Sam remove it to the truck. She asked for the sewing machine that she had given Winnie years before, and a blanket that once belonged to her. As they were leaving, Winnie heaved the red tricycle across the floor at them: "Here, if you want this so badly, take it." Winnie was especially upset that of all days to show up, they happened to choose Mother's Day.

Another letter arrived, this time from a lawyer. "I can't believe it," Winnie told John. "I'm being sued by my own father and mother." The suit demanded repayment of $1,500. On the advice of another lawyer, Winnie countersued, demanding equivalent back rent and grocery money from them both.

Both suits were dropped.

As Chan Sam faced the reality of his closing years, he had some loose ends in China that he wanted to tie up. He asked Yuen to contact a man in Chang Gar Bin who had a brother-in-law of Yuen's age, who was apparently interested in coming to Canada. The Canadian government, in an ever-softening attitude towards its resident Chinese, had raised the age limit of dependent children of Chinese Canadians allowed entry into the country. As a consequence, as far as Chan Sam was concerned, his son's identity was suddenly tradable. He was matter-of-fact with Yuen about selling his identification: "The sale of your entry document into Canada would be of great help to the family," he said.

Dithering from the Chinese side forced Chan Sam to make concessions on price. He'd hoped for two thousand dollars; he would only get half after the take of various middlemen. He grew anxious, explaining that the entry document would expire when Yuen turned twenty-one. The terms were finally agreed upon. The stand-in for Yuen then made the mistake of filing a deposition with immigration authorities under his own name and his own birthplace. Chan Sam, furious at such stupidity, had no choice but to call the deal off.

What dealt the body blow to Chan Sam's hopes and dreams for his family was news from Yuen that the villagers of Chang Gar Bin had gone further down the collective road and were now part of a "people's commune." Kwangtung was one of four provinces where Mao set up communes as pilot projects. Dozens of collectives comprising several tens of thousands of acres and as many as twenty thousand households were merged into one commune. Not until the following year would he extend the commune system to the rest of China's seven hundred million peasants. Everything came provided by the commune, but everybody also contributed to the commune. Ironically, Mao's socialist experiment, which deliberately undermined the institution of the family, also provided Yuen with his first job—he slopped out the pigpen. Of course, Huangbo and Yuen did not ask for any more remittances from abroad, and Chan Sam did not send any. Instead, his letters home polished new Communist rhetoric: "My wish is that everyone will have enough to eat, that production will go up, and the country will be reconstructed to become rich and strong, so the people can live and work in peace and contentment."

As if there was nothing else left, father and son traded shame, remorse and regret. Yuen apologized for his crippled feet. He was ashamed that they had prevented him from finding work. He was sorry for every grain of rice he'd eaten that should have been made into rice gruel: "*Baba*, I would have been happy to eat *jook* every day for the rest of my life, if only you could have come home." His father's sighs hung on the page. He apologized for having failed his wife and son. He said that he couldn't live with the thought that he and Yuen's mother had not seen each other in almost twenty years. He said he should have gone home long ago, but now he was bankrupt and stranded abroad. He said he had worked hard and lived frugally in hopes that a few *mau tin* would give the family a few bowls of rice. He wrote of forty years of toil abroad having come to naught: "Never did I dream my life would turn out so."

As if he were bequeathing more than money could buy, Chan Sam sent a letter telling his son how he had tried to live his life. It contained a litany of Chinese proverbs:

When I see how fast the changes are in the world, I realize in the end that everyone has to die. If someone manages to live beyond sixty and dies in his bed, that is enough. If someone dies unexpectedly and doesn't manage to write his will, that is to die with one's eyes unclosed. What I hope for now is that I may live for a long time, and that you and your mother will be happy and live long, in peace and happiness. Heaven gives very few people a good fate; the majority of people get no help from Heaven. Goodness has a good recompense, wickedness has a bad recompense. If there is no recompense, the time hasn't come.

Looking back over life, there is no one who has not made mistakes. If one makes a mistake and it is not corrected, then one would go in the wrong direction and would never get back onto the right road. It is very clear what is good and what is evil, so to correct a mistake is easy...

Man's fate is rough. If you have money and power, you need have no fear of having no friends. But if you are bankrupt and have no power, you can catch sparrows on the doorstep. In one's life one should not ride one's horse to the death; one should not try to be clever and show stupidity, but should bear in mind that former events forgotten may be the teachers of later events.

When one is on this earth, one should never get into point-less fights, but should yield to others, turn big things into small things and little things into nothing. In life you may run into cold looks and hard words, but you should not take too much notice. Everyone should have humanity in their hearts and he who cannot regulate himself will not be obeyed by others. Another thing is people should live simply and should not covet luxury. They should not be wasteful and should be able to be independent. At the same time they should be healthy and sound in mind. They should be clear about what they love or hate. Sun Yat-sen said, Knowing is hard, doing is easy...

In my opinion, sons and daughters should all marry when they grow up. They should become husbands or wives, also fathers or mothers. A man should take the same attitude towards caring for his parents, his wife and his children...

What I have talked about today about humanity and morality finishes here. It is up to you to decide whether you believe it or not.

Yuen made a last effort to secure his own footing on the family's broken staircase. He asked his father where he could write his sister in Canada. Chan Sam sent him the address on Gladstone Street, but accompanying it was an ominous charge that the third daughter had been "unfilial," of which he said he would say more in a later letter. There would not be another letter.

❦

It was illness that would close the rift between Winnie and her parents. The lawsuits were forgotten.

Her father was the first to fall seriously ill. He asked Winnie to accompany him to the hospital where he'd been sent for tests. Chan Sam was diagnosed as having cancer and was admitted to Mount Saint Joseph Oriental Hospital, first established by nuns from Montreal decades ago for the care of elderly and homeless Chinese men. On the heels of his diagnosis of cancer, May-ying, looking thin and drawn, was admitted to hospital for tests. She was diagnosed with tuberculosis, which she suspected she'd caught from the coughs and sneezes of other transients filtering over the half-partitions in the makeshift lodgings she had ended up in.

I remember standing outside the gates of Pearson Hospital where my grandmother was spending a six-month convalescence. Father would tell my sister and me to wave to the tiny figure standing in the doorway beside Mother. As she did for her father who was in the hospital at the same time, Mother visited May-ying three or four times a week, bringing rice and soup. She got none of her father's appreciation. Instead, her mother complained that Winnie did not come often enough, taking the opportunity to berate her for her failings as a daughter. Mother returned to the car obviously upset.

She was much more distraught the day she arrived to find her father's room empty. He'd been transfered to the Vancouver General Hospital. She found him in the basement, sitting on the floor in a barren room, his arms bound across his chest in the kind of strait-jacket that she herself had once used for the violent patients on "J" ward at Essondale Hospital. The nurses said the cancer had gone to her father's brain. Two weeks later, he was dead.

My grandmother was in hospital and wasn't allowed to attend my grandfather's funeral. In the sparse crowd, mostly the pallbearers from the Chan Society, the only person I recognized was a gentle man who my siblings and I addressed as Noong *Sook*—the man named Jang Noong—who my mother and grandmother often took us to visit in Chinatown. There was no weeping. There were some prayers, people threw dirt on the coffin, and left.

The secretary at the Chan Society on Pender opened the black book bound with a red leather spine, found Member 1,091, dipped his brush in red ink and wrote "Deceased, September 15, 1957."

After what had been months of silence, Yuen received a letter from Canada. In it was a funeral home notice from *The Chinese Times* announcing the death of his father at seventy years of age. Yuen saw his own name among those listed in mourning, along with his mother, the concubine and the other son, Gok-leng. No daughters were mentioned—the two surviving daughters, Ping and Hing, were married and therefore considered to be out of the family. There was also a brief note offering condolences, with the concubine's name at the bottom. Some weeks later, the Chan Society sent a remittance of the equivalent of twenty Canadian dollars—presumably what was left of Chan Sam's savings once the funeral had been paid for—in what would be the last letter to come from Canada.

# CHAPTER TWELVE

M Y MOTHER WENT from one rooming house to another in Chinatown looking for accommodation for my grandmother upon her discharge from hospital, only to discover that news of May-ying's "spitting-up blood disesase" had preceded her. One landlord after another refused to rent her a room. Mother couldn't take her in because the doctor had warned her that young children—the youngest of us, Chris, was born when my grandmother was in hospital—should not be exposed to the risk of tuberculosis. Eventually, Mother found a hotel a few blocks from Chinatown near the railway station that didn't ask questions of its transient guests.

Within days of being discharged, my grandmother asked Father to pick her up at the hotel to drive her to the cemetery where her husband was buried. She required the older grandchildren's presence: "It's only proper; they must worship their grandfather." When Father arrived, she had ready a thermos of tea, a bottle of whiskey, porcelain bowls of hot steamed rice, a whole steamed chicken and barbecued pork from a suckling pig, packed in a cardboard box along with cups for the tea and whiskey. Not understanding the rituals of worshiping the dead, I was astounded when she left it, dishes and all, in the shadow of the tombstone.

The recent death and illness of her parents left Mother with the feeling that she wanted to make a break with Vancouver. Father was also looking for a change. He decided he wanted to get out of the dry-cleaning business after he collapsed one day, in part from overwork and in part from the heat and fumes of the gas boiler that fed the steam press. He saw an advertisement for radio operators to direct landings and takeoffs at federal airports and to guide pilots overflying them. What interested Mother was that the successful applicants would be posted in communities outside Vancouver. The pay was low, but few Chinese had the security of an employer like the federal government. Father, already a ham radio buff, went to night school to get the necessary radio operator's licence. He then applied and was accepted for training at Vancouver Airport. When he was transfered to Prince George, a town of eight thousand, five hundred miles north of Vancouver, where temperatures often dropped as low as thirty below zero in the winter, Mother was enthusiastic. She quoted a celebrated public radio host who had traveled to the northern interior: "Go north, young man. Work hard and opportunity is yours."

"As long as you're happy, Win, that's the most important thing," said Father. Felix Cleaners was sold to one of his best customers, the Gladstone Street house to our milkman. Father enrolled his mother-in-law on social assistance. May-ying, like other Chinese, no longer saw welfare as shameful, as it had once been when it was seen only as a white handout rather than a benefit and right due any Canadian resident. "Grandma's got to start taking some responsibility for herself," Father said.

Mother had her own unfinished business to take care of. When she had last seen Leonard in London, Ontario, she had talked of him coming out to Vancouver. They had kept up a faithful correspondence ever since. He had since quit school, and at nineteen, he was working as a short-order cook in Windsor, Ontario. Mother wanted to do right by her brother. Knowing he was full of praise for Mrs. Henry, his foster mother, and afraid that he was embittered about his relationship with May-ying, she thought that knowing he was adopted might help. At first, Leonard didn't believe it. He wrote back saying his birth certificate proved otherwise. Mother explained the truth and urged him to take responsibility for his own future.

In the pre-dawn of Christmas Eve in 1958, Mother and Father bundled four children—aged one to seven—into their 1949 Meteor for the long drive north on the Old Caribou Road. The seascape changed to winding canyon hugging the Fraser River; the canyon gave way to rolling ranching country, the ranches to thick forests of spruce and fir. Rain became snow, bare road hazardous black ice.

Fourteen hours after setting out, Father pulled into the grounds of Prince George Airport. We drove up the main road, and on either side were large houses set in large yards, each adorned with Christmas lights. Disappointingly, ours was not among them. Our house was at the other end of the airport, nearest the woods, among the "substandards," a cluster of box-like houses built for extra personnel during the Second World War. We would live there for a year before we upgraded to a house on the main road.

We arrived to find no heat. A parka-clad neighbor took a blowtorch to the frozen water pipes, and we went looking for dinner in town five miles away, the route marked by plumes of smoke rising from the beehive burners of sawmills along the banks of the Fraser. Father cruised the deserted downtown and saw a sign for "The Shasta" advertising "Chinese and Canadian food." The door was locked, but he knocked anyway, because he could see people eating in the back. The proprietors, Wayne and Eleanor Chow, were having dinner with their staff. So startled were they to see an unfamiliar Chinese face—they knew every Chinese in town—that we were invited in.

Life changed dramatically in our new home. We had to adjust to living next to taxiing planes, to windows rattling from planes taking off and landing and to the nighttime sweep of the beacon looking for the cloud ceiling. All city-born, we now contemplated the sight of cows and sheep grazing on the adjacent federal experimental farm, and everywhere, forests. But we found comfort in the feeling of a company town. The fathers of the twenty-one families who lived on the airport were either radio operators, meteorologists, mechanics, firemen or maintenance workers, and all worked at the passenger terminal, the hangars or the garages. The government furnished and maintained the houses. The government collected the garbage, fixed the furnace, did the plumbing, even lent lawn mowers. Everybody attended socials at the airport clubhouse. Most children's first school was the airport's one-room schoolhouse, for grades one to three. To complete the sense of idyllic isolation, most of the time even the winds blew in our favour, driving the stomach-wrenching stench of the pulp mills near town in the opposite direction from the airport.

Mother grew up within the walls of rooming houses, smoke-filled mah-jongg parlors and dank alleyways. My siblings and I had country lanes to ride our bicycles on, snowbanks piled like mountain ranges to frolic in, a backyard that Father and Mother flooded in winter for us to skate on. Mother had no brothers or sisters to play with; we four were inseparable. She was punished if she played too much; we were allowed to play to our hearts' content. We had to clear just one early hurdle—neighbors not used to "Orientals" on the block. Taunts chased us to school: "Chinky, Chinky Chinaman, sitting on a fence, making a dollar out of fifteen cents." At recess, children threw stone-laden snowballs in our direction; after school they waited in ambush to knock us off our bicycles. Mother's advice to feign deafness worked, and she and Father made it clear to other parents that they wouldn't put up with abuse. Acceptance and friendship soon followed, and we ourselves soon forgot that we were any different from our white playmates.

Perhaps because I was starting school, learning to ride a two-wheel bicycle, hoping to graduate from my orthopedic shoes to the buckle shoes every other girl wore—in other words, old enough to have a concept of growing up—I became curious about what

Mother was like when she was my age. For the first few years in Prince George, from the time I was five until the age of nine or so, I was fascinated by the differences between the little girl she'd been and who I was.

Often there were late nights when the house was quiet but for the whir of the Mixmaster or Mother's sewing machine—she brought in a few extra dollars sewing. Only she and I would be up. Father would be either on shift at the terminal or working downtown; he had a part-time job stocking groceries. Mother would talk, I would listen.

There was nothing ordered about the vignettes from her past. At the time of the telling, I did not know that the years of her childhood that paralleled mine coincided with a period when her mother was having affairs with men, drinking and gambling, while still trying to prove she could be a good mother. I looked only for the happiness and the sadness. There was so little to laugh about that I would often ask her to repeat my few favorite stories. I liked best the one about how Mother actually got to name herself and chose the name Winnie.

There was a lot to cry about. Though Mother's tears did not fall again, her face mirrored the anguish she still felt when her mother dressed her as a boy, when she spanked her and ordered her to kneel in obedience afterwards. I remember laying out a sewing pattern with Mother when she told me how she'd had to fetch the stick she was disciplined with. Her pen traced the path on the tissue pattern between the shed where the kindling was kept and the house where her mother sat waiting for her. As Mother's pen went back and forth, tearing the tissue to shreds, she relived her terror, and so did I.

I didn't question why any of this happened. I knew that my grandfather, as Mother would say, was "out of the picture," and that my grandmother's profession, as "nothing but a *kay-toi-neu*," won Mother no friends. How I wished I could have been either of the two sisters that Mother never met, to provide the company and comfort my siblings and I gave each other. But the lasting impression I had from all Mother's stories came from the words they always ended with: "I had nobody."

It was only in front of the cedar chest upstairs in my parents' bedroom that I could begin to sort through the pieces of my mother's family. I would go through the pile of black-and-white photographs lying loose in the bottom drawer and bring together the images of father, mother, two daughters in China, a third daughter and an adopted son—my mother and Uncle Leonard— in Canada. I knew in real life that the family had never been together, and that the two halves, one in Canada, one in China, had never been one.

The Chinese side was a mystery to me. The first book I read about China was one my mother borrowed for me from the library, when I was eight years old. It was a book she had enjoyed herself. What I remembered most about *Moment in Peking*, a tome of more than 800 pages, was that women and girls, blamed for their own misfortunes, routinely committed suicide by either throwing themselves down wells or into reflecting pools. All that seemed beyond the reach of reality. To me, China was what was left behind when the boat carrying my grandmother, pregnant with my mother, docked in Vancouver. China was the soil underfoot in the photograph of the two sisters who, as I thought then, would never meet the third, my mother. China was where you'd find yourself if you dug a hole deep enough to come out the other side of the Earth.

❦

Friends and relatives in Vancouver weren't going to come up to Prince George for a visit; the thought of going somewhere where winters were so cold had no appeal. So, invariably, we made several trips to Vancouver during the year, combining visits to relatives with shopping for school clothes. In and around Vancouver, there was a multitude of aunts and uncles on Father's side to call on, and we were sorry if we missed any one of them. We went from house to house, ate from mounds of sandwiches, picked up boxes of hand-me-down clothes from our cousins and took pleasure in how Father could make everyone ache with laughter with his stories and observations of daily life.

Calling on my maternal grandmother was another story. As if bad news was best swallowed without proscrastination, *Po-po* was our first call upon arriving in Vancouver.

Chinatown had become a rather gloomy place. Investigations and crackdowns on immigration fraud had turned Chinatowns into communities under siege. In the mid-1950s, American authorities in Hong Kong had revealed that U.S. identification and citizenship rights were being bought and sold. The Canadian government followed with its own three-year investigation. One Sunday morning in May 1960, the Royal Canadian Mounted Police, aided by police recruited from Hong Kong, staged simultaneous raids in Chinatowns across Canada, entering offices, businesses and private homes to seize evidence. Because of the difficulties of deporting thousands of Chinese, Canada, like the United States, declared an amnesty, but ignorance kept many in hiding.

We had our own reasons to feel anxious. As Father pulled up to whatever rooming house *Po-po* was living in, dread weighed in everybody's stomach. Mother waited curbside in the car, unable to brave being the first to find out what condition her mother was in. Father and one of the children would climb the stairs. We'd find the right door along the dimly lit hallway and knock. If a slurred and reproachful voice answered, "What? What's your business with me?" we knew to come back later. That's what we also told Mother; nobody needed to say that *Po-po* had to dry out first.

When we did try again, there was no telling what was going to happen. If my grandmother was at her worst, morose and hectoring, guilt and recrimination swarmed over all present. If she was at her best, alert and animated, her girlish laughter chasing her lightning-quick wit, we invited her to join us on outings. We'd picnic in Stanley Park, looking across at the floating marine gas stations and the city skyline, my grandmother's favorite view. Mother would bring along *Po-po*'s favorite French doughnuts from Woodward's food floor. If the Pacific National Exhibition was on, she'd watch us go on the amusement rides. There was always one meal out, usually at Chinatown's Ho Ho Restaurant. There she took charge, ordering from the waiter and not allowing us to drink or eat before she'd scalded the teacups and chopsticks with tea. We knew enough never to take the last morsel of food on any platter for ourselves. We would offer it to *Po-po*, knowing that to give food to someone else was a sign of affection.

Beyond addressing my grandmother upon sight—"*Ah Po*"—I found it hard to work up the courage to open my mouth in front of her. It took more than one empty swallow before the most rudimentary Chinese escaped. More often than not I sat in silence. I would sooner ignore my favorite dish, black bean spare ribs, if the platter was out of my reach but within *Po-po*'s than ask her to reach me some. At the same time, I fervently hoped she'd offer; by my rules, nodding in reply counted as conversing with her. Even so, I chanced being stung with some unkindness. "Odd that Number Two Daughter eats so slowly," she once said to Mother. "You should take her to a doctor, check to see if there is something wrong with her." She knew I understood her every word, that she was implying I was a bit stupid. Mother's silence spoke in my defense.

I tried to avoid being one of the children left behind with my grandmother when Mother and Father went on errands. It wasn't just my unease in her presence; it was the rooming houses and the *Baks* in them that I found unnerving. There were always a few old-timers in the communal kitchen. They sat there straddling chairs turned backwards, asking us questions that seemed to test our ability in Chinese. They asked our names, ages and the name of the village Father's side of the family came from. It was just as nerve-racking if *Po-po* happened to leave us alone even for a few minutes in her room, where the silence was broken only by the tick-tock of the Big Ben clock on the dresser or a mouse skittering across the floor.

It was with relief and remorse that we abruptly stopped going to call on my grandmother. Mother called a halt to the visits for a while, after an incident when *Po-po*, still recovering from the night before, started hectoring her. Mother, afraid of an argument starting, ended up stomping off. I remember Father pulling away from the curb in front of *Po-po*'s rooming house, leaving her yelling and gesturing after us. It took a while before I could look out the rear window of our car and not see that image of her.

⟡

Though it would be more than a year before we saw her again, there were reminders of her presence in our lives. I noticed in my daily run to the terminal to check the mail and to post letters that there was the occasional one from my mother addressed in Chinese to a Chinatown rooming house. I first realized those envelopes to *Po-po* contained money when Father was compiling his annual income tax return and I heard mention of her as a dependent.

Our self-imposed exile from her came to an end after Wayne, the fifth child, was born. He arrived to great excitement—there hadn't been a baby in the house for five years. A new grandson was enough to entice *Po-po* to take the bus up to visit us after the strawberry-picking season ended. Now in her mid-fifties, she picked berries, and sometimes vegetables, to supplement her welfare check and whatever extra dollars my parents managed to send her.

The tiny figure who stepped off the bus presented a picture of quiet dignity. She was dressed in a hand-knit cardigan in navy and burgundy pulled down over narrow black pants. Her face was browned from working under the sun; there was a flash of gold in her ears. She opened her purse to present gifts to her grandsons: a bag of gold-foil-wrapped coins of chocolate for Greg and Chris, and a wind-up bear beating a tin drum for Wayne.

During her two-week visit, she seemed never happier. There were no unpleasant scenes. She tried to tempt Father, who had given up smoking, with offers of a cigarette, but that was all. Her favorite place to sit was next to Wayne's crib. He draped himself over the rail to look at her. The two liked to mimic each other, turning their heads this way and that, clapping their hands, playing peek-a-boo. She liked to bounce him on her knee. When he went to sleep, she went back to knitting, pulling technicolored yarns from her paper shopping bag for a new sweater for another one of the children.

She brought with her to Prince George a cardboard box of groceries from Chinatown—fresh greens, sometimes oolichans that she'd bought at the fishmongers and already fried, and a variety of preserved vegetables and sauces that she would use when she cooked for us during her stay. We used to have such square and rectangular tins and earthenware jars of food from China on our pantry shelves, but eventually, they sat there collecting dust. Mother felt that her children ought to eat to be as robust as their playmates. So she cooked Chinese-style only infrequently and instead put roasts on the table, enriched the milk in our glasses with extra cream and introduced cheese into her cooking—in Mother's childhood cheese was what was used to bait mousetraps. Lasagna, along with cinnamon buns, pound cake and apple pie, became one of her specialties.

The visits with *Po-po* served as a reminder that we were Chinese, yet her Chineseness could take us by surprise. On our weekly egg-buying trip to Veeken's Farm, she asked Father to buy her a live chicken. As it waited in a sack in our basement, we children turned the air hole in the sack into an escape route. To our wild amusement, Father ended up having to chase the chicken around the oil furnace, finally tripping it up with the crook of an outstretched wire hanger. We couldn't have imagined what followed. Father brought the chicken upstairs to *Po-po* in the kitchen, which was hot and steamy from the pot of water boiling on the stove. She wielded a Chinese cleaver across the chicken's throat; blood splattered, staining the Dutch Lady curtains above the sink. In Chinatown, when a customer selected a live chicken, the butcher at least slaughtered it out of sight, delivering it plucked and cleaned, ready for the pot.

What Chinese pastimes we did adopt in our home were shaped by western sensibilities. We inherited from the handful of old-timers in Prince George used mah-jongg sets; they became blocks for building roadworks and whole cities for my brothers. I actually pretended ignorance of a connection with China when one of my airport chums came calling during another of *Po-po*'s visits. Seeing that my grandmother didn't speak English and that she wasn't white, and forgetting that we Chongs were also different-looking, Diane asked where she came from. "My grandmother was born in Ladner," I said, retrieving a conveniently remembered detail from my mother's stories about a Canadian birth certificate that my grandmother had used to enter Canada. "Where's that?" Diane asked. I explained that it was a small town near Vancouver. Everybody on the airport at least knew where Vancouver was, even if they hadn't been there.

Since *Po-po* seemed to have changed for the better, Mother was more relaxed around her. On subsequent visits to Vancouver, she had allowed Louise several times to stay overnight with her grandmother. These stays had been without incident, and Mother thought she was helping with her mother's drinking problem by showing how she trusted her. *Po-po* was emboldened enough to drop persistent hints that she would like to have Greg on his own. Mother relented.

Greg, then seven, didn't mind at all that *Po-po* paraded him through Chinatown, calling out to anyone she knew, "This is my grandson, Hing's Number One son." She took him into several novelty and curio shops. "Whatever you want, you tell *Po-po*," she said, going up and down the aisles. He refused to choose anything; none of us thought of her as having extra money to spend.

That evening, after supper, they went out. He did as he was told and sat quietly by her side while she played mah-jongg. He ate from his roll of *san-ja-goh*; *Po-po* had bought two rolls of the crimson candy, instructing him to save the other for Chris. When her game was over, they returned to her room. When the string was pulled to turn off the light bulb above the three-quarter bed, the flashing neon sign outside the window bounced off the walls like a strobe light. "Don't be scared, don't be scared," *Po-po* whispered. If Greg had known enough Chinese to say so, he would have said that he was never scared with her. When we came to collect him the next morning, he was his usual smiling self. Mother noticed he was scratching at his scalp. *Po-po* confessed that she had washed his hair, and being out of shampoo, she'd used Lux soap flakes.

It was the next summer that the family was passing through Vancouver again on our way back from a month-long camping trip to California to take in Disneyland and the San Diego Zoo. Louise, fourteen and anxious to start saving money for university, asked to stay behind to join *Po-po* for the three-week-long strawberry picking season. She and *Po-po* had already talked about it; Mother gave her permission.

The pickers' day began in darkness. *Po-po,* up long before Louise to prepare rice and a cooked lunch they would bring, would wake her and put a bowl of thick *jook* before her. By half past four, they were at the corner of Gore and Pender to meet the truck that picked up workers for the ride to the farm. Louise was impressed by *Po-po's* sense of right and wrong. Her grandmother did not like the way some women—the same ones who arrived late and had to run after the truck—shoved to be first off, so they could plant themselves in the rows with the biggest, reddest strawberries. From time to time, she would call out to Louise, working in the next row over: "Remember, no rotten berries and no green berries, and no stealing from other rows." Louise, being the faster picker, helped *Po-po* fill her flat so they could each earn a dollar before stopping for lunch. *Po-po* laid out a picnic, pouring tea from one thermos and prying from another with a pair of chopsticks the hot lunch she had prepared, which she served in specially bought aluminum dishes.

When the truck dropped them off back in Chinatown, the two of them went shopping to buy fresh food for supper. *Po-po* told all who would listen that her granddaughter was going to university one day. Her pride was rewarded: "Oh what a smart girl, and so pretty, too!" At supper, *Po-po* introduced each dish as the favorite of one member of the family; steamed minced pork was Louise's, lily-root soup her younger sister's. There were treats—the banana jellies that were her sister's favorite, *san-ja-goh* that was her brother's. When the dishes were done, the two would sit on the bed. While *Po-po* combed Louise's long hair, she would talk of the virtues of good grooming, cleanliness and of keeping one's things neat and tidy. She emphasized the importance of being a good girl, of respecting one's parents. "I'm telling you this because that's how I raised your *Mama*," she said. Louise gave her a nightly English lesson. They giggled their way through "Good morning. How are you?" and the opening line to the national anthem, "O Canada, Our home and native land..."

By the second week, *Po-po* and Louise were not so inseparable. Before supper, her grandmother would suggest that she go to Woodward's to buy herself an ice cream cone, or else go call on a girl her age, the daughter of the storekeeper on the corner. Louise's suspicions that *Po-po* wanted her out of the way were confirmed when, after supper, she was ordered to stay in the room while *Po-po* went out, without saying where. Louise spent the time perusing her grandmother's pretty things. She used the tortoise-shell combs on her hair, tried on the beaded slippers; she opened the hand-painted fans, unfolded the embroidered handkerchiefs.

After several nights of this, Louise, bored, decided she was going out. She wandered the halls of the rooming house, then ventured further out to the street. She headed for Sing Kee Confectionery, where she knew *Po-po* played mah-jongg. Her grandmother, seeing her, dismissed her: "Don't bother me! I'm thinking."

*Po-po* started staying out later and later. Her moods would swing. Louise recognized the signs that her grandmother was drinking again and prayed that she wouldn't see her drunk. To Louise, the darkest side of *Po-po's* old ways was the tension it produced between her mother and her grandmother—the insinuation of guilt, the fear of accusation. Louise tried to ignore the first slur in her grandmother's words, the wandering focus of her eyes. Both were undeniable the day she accompanied *Po-po* shopping and observed her unsteady on her feet in front of some greens, indecisive about what to buy. A passerby called her a drunk.

Back at the hotel, *Po-po* passed out before supper. Louise went to find a pay phone. She had already made that week's call to check in so Mother was surprised. "Louise? What's wrong?" "Everything is okay, Mom," Louise said. Her faltering voice and tears betrayed what Mother feared most. She cut the call short, telling Louise to get on the next bus home to Prince George. Nobody commented on the fact that Louise came home earlier than expected.

We made up with *Po-po*. We even took her on vacation with us when we went camping in the sunny Okanagan Valley the following summer, and she came up to Prince George again. But we'd had to make up on her terms; she let us know that it was *she* who was annoyed at *us*. That first time we stopped in at her rooming house in Chinatown, she made as if she was too busy to see us.

We thought it was a deliberate pretense, because it didn't seem to ring true that there could be much better on offer for her in Chinatown. By the late 1960s, Chinatowns that hadn't disappeared clung precariously to life, fearful of what city councils were planning next in the name of urban renewal to hasten their demise. In Vancouver, bulldozers demolished a fifteen-block area adjacent to Chinatown for a public housing project; in Toronto, two-thirds of Chinatown had been leveled for a new city hall. Canadian immigration authorities in exercising their discretion over country of origin, favored Europeans over Asians. Chinatowns, cut off from new blood and commerce, were dying. Derelict buildings were condemned. Vancouver's city council enacted bylaws to sanitize the squalor and ordered commerce off the sidewalk—gone were the squawking chickens in cages, the barbecued pork and duck that once hung for the customer's perusal. The gambling dens that used to be my grandmother's livelihood and entertainment had already disappeared; the last one had been padlocked long ago by city police. Now when we went to Chinatown, I couldn't help but feel, as its walls seemed to close in, that we were walking through the debris of my mother's past.

One bright, wintry Saturday morning in Prince George, barely into the new year of 1967, Uncle Leonard was on the telephone from Kamloops, where he'd taken his first nursing job. At Mother's persuasion, he had applied to the nursing program at Essondale and had graduated as a psychiatric nurse.

Only I was home; the rest of the family was shopping in town. He said Mother should call him as soon as she got back, because he had "bad news about Grandma." I waited with dread.

"Oh no, oh no! It can't be. It can't be," Mother kept saying.

She could hardly manage to put the receiver back on its cradle; *Po-po* was dead. She had been killed in a car accident.

Mother's words were almost washed away in her tears, which were coming down in torrents. "I always worried about my mom crossing the street. I always worried she might get knocked down by a car," she said. "Whenever I would hear reports of car accidents on the radio, about people being hit, I worried it might be my mom."

Her first thought had been that *Po-po* had died as a pedestrian. Instead, she was a passenger in a car struck by another. It seemed odd; we knew *Po-po* didn't much like riding in cars and rarely did, trusting only Father to drive her.

That night, Mother and Father lay in bed talking. "The kind of feeling I have," Mother told him, "is as if my whole world has suddenly caved in on me."

A day or two later, Mother went to the cedar chest, opened the bottom drawer and took out the pile of black-and-white photographs of her family. Whenever she went through them, the one portrait of her father, the eight-by-ten in the cardboard frame, always made her weep, and she never knew why. This time was no different; it was that one, not the ones of her mother, that bothered her most. Mother removed the offending photograph from the pile; she wanted never to look at it again.

My parents took the two older boys with them to Vancouver to attend the funeral, and Louise and I, teenagers both, stayed behind to look after Wayne. During the week they were away, *The Vancouver Sun* reported twice on my grandmother's death. The first item reported her death as the city's third traffic fatality of the new year. The name was wrong, and so was her age; only the address of her rooming house was correct. The second item issued a correction to her name—but still didn't get it right—and reported the coroner's ruling of an accidental death.

For what seemed the better part of that week, I lay on my stomach on the brown, scratchy sofa in the living room watching my tears drain in rivulets along the nubble of the threads. On my grandmother's last visit to Prince George, I'd had my first, and what would be my last, comfortable conversation with her. I had offered to help her peel broccoli for that evening's meal. I prided myself on peeling the stalks as methodically as she did, without disturbing the florets.

"*Po-po,* what kind of vegetables have you picked?" I ventured.

"I usually pick green beans," she replied. "But they are not easy to pick; you have to be careful to pick them below the ends."

I dared another step. "I'd like to go pick green beans with you some time." "Sure, you can come with your *Po-po.*" She laughed and called out to Mother what I had said.

I recalled a line of Mother's from the stories she told when I was little: "My mom only talked to me when she wanted to bawl me out." An image came to mind of a day at the Gladstone Street house, when *Po-po* had brought back a live turtle. She freed it from the basin of water and laughed as Louise and I squealed in delight to see it explore the linoleum tiles while it awaited the soup pot. I remembered Mother telling me that *Po-po* fed me turtle soup when I arrived off the train in London, Ontario, sick with dysentery. I remembered a game of Chinese solitaire my mother learned from her mother, and that she in turn taught me and my siblings, where mah-jongg tiles are arranged in the shape of a turtle and where winning, by removing all the tiles, is rare. Mother had explained the significance of the turtle to the Chinese: "Turtle means long life." I thought of how it wasn't to be for my grandmother.

❦

Seventy-six-year-old Mr. Pang and his wife had invited three people, May-ying among them, to his home in Vancouver's east end. Mrs. Pang cooked fresh clam chowder and noodles and the other four played a round of mah-jongg. The game ended before midnight; Mr. Pang and his wife didn't like to stay up late and he had to drive his guests home.

His was the only car stopped at the light at Main and Prior, four blocks from the Garden Hotel, where May-ying lived. When the light turned green, seeing no oncoming traffic, he began his left turn. In a car coming in the opposite direction was a twenty-four-year-old driver and his chums, high school students. After driving around for a couple of hours to put some miles on a newly rebuilt car engine, they'd decided to head home, to their parents' homes on Vancouver's west side. The driver, seeing the red turn to green, shifted from second to third gear.

The collision threw May-ying to the floor in the back seat of Mr. Pang's car. "Take me to the hospital, take me to the hospital. Quickly, quickly," she said. An ambulance took her to the Vancouver General Hospital where, an hour later, she was pronounced dead.

At the scene of the accident, Mr. Pang's son arrived to translate for his father. The investigating officer took Mr. Pang's statement that night: "I turned the corner slow," he said. The officer took the other driver's the next day—he was called into the police station because of the fatality. He said the other car turned suddenly, that he hadn't seen any flashing turn signal.

The coroner's inquest was brief, impersonal. "The body was that of a tiny woman who measured only fifty-seven inches in length and weighed approximately ninety pounds," said the pathologist. He put up "Exhibit 2(f)," a photograph of the body in the morgue. Mother, from the seat she had chosen at the back of the courtroom, thought at first it must be a model, a doll—it was so tiny, so perfectly proportioned.

The cause of death was attributed to a punctured lung and multiple rib fractures from being spun about. Mention was made that scar tissue from abdominal surgery and one nonfunctioning kidney had left the body more rigid, less able to absorb the impact of the collision. No one else involved had sustained more than a bruise.

Mother hardly paid much attention to the proceedings after the first, unexpected question from a juror to the pathologist: "Was there any evidence of alcohol in the deceased woman's blood?" The answer, "No," reverberated in Mother's head. Before retiring for its verdict, the jury asked to be reminded of the age of the driver of "the Chinese car," in a pointed suggestion that his slow reaction time might have been to blame. The death was ruled "unnatural and accidental." The inquest was over; the body was released for burial.

⊷⊶

"She still looks beautiful," Father's sisters whispered to Mother as they filed by the casket.

"They're just saying that," Mother thought to herself. "My mother was a very beautiful woman. I've never seen her so ugly in my whole life." She was right; the impact of the crash had marred her mother's face, puffiness hid its fine bones.

Mother didn't cry at the funeral, but she did when Father collected the brown paper bag of her mother's "personal effects" from the police station. In it was her coat and purse, and a round tobacco tin, which the police had taken from her room because it was considered to contain "valuables." Inside were coins totalling $40.94 and a receipt from B.C. Collateral.

Mother couldn't face going to the pawnshop. "Pay whatever it takes to claim back her jewelry," she told Father. He returned with four pieces. But for one, a bracelet, Mother knew every piece only too well: the dangling earrings and the pendant which her mother had left China with, the diamond ring she got from Chow Guen.

"They're so symbolic of my life growing up with my mom," she told Father.

"Do you want to keep any of it, Win?" Father asked. "How about the ring? You don't have one."

Mother had sold the engagement ring Father had given her to her old friend Jang Noong years ago when news came of Father's posting to Prince George. Mother had wanted to buy the children snowsuits for the cold winters there. Days later, regretting having sold it, she had asked for it back. Jang Noong said he didn't have it, that he had already sent it to China for his son to give to his wife.

My grandmother's ring wasn't Mother's to keep. By coincidence, two weeks before she died, Leonard had telephoned

Mother to see if she might help ask my grandmother if he could have her diamond ring. He wanted it for his fiancée, a Japanese-Canadian girl, a nurse. "Sis, you never know with our mom. She might gamble that ring away," Leonard had said. Mother had backed away from his request: "How am I going to get it off her, Leonard? What am I going to say? She doesn't wear it; she uses it for collateral." Leonard had persisted: "Mom's health is so frail. If she dies, what will happen to her ring?"

Mother told Father she wanted nothing to do with her mother's jewelry. "I'm not going to be cursed by it," she said. "It's not a happy thing to have." She got in touch with Mr. Pang: "Would you like to take some of my mom's jade and gold off my hands?" She wanted only enough money in return to pay the modest funeral expenses.

Mother and Father made one last visit to the rooming house to clear out my grandmother's room. Some uncooked greens were on the table, cooked chicken sat outside on the window ledge, and underneath the bed were jars of dried herbs for soup. There was no whiskey. Of her clothes, only a hardly worn cashmere sweater that Mother had given her the past Mother's Day might have been worth keeping. Mother took only a chenille bedspread, last year's Christmas present, unused, its original tags attached. Woodward's would take it back. "You dispose of everything else," she told the building's caretaker.

⋯⋯

The past lingered as the cast of supporting men in *Po-po*'s life made their final entrance and exit. Mother had notified both Chow Guen and Jang Noong about her mother's death. Guen had just moved to Prince George and was living with other Chinese old-timers. He showed no emotion upon the news. Mother remembered May-ying telling her that just after their relationship ended, he had said to her, "I wouldn't lend you money even if you were down to your last penny." He gave Mother fifty dollars to put towards the funeral expenses, and he said he wouldn't be going. When Jang Noong learned of my grandmother's death, he cried, said he had lost "the only loyal and true friend" he ever had.

Having recently suffered a stroke, he was in a nursing home in Vancouver, but he came out for the funeral. He died a few months later and was buried a pauper. Guen subsequently befriended our family until a stroke, three years later, left him incoherent and uncomprehending. He was to live out his life at a nursing home in Prince George, leaving enough money to pay for his funeral upon his death, and to send four thousand dollars back to his family in China.

As a family, we moved more and more to the rhythm of our own lives. In the year of *Po-po*'s death, I made it as far as the provincial finals of a piano competition in celebration of Canada's centennial, and the following year, before the eldest of the children left home, my siblings and I put on a piano concert in the city's newest auditorium. When not driving the children to piano lessons, Kiwanis Music Festival competitions, examinations with the Royal Conservatory of Toronto or other special recitals and workshops, Father was driving us to and from the ski hill, or our part-time jobs in town as we each began saving for university. When the youngest started school, Mother herself found a part-time, and then a full-time job.

One by one, the children left home for university and after that, jobs. There were family gatherings in Vancouver, but our lives bypassed Chinatown. On rare occasions, we tried a new restaurant there.

Vancouver's Chinatown had a new face. After 1967, Canada, following the lead of the United States, put prospective immigrants on an equal footing, taking away the discretionary power of the authorities to exercise a bias with respect to country of origin. Consequently, Chinatowns were resuscitated by the capital and patronage of a new wave of immigration from southeast Asia. New immigrants from China would not begin to arrive in Canada until after 1972, and in the United States not until after 1979, upon their respective governments' official recognition of the People's Republic of China.

Some twelve years after *Po-po*'s death, we were posing for a family picture in front of a new *dim sum* house in Vancouver's

Chinatown. Mother noticed a broken end of a water pipe jutting out from a building and pointed out that this was the pipe she had run into when playing jump rope as a child. I remembered her telling that story to me when I was a child, and I remembered seeing the scar on her thigh to prove it. I thought to myself: "Somebody ought to have fixed that pipe by now." That was the first time in years that Mother had made mention of her past.

In the first years after *Po-po*'s death, there had been inadvertent reminders of Mother's sad history. They would serve as notice that there was still hurt there in need of repair, rather like that broken pipe in Chinatown. Two incidents came to mind. Once Mother came across the kitchen trash bin full to the brim; one of us children had neglected to empty it. She turned it upside down, scattering wet peelings, egg shells and tea leaves across the floor. We mopped it up, looking at each other in disbelief and disgust at what Mother had done. Mother, watching us, threw onto the trash these words: "It's scary. My mom once did the same thing to me." Another time, I forget what I had or hadn't done, I remember only that Mother grabbed the closest thing, the hollow extension to the vacuum cleaner. I was fourteen or fifteen, too old to be spanked. My sister yelled at her to stop. I began to hyperventilate. Mother froze upon her own words: "I used to cry like that. My mom used to strike me for no reason."

There were other times when Mother would unexpectedly spill tears upon something Father did or said. He and I would exchange knowing glances and put a hand around each other's shoulders out of Mother's sight. "Denise, you know how Mom is," he'd say. "She had a tough life." There was a shared sympathy, an unspoken understanding that she was still hurting from her past. Later, as if any row was his fault, Father always went to Mother, kissed her and apologized. As ever, it was his laughter and humor that once again wrapped the house in love, the surest sign of which was the murmur of my parents' voices from behind their bedroom door.

On one of my visits home to Prince George, when I was working in Ottawa, I went to the cedar chest. It had been years since

I'd opened the bottom drawer. In it were scrapbooks that Mother had compiled chronicling her children's accomplishments—news clippings of piano competitions, a program from the family concert, academic certificates. I found what I was looking for, the black-and-white photographs that had held my gaze as a child. They had long since been put into an album. I knew I would not find the portrait of my grandfather, but just as I'd never mentioned its disappearance to Mother, I knew not to ask why others had been scissored from their backgrounds before being pasted down. I flipped the pages of the album and thought how I'd preferred looking at the photographs when they were in a pile, unsorted.

# CHAPTER THIRTEEN

THE AIR IN Hong Kong had turned hot, heavy and humid—earlier than usual this year. It was spring of 1987, and Mother and I had just returned from celebrating her fifty-seventh birthday in the Verandah Restaurant at the Repulse Bay Hotel. With its graceful half-moon windows, shutters and wicker furnishings, the restaurant, part of the original hotel, was one of Hong Kong's few vestiges of British colonial architecture (the original hotel was the headquarters of the British in Hong Kong during the Second World War). Mother had flown to Hong Kong from her home in Prince George and I had come from mine in Peking. From there, we would begin a three-week trip together in China. I considered myself lucky she'd come; even though I knew she was the kind of person who made a decision and stood by it, I'd worried that she might change her mind.

I had been living in Peking for almost two years. My companion, Roger Smith (we would later marry), was a Canadian television correspondent, and when his network sent him from Ottawa on a two-year posting to Peking in 1985, I decided to join him. He'd always been interested in China; his grandfather, an

Anglican minister, and his wife taught in China for six years, before political chaos forced them to leave with their children in the mid-1920s. To me, China offered a welcome change of scene, and also a long-awaited opportunity to write; I had spent a decade in the turbulent waters of government and politics in Ottawa, working as an economist in the finance department and then as a senior economic adviser to Prime Minister Pierre Trudeau.

It was passing faces in the crowds in China that stirred awake a curiosity from my early childhood. The photograph of the two young girls, my mother's two sisters, that lay among the pile in the cedar chest kept coming to mind. A feeling that I had to stand on the same soil dogged me. It was not a sense of "Chineseness" I was after; I had stopped trying to contrive any such feeling following Mother's early advice—"You're Canadian, not Chinese. Stop trying to feel something." I didn't know why I wanted to, only that I could not leave China without going to the village of my grandfather's birth. I also knew that Mother had to accompany me. Persuading her was the hard part.

I told Mother the purpose of going to the village of Chang Gar Bin would be to take some scenic snapshots for the family album and talk to local authorities to fill in some blanks on the family tree. I told her the chances were remote that we'd find any relatives of her generation. Over the decades, China's political turmoil, if not a flood or famine, would surely have claimed them. Even if mother's sister, Ping, was alive, I saw little hope in trying to locate her; I assumed she had left the village upon marriage.

Our posting in Peking was nearing its end, and Mother had still shown no inclination to brave her complicated feelings about the past. When I had only a few weeks left before I was to return to Canada, I finally pleaded. If she wouldn't come for my sake, she should come because of what Father had once said: "After I die, Win, spend your money and travel—go to China." A sudden, brief illness had taken his life in 1982.

To help convince Mother to come, I planned the trip to the village as only the first leg of a much longer trip in China. Finally, she agreed. I wrote to the Chinese foreign ministry in Canton to explain the purpose of my visit and to get help making some travel arrangements. Between the time Mother decided to come and the time we were to rendezvous in Hong Kong, I had not received a reply.

For two days we played tourist in Hong Kong while we awaited word. We avoided talking about the trip to the village. Instead, I talked only about the onward trip I had planned. I spoke of the great cities like Canton, Shanghai and Peking. I told Mother she would be romanced by the beauty of Hangzhou and Suzhou. We would get off the beaten track, stop in Qufu, the birth place of Confucius. I warned her about the harsh realities of traveling without a government guide, of the elbowing needed to hold a place in line to buy train tickets, of having to explain to hotel clerks what "reservation" meant, of getting cold water from hot and cold taps, of restaurants that ran out of food. But I promised she'd love every moment.

"My mother is interested in tracing her ancestry," was how I had begun my letter to the Chinese authorities. I supplied details, obtained from Mother, of the names in Chinese characters and the approximate birth dates of my grandparents and my mother's two sisters. I said that my grandparents had left China in the spring of 1930, a date easy to pinpoint because I knew my grandmother was pregnant with my mother. I also told them that in addition to the three sisters, there had been a younger half-brother.

Never did I imagine what Mother and I were to hear back. It came second-hand. The terse message had been taken down by our interpreter in Peking and was relayed by Roger: "Go to the Chinese side of the border with Macau in two days. Officials will meet you there at 9:00 a.m. with your mother's two sisters and brother. Look for a white van."

Before I had even hung up, I was calling out to Mother: "Mom, they're alive! They're alive—your sisters are alive!"

For Mother, the news of having family still alive left her speechless. Twenty years since her mother's death, thirty since her father's, she had come to think of herself as the last of her family. Suddenly, she was to be presented with flesh-and-blood siblings.

But *two* sisters? The vision of that photograph come alive made me nervous with excitement. Not Mother. She was overcome by shock, jubilation, then disbelief and, finally, fear. As she tumbled backwards into her past, she could no longer sort fact from hearsay, from wishful thinking, or, dared she think, even lies? She wanted to believe that Nan was not dead, yet she remembered her father bringing her mother a letter from China with the news.

There were no answers, only questions. Had Nan's death been fabricated? Could the wife in China have invented her death as a cover to sell her out of the family? Did her father know the truth, or was he an accomplice to deceit? What hurt Mother most was the thought that if Nan had not died, then her mother had been misled. "Death is final, and easier to accept," Mother said.

I began to have my own doubts. I wondered if the authorities had dredged up fictitious relatives. Deng Xiaoping's policy of opening China to the West and liberalizing its economy had spawned the "red-eye disease" of jealousy. In the south, where there was easier access to foreign-made goods from nearby Hong Kong and to foreign tourists and businessmen, fraud, counterfeit and smuggling were rampant among Communist officials and individuals alike. Foreign currency was the entry ticket to state stores selling luxury goods and to discotheques, bars and restaurants in foreign-owned hotels. Could Mother and I be the victims of such economic crime? Who in China wouldn't be happy to lay claim to an overseas relative? Who was to know who was authentic?

I speculated that this was why the message said a van was being sent for us. It was a well-known travelers' tale that poorer Chinese relations cared less about blood ties than about the foreign-made color television, the VCR, maybe even a washing machine or refrigerator that their "rich" overseas relations could bring in as part of their special duty-free exemptions. The bigger the gift, the more money it cost, the happier were the Chinese relations. Mother invoked more deep-rooted suspicions: "Somebody could be fooling me, trying to get me to go to China." She was afraid: "I was brought up to hate the Communists for what they were doing and what they represented. My father sent money to chase them out." I knew she no more wanted to trust the Communists today than her father had in his time.

Far into the night Mother paced the floor. She tried to make sense of what she had known about the Chinese side of the family. Some I remembered from stories she'd told me when I was a child, but I'd never before tried to put any chronology to it. It had been intended that she herself would join the family there for her schooling, but her father had gone without her. She knew he went to build a house; she could remember he ran out of money part-way through. She wrote letters to the family there, but that came to a stop when her parents separated. Her father himself cut off contact after the Communists took power because of some suspicious letters, including one supposedly from Ping, the last surviving sister. Mother knew there had also been a half-brother; she could remember her father saying, "He walks like this—" which she understood to be the gait of a club foot.

I left it to Mother to decide whether or not we would go. She found it difficult to imagine coming face-to-face with siblings for the first time. The longing for company when she was growing up meant nothing now. But more unsettling than anything, the news of family had exposed Mother's unresolved feelings about her past. She harbored confusion and regret that neither of her parents had shown much care or love for her. If she had any remorse, it was that she had not honored her mother as she had promised she would; she had not gone to worship at May-ying's grave—nor had she been back to Chan Sam's.

In the morning, Mother gave her verdict: "It's so true, curiosity killed the cat." And so, I knew we were going. We took the jet-foil to Macau, an hour's ride from Hong Kong, and overnighted there. Still uncertain that the relatives we were to meet were genuine, we bought only token gifts: a few cartons of Marlboro cigarettes—if Mother's siblings didn't smoke, they could resell them for profit—some candied fruit and several tins of biscuits. We had decided to go at least as far as the border, to meet these so-called relatives before deciding whether to go on to the village of Chang

Gar Bin. That evening, we occupied our minds by trying our hand at some slot machines and at *fan tan* in the casino at the Lisboa Hotel. I felt as if our predicament was all my fault; here was Mother, in sight of the Chinese mainland, trapped on the threshold of her family's past—too scared to step across, too scared to turn back.

At the border on the other side of Macau, we were met only by hucksters—taxi drivers of small cars and three-wheeler mini-trucks bargaining for our fare, and money-changers offering black market rates for our foreign currency. An hour after the appointed meeting time, a white van pulled up to the immigration and customs building. The two young women from the Chinese foreign ministry had no one in tow. They made no apology for their lateness and no mention of the absent siblings. Our bags were loaded into the back of the van. Chang Gar Bin, they said, was a three-hour drive away. The driver would know where to go; the women were from Canton and had never been there.

The paved road wound along the estuary of the Pearl River. We rolled through scenes of timeless China. Women, their pant legs rolled up, babies tied to their backs, labored knee-deep in rice paddies; their men worked ploughs drawn by water buffalo. Abruptly, this peasant landscape was interrupted by the chaotic construction of the new China. Low-rise brick factories, hastily thrown up to capitalize on south China's economic growth, encroached on the rice paddies. Occasionally, more ambitious buildings fronted with fake marble spoke of the return of overseas Chinese investment. Mother stared out the window in silence. I made nervous small talk about the passing scenery. The officials responded with perfunctory replies: "Yes, the factories are taking up land for rice, but they are bringing new wealth." "The peasants are much better off now than before." Both checked their watches often, which I interpreted to Mother as a sign that they were concerned about missing lunch.

At noon, one of them excitedly pointed out what they'd been looking for—what looked to be a roadside garage. Inside were a few tables, all uncleaned. It was a seafood restaurant; the foreign ministry treated. By the time we were back on the road, it was two hours later, and Mother and I, at first wary, then exasperated, began to worry about what awaited us in Chang Gar Bin.

After another hour's drive, the driver, a man wearing white gloves, veered off the paved road onto a yellow dirt lane. He leaned annoyingly on his horn as peasants on foot and on bicycles grudgingly made way. We came around the backs of adobe houses, lined wall to wall. The lane opened onto a small square shaded by an enormous banyan tree. The driver took one of the three streets off it and turned through the gates of a walled compound. A plaque outside said "Chang Gar Bin Overseas Chinese Office."

We were ushered into a one-room building, furnished with a few chairs and a desk, old and scratched. The half-vases of plastic flowers mounted on the walls were the only effort at decoration. Someone went to fetch the local official-in-charge. Tea appeared, glasses were filled all around. The local official made small talk, mostly with the officials from Canton while word of our arrival was being sent to Mother's siblings.

We heard him before we saw him. The rhythmical slow, sweeping sounds were the footsteps of a thin man, clad in dark-blue baggy cotton. As he limped into the room, both his feet looked to be on backwards, like a broken doll whose legs had twisted round and stuck.

"Elder Sister," he said, nodding to Mother. His deformity was worse than we had known: how could this be contrived?

"*Ah* Yuen," Mother said as she rose and embraced her brother, feeling the sorrow of his crippled feet but also the joy that they swept away any doubt that he was an imposter. "How did you know who I was?" she asked. "I recognized your face," he said. Yuen had a face that reflected the quiet strength and squareness of my grandfather's. "*Baba* sent photographs."

Yuen answered the question of Nan. She had died many years before; the officials had got it wrong.

Out in the dirt courtyard, as we were taking our leave of the officials to go to Yuen's house, a woman in baggy pants and layers of cotton blouses appeared. The quickness of her movements, the proud lines of her face and her girlish smile were my grandmother reincarnated. Mother hugged her sister, Ping, for the first time. Through tears, both sisters fumbled for photographs. Mother had the one of her sisters, and another of herself and Leonard posing with their mother. Ping unwrapped yellowed cellophane from the one she had brought for this moment. She pointed to the baby in the arms of a young mother: "This is me." She turned the photograph over and ran her finger under the print at the bottom: "Made in Canada" it said. "You and I drank the same mother's milk," she said to Mother.

"I can see *Mama* in you," Mother replied. "Even your voice is like hers."

Strangers from a gathering throng—as it turned out, relatives, first and second cousins—loaded our bags on the backs of bicycles. "It's a good thing we can speak the same dialect," Ping said to Mother, "or it would have been like playing piano to a cow." Her laughter chased her wit, the same way my grandmother's did.

Like schoolgirls, the two sisters walked arm-in-arm, their younger brother riding his bicycle ahead. We passed a bicycle parts shop where Yuen kept the books. We wove our way among black pigs scavenging for scraps in the market, past the stalls where Ping's second son and his wife sold freshly slaughtered pork and where Yuen's two sons sold fresh fish from baskets strapped to their bicycles. Our progress was slowed by Ping stopping to show off Younger Sister: "This is my *Mui-mui!*" Stooped old ladies, holding black umbrellas to shield themselves and the babies tied on their backs from the sun, shook their heads, said they could remember a last sight of the concubine leaving pregnant for the boat. Few had believed mother or baby would survive.

We skirted a squat tower. Its door was sealed shut, and its outside walls bore traces of red-paint stencils of Mao Zedong's face and slogans like "Long Live Chairman Mao." We turned off the main path down a footpath, passing by houses jammed tightly together, a few of decades-old gray brick among the timeless yellow adobe of most of the others. Each path we turned onto was narrower than the last. We came to a gate. Mother and I passed through, then stopped. It was if we were viewing an enormous painting for the first time; to take it in, we had to stand back.

Across a cement courtyard stood an imposing two-story house, with a surrounding second-floor balcony. The front of the house was chalk-blue, on the side the bricks were bluish-gray. A crude brick wall divided the courtyard and the house in two. On the other side of the wall, and therefore inaccessible, was one doorway; on this side were two. The porticoed entrance was the grand entranceway; it was thrice our height, its cinnabar twin portals hewn from massive timbers. With each step we took, more detail came into focus. Above the smaller doorway was a bas-relief of flowers. Sculpted in the half-moon above one window was a vase of flowers, above another, a chicken with grain. Everything was faded and in need of repair, but the workmanship was still to be admired.

We had to negotiate around a pig too pregnant to move from the shade cast from a laundry stand, next to a well that looked to be dry. Near that, judging from the smell, was the outhouse. We stood in front of the main entrance to the house, pushed through a set of swinging doors and stepped inside. "Heaven and earth have eyes," said Yuen, as he and his two sisters laughed and cried at the triumph of standing under the roof that their father, my grandfather, had raised with such pride over his family.

As I looked about the room, I saw under glass on one wall old photographs of my mother. In one, she was wearing the dress with a mirrored neckline that her mother bought her for graduation day at Strathcona School, in another, her nurse's uniform. There was one of her and my father on their wedding day. But my eyes came to rest high overhead, on a side wall above a mahogany wall clock. There, in a starkly rendered drawing, was a larger-than-life double portrait of a woman and a man. The woman's face was plain, but kindly. The man's was the likeness of the photograph of my grandfather that had disappeared from the bottom drawer of the cedar chest in Prince George.

When Chan Sam's death notice came from Canada in the autumn of 1957, the widow Huangbo put into safekeeping the small pile of what was left of her husband's letters, in hopes that they would one day remind Yuen of the father who nurtured him. For the son and daughter who survived Chan Sam in China, any hopes left of a better life came to rest on another father figure, Mao Zedong.

At first, it seemed the cult of Mao more than filled the breach. In the spring of 1958, Huangbo, Yuen and Ping were called to meetings organized by their commune to hear Communist officials explain Mao's newest plan to harness the whole of the country's population to turn China into a modern industrial power. His goal was to raise the country's steel production several-fold, to overtake the United States' and Britain's within fifteen years. Some peasants would be sent from the fields to steel, coal and electric-power factories in the cities, others to build new dams, reservoirs and roads. From now on, the sole economic objective of the commune was to meet its monthly quota for steel production. The voice on the loudspeaker, accompanied by uplifting music, blared out the same message as the banners and the huge slogans on the walls: "A country without steel is like a man without bones." The people shouted "Long Live The Great Leap Forward!" and set out to prove that they had the sheer stamina and determination to make Mao's dream come true.

Like everyone else, whether they worked in the fields or on the new labor brigades, Huangbo, Ping and Yuen toiled day and night to the point of exhaustion to make steel. Despite the neglect of the fields, the leadership of their commune was claiming miraculous steel production *and* bountiful harvests. So was every other commune in China. The country's official Communist newspaper discussed "the problem of producing too much food." In this heady, frenzied mood, Mao, in late 1958, launched the "backyard furnace" program. In Chang Gar Bin, so many peasants built small brick furnaces to make iron that the skies glowed red. To keep the furnaces going round the clock, the peasants burned whatever fuel they could find, even stripping the hills behind the village bare of scrub. Communist officials looking for iron to melt down went from house to house to confiscate kitchen utensils like woks; they declared these unnecessary now that people were eating in communal canteens. In Huangbo's house, the officials found a bounty of iron in the wrought-iron gate, the gratings over the windows and the locks in the doorways.

Despite the official propaganda, it was already apparent that a food shortage was coming, for the commune had been too busy making iron to get the harvest in. The backyard furnaces had produced heat and little else. All of China was in the same calamity and chaos. In the summer of 1959, Mao finally abandoned the Great Leap Forward. But there was no stopping the momentum of damage from the neglect of crops and the misguided projects, like building dams. That same year was the first of what was to be three years of bad weather. China was gripped by the worst famine in its history, with a death toll worse than any war. From 1959 to 1962, untold numbers—perhaps twenty to thirty million—would succumb to starvation and malnutrition, tuberculosis, hepatitis, edema and various parasitic diseases of the blood and intestines.

Even in Guangdong (formerly known as Kwangtung), one of the richest provinces, rice was rationed to the most meager portions. It went to the cities first, the countryside second. Black markets began in food not normally eaten, like the tops of root vegetables, but eventually in all manner of food and goods. Everybody with anything to sell for food patronized them. Ping traded sentimentality to feed her children and sold the Big Ben alarm clock her father had given her when she was a child. She was less distraught when she sold the baby clothes, hand-knit by her mother overseas, which her father had included in a care package for her firstborn; the clothes had been handed down as far as they could go. Yuen and Huangbo, reluctant to part with the few possessions from Chan Sam, sold the glass in the windows of the house.

When Yuen saw goods from Hong Kong, like cigarette-lighter flints, appearing in the black market, he decided he should try to use his overseas connection. His father had once said that the sister in Canada could not afford to send money, but Yuen reasoned she could send a care package of merchandise that he could sell for profit on the black market. He wrote to the address his father had given him for her. No reply came. He presumed Hing had moved away to the United States—he remembered his father's description of riches enough there to build roads eight automobiles across. When he heard of friends of friends going to the United States or to Canada, he asked them to look for his sister and her husband. He knew only that she was a nurse and that he was in the laundry business. No word ever came back.

As the famine worsened, Ping's husband fled to Hong Kong to join his mistress there, leaving Ping with four children, the youngest but a baby. Ping, depriving herself, fed her family's daily ration of rice to her children and was still unable to satisfy their hunger. Like others in the village, she, Huangbo and Yuen searched for extra sustenance in banana stalks, and when those were gone, in wild plants and bugs and worms—sources of protein that the regime itself urged people to experiment with. Ping, as she toiled in the field and grew weak from stomach troubles, lamented aloud that things could have turned out very differently: "If only my mother and father had come back for me, if only they had brought me to Canada." Other villagers had no sympathy: "You must deserve to have been left behind. You deserve to toil and sweat. You deserve to suffer and die here." "It's not fair. I don't deserve it," Ping protested. "I wasn't born here. Other people born abroad have left. Why can't I? I cannot accept this and I never will. My heart will always be bitter."

Ping's regret did not mean that she worried any less about the mother who raised her. Concerned that Huangbo's failing health might confine her to bed, and that she would need a woman's attention, Ping decided it was time for Yuen, now aged twenty-five, to take a wife. There were two unmarried women whom he worked with minding the commune's stores. Too timid to make a choice, Yuen asked Ping to inspect them. "Choose the tall one," she advised. "She looks stronger." To mark the marriage, a handful of villagers assembled at the house. Each came bearing a few grains of rice in their palm as a symbolic wedding gift. It amounted to less than one mouthful, but it was all they could spare in the continuing famine.

Three years after the famine had subsided, a frustrated Mao was again to betray his impatience with the lack of progress in achieving his brand of communism. In 1966, he unleashed the Cultural Revolution, ostensibly to mold a new generation of youth. He urged Red Guards to "spread disorder" and instructed Work Teams to rout out "old ideas, old culture, old customs and old habits." Aided by his actress wife, Chiang Ching, who used her position in charge of productions of new Chinese operas to grab more power and influence, Mao's campaign became another of China's sweeping political dramas, marked by fanatical violence, denunciations and killings.

In Chang Gar Bin, Red Guards destroyed the temple near the village, shut down the schools and attacked the teachers. Work Teams went on search-and-destroy missions. Books, works of art, luxury furniture like typewriters and radios, fashionable clothing, even certain hairstyles, were banned as "bourgeois." Mao also named "Seven Kinds of Blacks": landlords, rich peasants, counter-revolutionaries, bad elements, rightists, monsters and freaks, and pro-capitalists. Yuen hastily took black oil paint and covered the calligraphy and paintings of western scenes on the porcelain panels in the house. He himself wasn't sure what they depicted but he feared they were dangerous. The Work Team, in their haste, did not bother to look that high overhead when they searched his house.

A year after the Cultural Revolution began, Mao intervened to restore order. Yuen cleaned off the black paint. He restored a place of honor in the house to his parents by hiring an artist to draw a double portrait of them to replace the one, painted in the year of his birth, that had once hung on a wall in the main reception room but had been vandalized and destroyed during the land reform. He provided the artist with a photograph of his father. It was one Chan Sam had sent, taken when he received his naturalization papers in Canada. Hardly had Huangbo finished sitting for the new portrait when her health took a turn for the worse. Yuen's wife could not care for her; she had three young children, the youngest a new baby. Ping took Huangbo to the hospital in Shekki. Because the family was not able to afford a nurse, Ping stayed at her bedside. In the spring of 1968, Huangbo died in Ping's arms and was buried on the hillside above Chang Gar Bin. Nothing remained to distinguish the family plot; the carved ancestral monuments and soul tablets erected by Chan Sam some thirty years earlier had been smashed to pieces by Red Guards.

As the years passed, Ping saw her four children married off; her two sons moved their wives in with her and began to have children of their own. Despite Yuen's desire that his children stay in school until they graduated, only his daughter, the eldest of the three, would. Though Ping and Yuen lived as though their hopes were no different from that of other peasants—for good weather and a good harvest, and less political turmoil—talk among them about the third sister last known to be in Canada never disappeared. Sometimes it was Ping who met her in a dream, sometimes it was Yuen or his wife, who had absorbed her husband's stories over the years. The three remained convinced that the lost sister was alive and well, and that her life abroad was better than theirs at home.

Decades came and went. In the spring of 1987, but days after the sister had again shown herself to Yuen's wife in a dream, the official from the Overseas Chinese Office came calling on Yuen and Ping. His office was investigating every family of the surname "Chan" in Chang Gar Bin and surroundings; they were looking for the relations of a Canadian woman. Yuen produced evidence that he was the half-brother and that his family had been divided between China and abroad: a bottle of quinine sulphate pills from Buckshon's Pharmacy in Vancouver, an American ten-dollar bill minted in the year of his birth, a Big Ben clock that had been Nan's and had passed to him and letters and photographs that his father had sent. Ping produced the photograph of herself with the concubine, pointing out what was printed on the back. Two weeks later the official paid Yuen a return visit. "You better clean your house from top to bottom," he said. "In a few days your sister and niece will be here."

The reunion was the talk of Chang Gar Bin and of neighboring villages. "So your sister is coming back. So many decades that you have not seen each other's faces and she still cares enough to come back!" people said. "Fifty years! Never has a village seen a family reunited after being separated so long." What others said helped convince Ping, Yuen and his wife that the sister would appear this time for real. Not since after "Liberation," when a Work Team came to take Huangbo away and to rectify the excesses of Chan Sam's house, had the family had such attention.

❦

Mother and I were given the room of honor in Yuen's house. He and his wife gave up the back bedroom, which was the same room my grandfather had shared with Huangbo, and moved upstairs with their three children. Yet there was little privacy. We had to contend with the pig pacing the adjoining kitchen and passageway, snorting and slurping as she went. Mosquitoes, oblivious to the acrid blue smoke of a repellent tablet smoldering atop a kerosene lamp on the cement floor, found their way behind the netting draping from the bed frame. At first dawn, dogs howled and barked next door, where the neighbor slaughtered the choice of the day for his restaurant. We waited for the sign our household was waking—the shudder of the board being drawn across the thick timbers of the main entrance, followed by the creak of the doors swinging opening to admit the day.

Our visit lasted four days. Yuen and his wife stayed home from work the entire time, he from the shop, she from the fields. "It doesn't matter whether I work one day or twenty days in a month," Yuen said. "I still get the same wage." He'd been keeping the books at the state-owned shop ever since he was reassigned there from the commune twenty years ago. Ping—now sixty-one and no longer working for wages—had only one obligation, to mind her second son's two young children and to prepare the day's meals for herself and his family. Only that son's family shared her house; the eldest—a district economic official—had moved his out when his work unit built new housing. But someone else would soon be arriving; after two and a half decades of silence, Ping's husband had written to say that his mistress had died, that he was ill and would be coming home for his wife to care for him.

Each day, Ping would come from her house to Yuen's, to join us in Yuen's main reception room. Sometimes it was just us four. Other times there was also Yuen's wife, her children, or sometimes an elderly cousin of Mother's—the daughter of my grandfather's brother, who went to Havana in the 1920s and was never heard from again. From their opening words, it was clear that the Chinese side of the family regarded Mother as the one who had to reclaim lost family history, not them, and that it was they who would do the talking, not us.

On the afternoon of our arrival, Mother passed around the photographs she'd brought. "Who's that?" Ping asked. It was May-ying, her own mother. We explained that May-ying had died in a car accident. In their lack of interest, we saw our own omission. Out of politeness, we asked when Yuen's mother had passed on.

Yuen wanted Mother to know that over the years he had tried, unsuccessfully, to contact her. Mother began an apology: "I hardly knew my dad, so I hardly ever heard the family at home mentioned. You knew my mom and dad separated when I was young? My mom couldn't look after me; she always boarded me out. She liked to gamble. She liked to play mah-jongg—"

"—and she was a drinker," Yuen's daughter said, repeating the stories that had been passed on to her. The Chinese side of the family finished Mother's sentences for her. It was as if they had rehearsed a play for this very moment. Said Ping: "I know what *Mama* was like. *Baba* said no man could keep up with her drinking and gambling. *Dai-ma* couldn't stand to live under the same roof as her; she was always very cranky." Yuen's wife followed: "Your father couldn't stand her arguing any more and that's why they separated." It was Yuen's turn: "*Baba* would say there was no feeling or love between your mother and him, no feelings of husband and wife. But my mother he had a lot of feeling for."

Ping, in her respected position as eldest sister, gave a synopsis: "I know we had three mothers: I know mine and Nan's is Number Three; Yuen's is Number Two. Mother Number One died, that's why Father got himself another wife, our *Dai-ma*. Then he got himself a third wife. They had three daughters. Two—myself and Nan—were brought back from Gold Mountain to China. Other than that, I didn't know my mother. As far as I was concerned, she was a 'foreign lady.' Only my father worried about us, that I do know."

There was a presumption that my grandfather would have told the Chinese side of the family everything of importance about the Canadian side. "*Baba* was very consistent about writing," said Yuen. "He wrote of everything in detail—one-one, two-two..." Our Chinese relatives were not interested in what Mother could add about what had happened in Canada. It seemed the last word on the family history was comprised of my grandfather's words from Canada, along with what happened to the Chinese family at home. For us, knowing that they were living with an incomplete version of the Canadian family's history was no more unsettling than looking at the surreal western scenes overhead on the porcelain panels that my grandfather had commissioned. The scenes of wealthy Hollywood, San Francisco's Golden Gate Bridge and the pristine sea and mountain-scape of Vancouver evoked none of the feeling of the dingy rooming houses of my grandparents' time, or of the frontier logging and pulp mill town that Prince George was when we moved there. But it did not matter, for we were not there to right any wrongs about my grandfather's house.

And so, as Mother and I sat in Yuen's front room, under the gaze of the double portrait of my grandfather and the wife in China and to the accompaniment of the Regulator clock marking time, we listened as the Chinese side of the family poured out their stories. As one relative spoke, another would illustrate by pointing to the courtyard where overseas crates were once piled high while the house was being completed, to the places where once stood overseas dressers, where once hung decorative mirrors, to the back bedroom where Yuen was born and Nan died, and Huangbo lived out her life. The future of the family was tied to the issue of getting the house to themselves again: under the new Communist policy of allowing limited home ownership again, Yuen could have it, if he raised the money to build the occupants on the other side of the brick wall a house of their own. "I am scrimping and saving for the pride of my father," he said.

Our Chinese relatives could not mention my grandfather's name without reverence and admiration. To them, what elevated my grandfather to heroic proportions was the tragedy of his hard life in Canada. They cried for the anguish my grandmother caused him, and the separation he had to endure from his wife and family in China. Yuen's words paid high tribute: "He was a model father and husband. I'm very much like my father. I work hard; I stay away from drinking and gambling, from all such non-senses that are good for nothing. My sons are the same."

In the face of such devotion to her father's memory, Mother held back the truths dawning in her own mind. She did not tell Ping and Yuen what she understood now that the two halves of the family's history had closed together to make one: that the house they cherished as a monument to her father had been built on her mother's back, on the wages and wits of waitressing and the life that came with it. She did not tell them that it stood for everything that had been so misunderstood about her mother, by them and by herself. She did not say what she felt, that her father's love and her mother's money had been siphoned from her to the family in China, that the money that Huangbo was swin-dled out of when she tried to turn baby Yuen's feet the right way around was money that Chan Sam had come to collect from May-ying in Nanaimo. For Mother to have said any of this would have undone what had sustained the Chinese family through hard and trying times, what had given them reason to carry on. Events had more than evened the score. She decided it was better to let them believe that her mother brought their father only unhappiness, and that the other mother who raised them had been the superior wife.

On the morning before our day of departure, the womenfolk among the relatives returned from the market with an armful of biscuits, and announced to Mother and me that we were going to call on "Nan's in-laws" because there was a new baby in the house and it was the day of the Full Month celebration. Mother and I exchanged looks of confusion. We had asked about the circumstances of Nan's death. "Somebody frightened her in the field," was all Ping and Yuen said. The pain and sorrow etched on their faces stopped us from asking more. But nobody had mentioned that Nan had been married! Yuen's wife explained: the family had always worried about what to do with Nan's unmarried spirit and were fearful that it would turn into a ghost. In the early 1980s, as the Communists gradually relaxed the ban against the practice of religion, customs and traditions, Ping and Yuen's wife had decided to act. They knew of a family that had lost two sons. Nan had known neither in life; Ping had, and pronounced them both suitable husbands. "Let the dead marry the dead," agreed both families.

The two brothers should have been asked who wanted Nan. But the other family agreed with Ping, that because Nan was "so smart," she could choose between them. The families sought out a *sun-po* (a woman who becomes a spirit medium after herself having survived several crises, typically the death of children and a husband). She put herself into a trance and sent her soul into the underworld, where she found Nan and the two brothers.

"How can we be sure she is Nan?" Ping wanted to know.

"She says your younger brother uses an abacus to earn his living," said the *sun-po*. It was something the woman, being from another village, could not have known.

Nan spoke through the *sun-po* about her death to her living relatives: "Yuen's mother liked me, but my mother never liked me and that's why I did not live long." Nan then rowed, with the husband of her choice, back along the great river of the underworld to rejoin the dead. After the seance, she officially left the family;

the two families went to the hillside where she was buried, dug up her remains and reburied them beside her dead husband's.

At the home of the in-laws, we gave our gifts of biscuits and sipped a pungent ginger-flavored soup in celebration of the new baby. Yuen's children arrived with their bicycles to give us a ride to the recently restored Dragon Mother's Temple near the village, where the womenfolk wanted to go next. We asked to make a small detour en route, to see where my grandfather's old house had been. Sandwiched by houses on all sides was a small patch of land. Weeds poked up through cement. The old house had long since been knocked down, and nobody had wanted to rebuild on a space so small. This was where my grandmother had lived during the brief time she lived in Chang Gar Bin.

The visit to the temple was their weekly trip; the womenfolk said they were going to give thanks for our visit. One by one, they approached the altar, lit incense and bowed three times in worship. The elderly cousin gestured to Mother to take her turn. She did what she had seen her own mother do many times in a makeshift temple in Vancouver's Chinatown and in the womblike temple on the third floor of the building in Victoria's Chinatown. I stood by, watching, wondering what was said between Mother and the resident goddess.

It was on our last afternoon in Chang Gar Bin that Ping was to catch Mother by surprise. She said that she and Yuen had something to give back to her.

When she was growing up, Mother had never thought of herself as having the luxury of possessions worth keeping. Whenever she and her mother packed up to move on, whatever they owned fit into her mother's metal trunk; anything else of value was at the pawnbrokers. When Mother moved out of her mother's rooming house into the nurses' residence at Essondale, her belongings fit into one small, white suitcase.

Upstairs, in the room that was once a guest room when my grandfather first built the house, there were only a few relics from Gold Mountain. The rusted crib frame, the phonograph, the broken crockery—nothing looked salvageable. Yuen searched and found something else, buried in one of the straw baskets.

In the sunlight outside on the balcony, the bundle of cloth, frayed and discolored, also looked like it had long outlived any usefulness. Then Mother's face brought the brown knit coat back to life, when it wrapped her neck in velvet and bridged the more than four decades of adversity during which the Chinese family hoped it could be united as one.

Our farewell banquet was held on our last evening in Chang Gar Bin. The relatives, numbering twenty-one, gathered at Ping's house. It was immaculate; even the cement floor of the pigpen adjoining the kitchen hearth was cleaner than any space in Yuen's house. Ping showed Mother and me to her quarters. She had only a small corner to herself, under the sloping ceiling of the second floor, consisting of a table beside a bed shrouded in mosquito netting. On the table was a tin box where she kept her valuables, including the photograph of herself as a babe-in-arms in Canada. On the bed were two pillows and a blanket. The pillows were her only luxury, stuffed with down salvaged from the inside of the comforter that had come with her from Canada.

Away from Yuen's house and from Yuen, Ping adopted a more sister-to-sister, confessional tone with Mother. Her voice dropped to a whisper. She voiced feelings of resentment that the Chinese ways left out the daughter, that the remittances from abroad, the family home and its contents had all gone to Yuen. "Because I am a woman, I have no say and I can't speak out," she said. Mother, wanting to give her sister something, took her watch off her wrist and put it on Ping's. She took off her shoes, which had rhinestones at the toes, to see if they would fit Ping's feet. They didn't.

The scene downstairs and in the courtyard was buoyant. Yuen's sons had bicycled to Shekki that morning for fish to sell in the market and had saved the largest one for tonight. Ping's second son had brought home several live chickens, their legs tied together and hooked over the handlebars of his motorbike. The eldest son brought some bottles of Coke and "One Hundred Happiness" beer on the back of his. Yuen's wife told Mother she planned to prepare dog as one dish. Mother asked if she would mind not cooking it. "Do you fancy cat, then?" Yuen's wife asked. Mother shook her head.

Every dish, as always, was mouth-watering, but our appetites were satiated; the visit had been filled in equal measure with talking and eating. In between meals we had seen bottomless cups of tea, never-ending piles of persimmons, Mandarin oranges, pears, papayas and hard-boiled eggs. And feeling a hankering for our western ways, Mother and I shared a glance of disapproval at the sight of the fly struggling to pull itself free from the eyeball of a fish, and at our relatives spitting bones and refuse onto the floor at their feet.

But the mood was jubilant, and there were toasts to everybody's health and to our onward journey. In return for their hospitality, I offered to buy something of their choice from a shop in Chang Gar Bin. I confessed embarrassment at having brought only token gifts. "It's enough to see each other's faces," Ping and Yuen said. Mother mentioned my speculation as to why officials had sent a van to the border: "Maybe they thought we were bringing you a refrigerator." "Next time you come," yelled Ping's pork-seller son, standing and gesturing with his chopsticks, "bring two!"

Later that evening, back in Yuen's front room, the three siblings had parting talks. Ping asked Mother to locate her birth certificate, to prove the truth of the memento of the photograph and what was printed on the back. Even though Ping had no desire this late in her life to leave Chang Gar Bin, Mother did not have the heart to tell her that their father had sold the document years before, and that another woman was living in her name in Canada. We asked Ping, however, if she'd like to visit Canada one day. "I'd like to see where I was born before I die," Ping said. Then, laughing with her eyes the way my grandmother did, she said to Mother, "Yuen can come too; he'll walk ahead of us. With his crooked feet, he can rake in the gold and you and I will follow behind and pick it up!"

Yuen had his own request. He wanted to get his children out

of China, one at a time. He thought his daughter, being educated—she had a job labeling cardboard cartons in a local factory—and still unmarried, had the best chance. She was twenty-four. Would Mother consider marrying off one of her three sons to her as a way of getting her into Canada? We gently discouraged that notion. We explained that his daughter could not emigrate to Canada on the basis of her job—she did not have a skill that was in demand—and a legal marriage would take some arranging. Yuen then disclosed that he was negotiating with a middleman to sell his daughter to a future husband in Panama. "What kind of man is he and what is his age?" I asked. Yuen said he didn't know what the man did and that "any age" would do; what mattered was that his daughter get out of China. From Panama, she could find her way, he hoped, to Canada or the United States, and once there, help get her two brothers out of China.

⁂

Most of the relatives rose early the next morning to see us off. As we waited for the bus to take us on to Canton, Ping kept pinching herself on the arm, as she had done repeatedly since we first arrived, to convince herself again that our visit had not been a dream. There was weeping all around. For Mother, it was as much for the realization that she had ended up the luckier of her siblings as it was for the parting of flesh and blood. What she saw and heard in China illuminated her own past. Instead of making her bitter, it lifted the burden of her shame. Her father had come to Canada to throw off the cloak of poverty at home, but the truth was that his penchant for showiness had brought the family members persecution, had left them victims of a regime driven by vindictiveness. For Mother, who had lived her childhood in a shadow of sacrifice for the Chinese side of the family, her parents' act of immigration to the new world and her mother's determination in pregnancy to chance the journey by sea had been her liberation, the best gift of all.

As I lost sight of my relatives in the yellow dust billowing behind the bus, the flickering hope on the faces of Ping and Yuen the evening before came to mind. I thought of how Mother, having left behind the rooming houses of her past, would return at the end of her travels to Prince George and to a life of her own choosing. Her five children were university-educated and living their own lives. Ping and Yuen could expect to die in Chang Gar Bin, the birth and burial place of generations of the family. They could nurture only faint hopes that their children or their children's children might escape a peasant's lot.

My uncle Yuen, worried before our arrival that we might not be able to speak their dialect, had written a letter in case that was all that could be said between him and his sister. As he and Mother said goodnight on our last evening in his house, he had pressed the letter into her hand. Its prose was poetic, explaining with sorrow who had passed on, how many there were in the generation that followed. It ended with echoes of my grandfather, as Yuen looked back on his own life and ahead at his children's:

...I, myself, born with two crippled legs, only resolved to work harder for the goal of life, and to turn sorrow into strength. When it comes to living in this world, one should know the significance of human life. One should suffer and then enjoy. One should rely on himself, work hard and practice economy...

As parents, who would not be concerned about the future of his or her children? I hope to get my children out of China to take root in Canada. Then, the roots of the tree will grow downward and the leaves will be luxuriant. We will be fortunate, the children will be fortunate and our children's children will be fortunate. The family will be glorious and future generations will have a good foundation...

It is my utmost hope that you will render your assistance, help and promotion. If there's a chance to get my children out of China, I guarantee that I will pay back the money involved. If that chance is realized, thousands of thanks, ten thousands of thanks, never forgotten...

Mother left the brown knit coat with the velvet-trimmed collar behind in Chang Gar Bin. It seemed that it still belonged in China, where the threads of my grandfather's hopes were still woven in his children's dreams.

## CHAPTER FOURTEEN

*T*HERE WAS NO signpost to identify Market Alley. Mother and I were looking for Number 79, where Chan Sam took the pregnant May-ying after stepping off the boat from China. We found ourselves in front of a boarded-up building. Above a doorway, the number and street address was inlaid in a half-moon shape, in tiles of red and green, colors of happiness and prosperity. Here were Mother's beginnings. This time, as we waded through the past together to recover more completely her family's history, she could no longer end her stories the way she once had: "I had nobody."

Filling in the blanks in the stories of the other children of the concubine required a second trip to China. Mother and I, accompanied by my brother Wayne, went back in 1989, two and a half years after the first visit. Though the massacre in Tiananmen Square was still recent, we arrived to find that Yuen had given up, for now, making plans to get his children out of China. He'd married off his daughter to a man in a neighboring village. The room of honor in my grandfather's house, the back bedroom downstairs, was now occupied by his eldest son, his wife and their baby.

As for Yuen, we found him busy "harvesting the silver tree." He would venture only one opinion about the latest political turmoil: regret that the clamp-down by Peking and subsequent international sanctions would dampen economic growth in south China. Deng Xiaoping's economic policies had made peasants rich like never before; virtually everyone was engaged in commerce on the side. Yuen and his two sons were in partnership and doing so well that they needed a heavy safe to keep their cash.

We were able to deliver the proof Ping wanted that she was born in Canada. There was no formality; we simply applied to the government for a copy of her birth certificate, enclosed the prescribed fee and received it in the mail. Ping's second son, disillusioned with life in the village—he had been fined twice, heavily, for gambling —eyed his mother's birth certificate as a ticket to get himself and his family out of China. He wanted Ping to try to use proof that she was foreign-born to get herself out first, then to find a way to get him out.

A trip with our relatives to Canton, to the duty-free shop, had already been planned so we could make up for the obligation we had failed to fulfil on our first trip. We used our foreign currency allowances and exemptions to buy them a television and motorcycle from Japan and a Chinese-made washing machine—Yuen's house now had plumbing. The next stop was a call on the foreign ministry, so that Ping, escorted by her second son, could argue that the birth certificate was reason enough to give her an exit visa. The ministry official, beleaguered by the rush to leave the country after Tiananmen Square, tossed the certificate back with hardly a glance. Ping put it back in her tin box of valuables, pleased enough to know that she had been born with both a Chinese name and an English name: "Mary Chan" it said on her birth certificate.

On the coroner's report into my grandmother's death, a "Mary Ho" was named as the next-of-kin who identified the body. Mother thought it could only have been "Mary Chan," the woman who bought her eldest sister's birth certificate; "Ho" had to be a married name. We went to the address on the report, not optimistic that the woman would still be there some twenty years on. Mother and the tall, moon-faced woman who answered the door recognized each other. They had met many years before, when we came calling on my grandmother on one of our visits down from Prince George. I myself remembered *Po-po* telling us to address her as "Auntie," and Mother addressing her as "Ping."

On the morning after my grandmother's death, the caretaker at her rooming house had directed the police officer to the house of her "daughter." Mary Ho explained at the morgue that she was only a stepdaughter, that the deceased had a son named Leonard, for whom a telephone number was found in May-ying's purse. Mary told the police to add the married name "Chan" to my grandmother's name, which explained the correction that appeared in *The Vancouver Sun.* Even so, my grandmother died under the false name and age on the birth certificate she used to enter Canada.

When Mary spoke of my grandmother, she had to dab at her eyes. In the last year of May-ying's life—at the same time that our family had puzzled over what was occupying my grandmother's time—the two had become friends. During that time, Mary was in and out of hospital with a stomach ailment. May-ying visited her in hospital and stayed at her home to care for her children. Mary felt as if she were being treated like a real daughter, like the one May-ying left behind in China.

I asked Mary if she had any mementos of May-ying to show me. Photographs perhaps? In reply, she brought up Nan's name: she and her "buy paper" sister each had the same set of two photographs. I expressed surprise that the false sisters kept in touch. Mary explained that she had few friends, partly because of her fear of being prosecuted as an illegal immigrant; not until 1985 did she take the amnesty available and become a bona fide Canadian citizen. Now, she and Nan saw each other only once a year, during the grave-sweeping festival of *Ching Ming,* when they went together to worship at the graves of Chan Sam and May-ying.

Mary went behind a beaded curtain into another room and

returned with two black-and-white photographs. She said she'd first laid eyes on them in Hong Kong when she was preparing to masquerade for immigration officials as the eldest daughter of Chan Sam and May-ying. "These are the photographs I have to remember my parents by," she had told the interrogating officer, showing him one of a man, another of a woman. "They were taken before they left my sister, Nan, and me behind in China, when they went back to Canada so that our younger sister could be born there too."

My quest into the past reached its symbolic end when these two photographs came into my possession. The one of my grandfather is a formal, full-length portrait. He looks youthful and handsome. His black hair is combed to the side, his shoes are shined, his western suit immaculately tailored. The tilt of his chin, the proud pose of his long, lean body on a chair, beside a table adorned with the props of a gentleman's study—a clock, an open book, a porcelain vase of peach blossoms—show none of the melancholy of the portrait taken many years later. The photograph of my grandmother is a close-up of her face. Her long hair is jauntily held back with a satin ribbon, curls tumble behind her dangling earrings. A girlish blush exists side by side with a confident maturity. It is a portrait of compelling beauty.

I put these two photographs into the family album and sent framed copies of them both to my Aunt Ping in China. My feeling was that I had found some nobility of purpose to the hard lives that Chan Sam and May-ying led. They had seen their family cleaved in two by misfortune and chance. If ever the surviving sisters—my mother and my Aunt Ping—were to be united, it would take a powerful sense of family to bridge the time and distance since traveled. The Chinese side had tried to make contact, and had failed. Mother's sense of family was fashioned in a more modern world of choice, where romantic love played more of a hand in fate. With my father's help, she had struggled free of the familial obligation and sacrifice that bound the Chinese side. Yet, in spite of these liberating differences, something made us revisit the past. I believe it was Mother's doing. A mother's stories to her daughter ultimately stirred a feeling in me that the life we lead begins before, and continues after, our time. I owed it to Mother, and to Chan Sam and May-ying, to find the good among the bad, and pride among the shame of their past. The lost history that Mother and I recovered gave the past new meaning, perhaps enough to be a compass to provide some bearings when her grandchildren chart their own course.

⊰⊱

An incessant rain is falling—a typical late-spring day in Vancouver. Mother and Wayne have been before me to Mountain View Cemetery to try to visit the graves of her mother and father. Mother tried to go by memory from when the coffins of Chan Sam and May-ying, ten years apart, were lowered into the ground. It was raining hard, and Mother and Wayne, cold and soaked, finally had to give up. Today, the custodian's office is open, and he's looked up the records, given Wayne and me a map and the coordinates for each grave.

Both are in the old Chinese section of the cemetery, where the tombstones face the layers of mountains on the north shore. Chan Sam and Leong May-Ying are buried rows and rows apart, strangers on either side. I have not brought anything to leave behind, but that is not why I've come. If they could hear from the grave, I would tell my grandfather and my grandmother that I have seen, for their dead eyes, the fruits of their labors. I would tell them they can now close their eyes in sleep.